Essentials of Clinical Supervision

Essentials of Mental Health Practice Series

Founding Editors, Alan S. Kaufman and Nadeen L. Kaufman

Essentials of Interviewing
by Donald E. Wiger and Debra K. Huntley

Essentials of Outcome Assessment
by Benjamin M. Ogles, Michael J. Lambert, and Scott A. Fields

Essentials of Treatment Planning
by Mark E. Maruish

Essentials of Crisis Counseling and Intervention
by Donald E. Wiger and Kathy J. Harowski

Essentials of Group Therapy
by Virginia A. Brabender, Andrew I. Smolar, and April E. Fallon

Essentials of Clinical Supervision
by Jane M. Campbell

Essentials

of Clinical Supervision

Jane M. Campbell

Featuring a Chapter on Ethics by
Barbara Herlihy

John Wiley & Sons, Inc.

Published by John Wiley & Sons, Inc., Hoboken, New Jersey.
Published simultaneously in Canada.

Library of Congress Cataloging-in-Publication Data

Campbell, Jane M., PhD.
  Essentials of clinical supervision / Jane Campbell.
      p. ; cm. — (Essentials of mental health practice series)
  Includes bibliographical references.
  ISBN-10 0-471-23304-8 (pbk)
  ISBN-13 978-0-471-23304-6 (pbk)
    1. Clinical psychologists—Supervision of. 2. Psychotherapists—Supervision of. 3.
  Counselors—Supervision of. I. Title. II. Series.
    [DNLM: 1. Psychology, Clinical—organization & administration. 2. Organization and
  Administration. WM 105 C188e 2006]
  RC467.7.C36 2006
  616.89—dc22   2005047499

Coventry University

Printed in the United States of America.

10 9 8 7 6 5 4 3 2 1

Dedication

This book is dedicated to all of the enthusiastic, involved, and committed clinical supervisors around the world who continue to do their best even in the most difficult and trying circumstances. The future of the mental and behavioral health professions is in your hands. Thank you.

Acknowledgments

Many of the case examples and Putting It Into Practice suggestions represent a compellation of ideas gathered from my supervision workshops and training offered across the United States these past 5 years. During these workshops, participants freely offered up creative and innovative ideas on how to solve day-to-day problems facing clinical supervisors everywhere and continuously validate the main premise of this book; it is the relationship supervisors build with supervisees that is core to effectiveness. I thank all of these nameless people who imparted their wisdom to me and to others in attendance at the workshops and wish to acknowledge their contributions to this book even if I am unable to thank them personally.

Jane M. Campbell
October 2005

CONTENTS

SERIES PREFACE

I n the *Essentials of Mental Health Practice* series, our goal is to provide readers with books that will deliver key practical information in an efficient and accessible style. The series features books on a variety of critical practice topics, such as interviewing, treatment planning, and outcomes assessment, to name a few. For the experienced professional, books in the series offer a concise yet thorough overview of a specific area of expertise, including numerous tips for best practices. Students will find here a prioritized assembly of all the information and techniques that must be at one's fingertips to practice knowledgeably, efficiently, and ethically in today's behavioral health environment.

Wherever feasible, visual cues highlighting key points are utilized alongside systematic, step-by-step guidelines. Chapters are focused and succinct. Topics are organized for an easy understanding of the essential material related to a particular practice area. Theory and research are continually woven into the fabric of each book, but always to enhance the practical application of the material, rather than to sidetrack or overwhelm readers. With this series, we aim to challenge and assist readers engaged in providing mental health services to aspire to the highest level of proficiency in their particular discipline by arming them with the tools they need for effective practice.

This text focuses on the basics of clinical supervision as both a training and a monitoring tool. Chapter 1 introduces the reader to the realities of clinical supervision in the twenty-first century and describes good and bad supervision practices. Chapter 2 explains the ethical and legal issues that are present in clinical supervision. Chapter 3 covers the current models for supervision and suggests a comprehensive model for practice. Chapters 4 and 5 go into detail about the major formats for delivery of supervision along with the most common methods and techniques. Chapter 6 stresses the importance of preparation in effective supervision and details for the reader how to set goals, plan best use of time, use proper documentation procedures, and structure evaluation in an ethical manner.

Chapters 7, 8, and 9 delineate the tasks, skills, and activities necessary at each stage of development of the supervisory relationship along with suggestions on how to solve some of the most common problems encountered by supervisors.

Alan S. Kaufman, PhD, and Nadeen L. Kaufman, EdD, Founding Editors
Yale University School of Medicine

One

INTRODUCTION TO CLINICAL SUPERVISION

C linical supervision is an increasingly important area of specialization in the mental health field. It has become the primary means by which the entire allied health field is now taught (Getz, 1999; Neufeldt, 2003; Storm, Todd, Sprenkle, & Morgan, 2001). Extensive graduate course work is followed by mandatory hours, even years, of clinical supervision both within and outside a degree program. After graduation, most states require several thousand hours of supervised experience in order to become licensed for independent practice. In fact, for those specializing in substance abuse treatment, most professional training occurs through supervision of on-the-job experience, and not in the classroom. It is under the tutelage of an experienced practitioner that professionals, regardless of their discipline, learn the skills necessary to become competent, ethical, and effective helpers.

Additionally, clinical supervision is increasingly at the forefront of malpractice prevention. Agencies, hospitals, schools, and private practice settings are concerned about liability, and thus many are moving to mandatory clinical supervision for all employees regardless of level of education or years of experience in order to assure the highest standard of care possible for clients.

Yet even as clinical supervision grows in importance, specialized training in this area lags behind (Kaiser & Barretta-Herman, 1999; Saccuzzo, 2002; Scott, Ingram, Vitanza, & Smith, 2000). Most are promoted to supervisor because of excellent clinical skills and ability to do the work rather than because they have formal training in clinical supervision. Moreover, few receive ongoing training in supervision or supervision of supervision by practicing clinical supervisors (Baronchok and Kunkel, 1990; Page, Pietzak, & Sutton, 2001). Instead, most supervisors today rely mainly on their own background and experience as supervisees and utilize the same structure and methods their supervisors used with them (Campbell, 2001–2005). Though this is a rich tradition, there is a growing concern that supervisors are simply perpetuating the mistakes of their own supervisors and that clinical supervision as a specialization is floundering (Campbell, 2001–2005; Steven, Goodyear, & Robertson, 1998; Whiston & Coker, 2000; Worthington, 1987). Without any training, supervisors may be unprepared for the many changes and demands now being placed on them.

THE NATURE OF SUPERVISION

Why should clinical supervisors require specialized training? Shouldn't the fact that supervisors are usually highly successful and skilled practitioners automatically make them effective supervisors? The answer is no. Just because one is a skilled practitioner with clients does not necessarily mean one can be a good supervisor.

Supervision is a different relationship than counseling and therapy. Succinctly put, the primary purpose of clinical supervision is to review practitioners' work to increase their skills and help them solve problems in order to provide clients the optimal quality of service possible and prevent any harm from occurring. Therefore, it is a teaching and training role as well as a monitoring function. Because the goal of supervision is to support ethical practice with clients, practitioners at all levels of education and experience can profit from supervision. The supervisory relationship may be voluntary (sought out) or involuntary (required by law), may extend over a definite period (as in the case of graduate internships or licensure), or be required indefinitely as part of employment. Always, however, the fundamental purpose of supervision remains the same.

What sets clinical supervision aside from other types of relationships, such as psychotherapy or consultation, is the presence of an evaluative component. Evaluation may be emphasized and central to the relationship or may be underemphasized depending on the context, purpose, and developmental needs of supervisees. For example, clinical supervision required of experienced licensed practitioners would have a different evaluative structure and purpose than supervision of prelicensed practitioners. However, the role of the supervisor is always to evaluate the quality of care being given to clients and to make suggestions for improvement when necessary.

Another important but frequently overlooked variable that needs to be considered is the fact that clinical supervision, for the majority of supervisees, is not voluntary. It is required to obtain a graduate degree, a certificate, a license to practice, to keep employment, and for malpractice prevention. The evaluative component along with the nonvoluntary nature of supervision cast issues of power, trust, safety, and control into the center of the clinical supervision experience and the supervisory relationship. This attribute also distinguishes supervision from consultation in that suggestions made by a consultant for client care are recommendations, not requirements.

Unique ethical and legal issues must also be addressed. Ethically, and by law, clinical supervisors are responsible for the actions of supervisees with clients. This fact turns clinical supervisors into not just teachers and trainers but also monitors of ethical practice in the mental health field and protectors of the

> ## DON'T FORGET
>
> The primary task of a clinical supervisor is to protect clients from harm while promoting the competency of supervisees. The nonvoluntary nature of the relationship along with the evaluative component makes supervision a relationship of unequal power.

community in which they live. They are responsible for overseeing the quality of client services and to prevent incompetent, impaired supervisees from serving the public. Accordingly, the role of the clinical supervisor is one of impressive responsibility and new challenges that should receive increased consideration as an area of specialized training.

FACTORS THAT CREATE DIFFICULTIES FOR SUPERVISORS

Clinical supervision is a balancing act between the needs of the supervisee and the needs of the client. This balancing act can be difficult and stressful or exciting and fulfilling depending on a number of variables. Such things as the purpose of supervision, level of competence, background and training of supervisees and supervisors, role clarity, organizational needs and organizational climate, and commitment of time and resources can all contribute to the ease or hardship of managing this complex relationship. Clinical supervision can be particularly daunting for new supervisors if they have no training or skills in clinical supervision and do not clearly understand their role, purpose, and function. Additionally, the amount and type of support given by an organizational system to clinical supervisors may help or hinder the supervisory process.

The first requirement for success as a clinical supervisor is to understand the function and purpose of supervision and how supervision is different from other relationships. Second, supervisors need to understand the ethical and legal issues that affect the supervisory relationship. Third, they need to acquire a model for supervision, learn to set goals, create structure, and use suitable methods and techniques, understand the pitfalls and problems inherent in supervision, and focus time and attention on building the supervision relationship. Last, supervisors have to find time for supervision.

This last task, finding time to supervise, is sometimes the hardest, particularly if the supervisor is still providing clinical services. Practitioners are constantly being asked to do more with less; at the same time there is increasing emphasis on the need for clinical supervision. Frequently, the clinical supervisor role is tacked onto the practitioner's routine job duties. It is hard for these overtaxed individuals to monitor the supervisees' quality of work and assist them to grow and develop while attempting to provide quality care to their own clients. In situations where supervisees are employees and are also receiving postdegree supervision for licensure along with their job, supervision can sometimes become even a more difficult and stressful balancing act. To find time for supervision, both supervisors and administrators have to understand the importance of clinical supervision and value it as a function not only in the organizational context but also in terms of society at large.

DIFFERENCES BETWEEN ADMINISTRATIVE AND CLINICAL SUPERVISION

Another factor that can add to difficulties and the stress level for clinical supervisors and supervisees alike is role conflict and role confusion. Dual relationships permeate supervision and are difficult to avoid. However, for countless numbers of mental health practitioners, the largest area of uncertainty and misunderstanding created by dual relationships is the overlap between clinical and administrative supervisory functions. Many clinical supervisors are required to serve in both capacities and sometimes knowing what to do is difficult at best as everyone attempts to sort out the various roles and relationships.

Although similar in certain respects, key differences do exist between the purpose and role of administrative and clinical supervisors. Understanding these differences will go a long way to clear up some of the bewilderment. The first point is to understand that administrative supervisors and clinical supervisors function under two separate models with different purposes, different missions, and different rule books. Administrators function under a business management model. The aim of an administrative supervisor is to keep an organizational system functioning in a healthy manner, accomplishing whatever is the organization's mission. Administrative supervisors are involved in hiring, firing, promotions, raises, scheduling, unions, and other personnel duties. The focus of administrative supervision is on productivity, workload management, and accountability. Decisions are made in terms of benefit or harm to the organizational system, not individuals. Local, state, and federal regulations, such as Equal Employment Opportunity Commission (EEOC) Guidelines and the Disability Act, govern their actions.

Clinical supervisors function under a different model. The purpose of clinical supervisors is to help practitioners develop skills, overcome obstacles, increase competency, and practice ethically with clients. It is historically a teaching, training, mentoring, and monitoring position with an emphasis on developing and maintaining competence. The focus in clinical supervision is on the individual supervisee's activities with clients. The vehicle for supervision is the review of client cases and the offer of suggestions and corrective feedback for improvement. Evaluation is ongoing and integral to the supervisory process as it is used to shape and direct learning. Even though a final summative evaluation is required in most types of clinical supervision, the essence of the supervisory process is continuous feedback throughout supervision, the intention of which is to help supervisees develop mastery and encourage ethical practice with clients.

In the administrative model, evaluation has a different intent and is mainly retrospective rather than formative. After a probationary term, the assumption is made that employees now have the necessary competencies to do the job. Once or twice a year, in what is titled a *performance appraisal,* employees are evaluated against a base line of these competencies and receive suggestions for improvement, warnings, or recognition for job excellence such as a promotion or a raise.

Another important area of potential confusion for clinical and administrative supervisors is differences between laws and ethical codes. As is well known to virtually everyone in the mental health field, ethical and legal standards frequently conflict. Clinical supervision as a specialized activity of the health professions falls under the ethical codes and standards for each discipline. Administrative supervisors, on the other hand, refer to laws, regulations, and management policy for their actions.

Obviously, a large area of overlap exists between the two functions of administrative and clinical supervisors, just as there is overlap between ethical codes and laws. Clinical supervisors are involved in a myriad of administrative tasks, such as documentation, time management, as well as monetary issues. Administrators, in turn, work extensively with their employees to help them increase skills. Both have to function within the laws of the community. Last, any unethical behavior on the part of a supervisee is cause for concern for both an administrator and a clinical supervisor.

However, there are many instances when the two functions contradict each other. Most prominently, successful clinical supervision is built on an important ethical premise that supervisees, in order to grow and learn, will be open, honest, truthful, and willing to admit mistakes. In return, clinical supervisors are expected to treat supervisees with respect and fairness; to maintain a commit-

> **CAUTION**
> ....
> There are differences in purpose and function between clinical and administrative supervision. Role conflict can sometimes lead to difficulties with supervisees.

ment to growth and development; and to avoid bias, exploitation, and impaired judgment. This is the basis of ethical practice in supervision.

In the administrative model, complete openness and honesty may take on a different meaning and have very different consequences. Both supervisor and supervisees have to carefully weigh the impact of complete honesty in an organization, especially if they wish to continue to draw a paycheck.

It is therefore evident, if the supervisee is both an employee and receiving clinical supervision for an outside purpose, such as a graduate internship or license, or if the clinical supervisor is also the administrator, these dual roles can create some serious problems in supervision if not treated with care. Extra effort will be needed to manage the delicate balance between encouraging supervisees to take risks and make mistakes in order to grow and the impact of that learning process on clients.

RESEARCH IN SUPERVISION

A further difficulty facing clinical supervisors is the fact that as a specialization, clinical supervision lags well behind other areas in quality empirical research that will validate many of its assumptions and accepted practices (Davy, 2002; Ladany & Muse-Burke, 2001; Watkins, 1998). For example, only a few studies have attempted to connect the practice of supervision to actual client outcome (Freitas, 2002; Patton & Kivlighan, 1997). Most of the research and theoretical writing in this field is primarily created within and for academic settings. In the majority of cases the studies in the field of supervision consist of surveys of beginning masters- or doctoral-level students in on-campus settings during their first experience as supervisees or supervisors, and they rarely venture beyond that pool of subjects for their findings. Many of these studies also involve small numbers of subjects and hypothetical situations.

There are also a small number of empirical studies of note that include supervisors and supervisees at a more advanced stage of development in settings outside academia (Borders & Usher, 1992; Neufeldt & Nelson, 1998; Storm et al., 2001; Weaks, 2002). Not much is known about the practices and needs of advanced supervisors and supervisees who face problems of delivering service in hospitals, agencies, schools, and private practice, and, as a result, clinical supervisors outside academia are left to figure out for themselves what to do to increase their effectiveness.

Significant differences exist between clinical supervision as practiced in academic settings and the supervision offered in agencies, schools, hospitals, and treatment facilities. The most important difference is one of control. The focus in on-campus practicum and internship sites, such as a college counseling center, is on supervisee training and development. A relatively small amount of time is spent on administrative tasks, such as paperwork, scheduling, and productivity. Usually the type and severity of client problems, as well as the number of clients for each supervisee, are also controlled. Supervisors are given time to supervise and have access to state-of-the-art equipment. Supervisees may receive several hours of individual supervision per client contact from several different supervisors using live observations, videotaping, as well as group supervision. There is usually abundant time for both supervisor and supervisee to contemplate, discuss ideas, and experiment.

In the world outside of academic settings, hardly any sites make training a central focus. Clinical supervision is usually an additional task added on to the supervisor's existing client load and results in an insufficient amount of time available for supervision. Further, clinical supervisors usually have little control over client numbers assigned to supervisees or the severity of client problems. Some supervisors even have no choice about being a supervisor, having been appointed to the job, and no input on the selection, numbers, experience, and background of those they supervise. As discussed previously, increasing numbers of clinical supervisors are also administrative supervisors, which can serve as another barrier to effectiveness. In other words, contextual issues dominate the practice of clinical supervision in these settings and make application of models, methods, and techniques from academic settings appear impractical.

SUPERVISOR COMPETENCIES

The paucity of research and lack of training in clinical supervision along with the impact of contextual factors and the multiplicity of roles required of supervisors have a direct impact on ethical practice of supervision. Ethically, one of the first demands for clinical supervisors is the necessity for them to be competent to supervise. This means that supervisors are fully trained and knowledgeable about the role and function of clinical supervisors; they have a model, skills, and strategies to effectively carry out the role. Added to that is an expectation that each supervisor is fully versed and competent in the areas of client service in which they are supervising.

DON'T FORGET

Supervisors should seek information on ethical standards and required competencies for supervision from their particular professional discipline.

A growing number of states and national organizations are attempting to assist supervisors to fulfill this expectation and become competent as clinical supervisors. For example, many states now require clinical supervisors of postdegree candidates for licensure to take a course on supervision in order to become certified. The length of these supervision courses will vary; the state of Texas demands a 40-hour course while Arizona recently instituted a 12-hour course prerequisite (with 6 hours thereafter). Both the National Board for Certified Counselors (NBCC) and the American Association

 Rapid Reference 1.1

Supervisor Competencies

Supervision Skills
- Knowledge of the role and function of clinical supervisors
- Knowledge of legal, ethical, and regulatory guidelines as they apply to supervision
- Understanding of the importance of the supervisory relationship and ability to facilitate that relationship
- Competencies in all areas of client care in which supervising
- Ability to set goals and objectives and create and implement a supervision plan
- Knowledge of the models, methods, and techniques of clinical supervision
- Knowledge of strategies for supervision and ability to be flexible in style and choice of strategies
- Knowledge of the role of systems, cultural issues, and environmental factors and their impact on supervision
- Familiarity with the methods of evaluation and ability to apply them fairly
- Understanding of the existence of dual relationships and their impact on supervisory objectivity and judgment
- Strategies to limit harm that may come from dual relationships in supervision
- Knowledge of multicultural issues and ability to respond to multicultural differences
- Documentation skills
- Awareness of the requirements and procedures required for licensure or certification if applicable

for Marriage and Family Therapy (AAMFT) offer an approved supervisor credential and a standardized curriculum to obtain it. Hopefully, as added attention is placed on the ethical and legal functions of clinical supervisors in the mental health field, more states and national organizations will tackle this vital issue of supervisor competence and training in the future.

More often than not, however, the only requirement for a clinical supervisor is a set number of years of experience, say 2 or 3, in their field. It is left up to the majority of supervisors to determine if they have the knowledge and skills to be competent.

Rapid Reference 1.1 provides a broad list of recommended competencies for all clinical supervisors. Depending on one's field or discipline, specific competencies pertinent to that practice should be added. Rapid Reference 1.2 contains an example of a more specialized list of competencies and skills required for counselors and psychotherapists. Those who are in substance abuse, nursing, or

≡ Rapid Reference 1.2

Recommended Counseling and Psychotherapy Skills for Supervisors

- Knowledge in the areas of practice—group, individual, family, couple, child and adolescence
- Relationship skills—ability to build rapport and trust
- Ethical judgment and decision making
- Knowledge and application of ethical guidelines and standards to specific cases and situations, particularly in crisis
- Crisis management skills
- Assessment and diagnostic skills
- Conceptualization skills
- Problem-solving and goal-setting skills
- Knowledge and experience in the use of the methods and techniques of counseling and psychotherapy
- Intervention strategies—knowledge and application of a variety of intervention techniques for change
- Written skills—documentation and record keeping
- Knowledge of and ability to understand systems and the interaction between individuals, setting, environmental factors, and presenting problems
- Knowledge of multicultural issues and ability to respond to those issues
- Understanding of the role of developmental factors in client problems

home services or those who work as case managers can adapt this list to fit their particular requirements.

QUALITIES AND CHARACTERISTICS OF EFFECTIVE SUPERVISORS

Beyond consideration of what knowledge and expertise is required for ethical practice of supervision, most supervisors, especially those new to the position, are interested in what qualities and characteristics are necessary in order to be successful and effective. It should be apparent that because of the complexity and the demands of the role, the answer to this question is not simple. For example, a study by White and Russell (1995) concerning the essential elements of marriage and family therapy supervision generated over 800 variables that influence the outcome of supervision.

As indicated in the previous section, researchers are just beginning to examine in a systematic way what factors are important in successful supervision outcome. Having said that, most studies in supervision, as well as anecdotal reports by supervisees about their experiences in supervision, continually point to the fact that qualities and attributes of effective supervisors mirror those for effective counselors and psychotherapists (Anderson, Schlossberg, & Rigazio-DiGilio, 2000; Chung, Baskin, & Case, 1998; Getz, 1999). Supervisees, regardless of education and level of experience, want and need support and acceptance from supervisors. To summarize, some of the personal attributes that have been consistently identified across the board as essential to effective supervision are trustworthiness, authenticity, genuineness, openness, tolerance, respect, empathy, and flexibility, along with an ability to confront, a concern for a supervisee's growth and well-being, a willingness to hear feedback, the possession of personal courage, and a sense of humor.

DON'T FORGET

Regardless of one's specific theoretical model or the level of training or experience of the supervisee, a supportive, facilitative supervisory environment is deemed critical to effective supervision and supervisory growth. Therefore, those personal qualities that contribute to creating a nurturing environment are the most essential.

Two other important variables in a successful supervision experience are the level of commitment by supervisors to the role and to the supervisees' growth and development. Anderson et al. (2000) concluded that the more available and involved supervisors are in supervision and the more open the supervisory environment, the better the supervisee's experience. Thus, supervisors who take supervision seriously, work to create an open and encouraging supervisory environment, and attend to the personal growth of supervisees along with their development of technical and conceptual skills are deemed most effective. A study of clinical supervision in a public rehabilitation setting also emphasized the importance of regularly scheduled supervision sessions along with proactive teaching activities in supervisee satisfaction (Schultz, Odokie, Fried, Nelson, & Bardos, 2002). Rapid Reference 1.3 provides a description of effective supervisory behaviors. This list represents a composite of responses given by hundreds of active clinical supervisors while participating in supervision workshops across the country regarding the qualities and characteristics of an effective supervisor (Campbell, 2001–2005).

≡ Rapid Reference 1.3

Effective Supervisory Behaviors

- Clarifies expectations and roles
- Is accessible and available
- Takes the role of supervisor seriously
  - Cares about the well-being of the supervisee
  - Provides frequent scheduled supervision
  - Is fully present in supervision session and not multitasking
  - Is invested in the supervisee's development
- Is able to create a safe learning environment
  - Recognizes and validates the strengths of the supervisees
  - Creates a relaxed learning environment
  - Encourages the exploration of new ideas and techniques
  - Is tolerant, open, and flexible
  - Open to ideas, thoughts, and feelings of supervisees
  - Fosters autonomy and risk-taking
  - Perceives growth as an ongoing process
  - Is curious
- Has the ability to communicate effectively
  - Works collaboratively
  - Is supportive and encouraging
  - Provides constructive criticism as well as positive reinforcement
  - Is genuine and congruent

(continued)

- Models appropriate ethical behavior
  - —Maintains consistent and appropriate boundaries
  - —Is competent and credible
  - —Is knowledgeable and up to date
  - —Has extensive practical experience in the area in which supervising
  - —Demonstrates how to get work done in the organization
- Is personally and professionally mature
  - —Serves as a professional role model
  - —Is aware of and accepts his or her own limitations and strengths
  - —Is willing to accept mistakes
  - —Is not easily rattled in a crisis
  - —Has a high tolerance for conflict and so is able to hang in on difficult situations and confront negative behavior
  - —Is courageous
- Has an awareness of personal power
  - —Is nonauthoritarian and nonthreatening
  - —Has personal integrity
  - —Is respectful and considerate of others, honest, truthful, and trustworthy
- Has a sense of humor and does not take him or herself too seriously

INEFFECTIVE OR BAD SUPERVISORS

No discussion of the qualities and attributes of effective supervisors would be complete without attention to the area of ineffective or bad supervisors. A small body of research is beginning to press the alarm button about the prevalence of bad or lousy supervision and its negative impact on supervisees (Chung et al., 1998; Gray, Ladany, Walker, & Ancis, 2001; Magnuson, Wilcoxon, & Norem, 2000). Shockingly, a number of these studies indicate that the rate for bad supervision experiences of some type is as high as 50 percent (Nelson & Friedlander, 2001; Worthen & McNeil, 1999).

While there are a number of descriptors for bad and ineffective supervisors, the foremost appears to be apathy or a "lack of investment in supervision" on the part of supervisors (Ellis, 2001, p. 404). This lack of interest in supervision can take the form of not being available, paying inadequate attention to supervision, being chronically late, canceling supervision appointments, failing to offer feedback or suggestions, working on paperwork or the computer during supervision sessions, allowing continuous interruptions, and being generally unproductive during supervision sessions (Ellis, 2001; Magnuson et al., 2000; Wulf & Nelson, 2001).

Other examples of poor supervisor behaviors run the gamut from lack of expertness, little support for autonomy, disorganization, excessively nondirective behavior, lack of attention to evaluation (such as not being forthcoming about problems with the supervisee's skills until final evaluation), excessive criticalness, unwillingness to ask for or respond to a supervisee's thoughts or feelings (emotional neglect), intolerance for differences in style or theoretical model, stereotypical viewpoint on multicultural differences, problems with boundary setting with supervisees (such as turning supervision into psychotherapy for supervisees), too much time spent on administrative detail and not enough on helping supervisees develop clinical expertise, or having the primary focus of supervision be helping the supervisor with his or her cases (Anderson et al., 2000; Campbell, 2001–2005; Ellis, 2001; Magnuson et al., 2000; Veach, 2001). Rapid Reference 1.4 summarizes qualities of ineffective supervisors.

These descriptors of bad or lousy supervision take the reader back to the initial problem identified at the beginning of this introduction: how clinical supervision is viewed today in organizations, how supervisors are selected and how much support is given to people in this role, and the importance of training supervisors. As long as the role and function of clinical supervisors is misunderstood or undervalued by organizations and administrators, such as when clinical supervision is tacked onto regu-

DON'T FORGET

Supervisors can vary in style, theoretical models, gender, race, and ethnicity and can even not be strong on the expression of warmth and still be effective as long as supervisees see them as attempting to be helpful and genuinely invested in supervision.

≡ Rapid Reference 1.4

Qualities of Ineffective or Bad Supervisors

- Unavailable
- Inconsistent
- Inconsiderate
- Dogmatic
- Closed
- Prejudiced
- Intolerant
- Inflexible
- Arrogant
- Critical
- Disinterested
- Disorganized
- Neglectful
- Untrustworthy
- Poor at setting boundaries

DON'T FORGET

....

Supervisees need to be encouraged to know their rights and responsibilities and to speak up about bad or harmful supervision.

lar job duties without reducing other work demands, and supervisors are selected by convenience or availability, not skill or training, poor supervision will continue to be a recurring problem (Campbell, 2001–2005).

THE IMPORTANCE OF TRAINING SUPERVISORS

If supervision is a different relationship than counseling or psychotherapy, everyone would ethically be bound to receive training in order to achieve full competency in the role. To be effective and successful as a clinical supervisor in today's world, supervisors need to understand the nature of supervision, what it is, and what it isn't. They need to take into account the hierarchical nature of clinical supervision and the factor of low or no choice that places issues such as safety and trust into the foreground of any supervision experience. Additionally, today's clinical supervisors have to be mindful of all of the contextual and systems variables that influence the supervisory relationship and develop skills and strategies to effectively manage their impact.

The importance of training supervisors needs also to be emphasized. No longer can supervisors rely merely on their experiences in supervision or their expertise with clients to be effective supervisors. Supervision training has been found to improve confidence and self-awareness, contribute to a decrease in dogmatism and criticalness on the part of supervisors, and in the case of a residential treatment center, even lead to a rejuvenation on the part of the staff (Foster & McAdams, 1998; McMahon & Simons, 2004; Steven et al., 1998).

In closing, clinical supervision is a complex topic with many issues that need to be addressed. With understanding, forethought, and planning, the role can be exciting and fulfilling. Through modeling, teaching, training, and mentoring, clinical supervisors have an opportunity to shape the future of the mental health field. The purpose of this book is to provide clinical supervisors with essential information and practical ideas to increase competence and effectiveness, promote ethical practice, stimulate innovation, and generate excitement for this important role.

HOW TO USE THIS BOOK

Writing a handbook for the field of clinical supervision is a daunting task. Clinical supervisors come in all shapes and sizes and from a range of backgrounds, disciplines, and education levels. Some have a vast body of clinical and counseling experience from which to draw, so, consequently, many of the ideas in the book will seem elementary, whereas others lacking that wealth of experience or training in counseling and therapy may wish for more elucidation. For some readers this book will provide a foundation and excellent source of new ideas, while for others it will serve as a review of previously gained knowledge.

> **DON'T FORGET**
>
> Supervision is supervision: The purpose of supervision is to review supervisees' work in order to provide clients with the highest quality of care and prevent harm. This purpose of supervision is the same, regardless of discipline, setting, level of education, and training level of supervisors.

The material should be applicable to all types of supervision circumstances regardless of the supervisor's discipline, practice, setting, and level of education. However, each reader will need to tailor the information to his or her unique needs in the setting in which he or she practices. For example, some of the suggestions are more relevant for those providing counseling and psychotherapy services than for those operating in a case-management format or providing psychoeducation services. Also, a number of core ideas are repeated throughout the book so that those who do not read the book straight through but wish to simply read one section or chapter will receive all pertinent material.

For the purpose of clarity and ease of reading, certain terms are employed in this book. The term *client* rather than *patient* was selected as a generic term

Putting It Into Practice

A Common Error in Clinical Supervision

Susan, a licensed social worker at a community agency, was appointed clinical supervisor. She was seen as a highly skilled therapist who did excellent work with clients. She was well organized, timely with her paperwork, and a good team member. Although she had received no formal training in supervision, Susan felt confident that with her expertise she could be an excellent supervisor and looked forward to the challenge. However, within a few weeks, problems began to occur. Susan was puzzled, confused, and unsure how to proceed.

Teaching Point: Although expertise in the area of clinical practice is a necessary component of effective supervision, the supervisory relationship is different in nature from psychotherapy and counseling. Success and competency in one area does not preclude success in the other. To be effective, supervisors need to understand the purpose of supervision and its nature and quality and seek out specialized training in this important field.

to refer to the person receiving services. *Clinical supervision,* rather than *counselor* or *psychotherapy supervision,* was selected for the same reason. The *supervisor* is the person giving clinical supervision and the *supervisee* is the person receiving the supervision. *Supervisee* rather than *trainee* was selected because in many instances, supervision involves practitioners far beyond the entry stage. The term *mental health field* is meant to encompass behavioral health specialties such as substance abuse, school counseling, and nursing along with social work, marriage and family counseling, and other social service providers.

🐾 TEST YOURSELF 🐾

1. **The role of the clinical supervisor is teacher, trainer, mentor, monitor, and evaluator.** True or False?

2. **If clinical supervisors have 3 years of experience working with clients, they can automatically be good supervisors.** True or False?

3. **There is a significant body of empirical research in clinical supervision to reassure all supervisors in their practice.** True or False?

4. **Two factors that distinguish clinical supervision from consultation and psychotherapy are**
   (a) the evaluative component and the nonvoluntary nature of the relationship.
   (b) there are no real differences.
   (c) clinical supervision is usually more fun to do because supervisees can ignore what supervisors ask them to do and do what they want.
   (d) supervisees don't have advanced degrees and only meet for supervision when there is a crisis.

5. **The qualities and characteristics of an effective supervisor mirror those of an effective psychotherapist.** True or False?

6. **There is little cause for concern that clinical supervision can ever be harmful to supervisees.** True or False?

7. **The primary cause of most lousy supervision is**
   (a) lack of attention given to the role.
   (b) misinformation about purpose and function of supervisors.
   (c) high criticalness and dogmatism.
   (d) only a.
   (e) only c.
   (f) a, b, and c.

8. **There are no significant differences between an administrative supervisor and a clinical supervisor.** True or False?

(continued)

9. **Clinical supervisors, in order to practice ethically, need only refer to their state laws and agency policies.** True or False?

10. **When appointed administrative supervisor along with clinical supervisor, you would need to**

    (a) work hard to establish clear boundaries between the two roles.

    (b) not do much because both roles are the same.

    (c) be glad for the promotion because putting the two roles together will be less work.

    (d) understand potential for harm that may come from role conflict and confusion with supervisees.

    (e) do both a and d.

    (f) do both b and c.

11. **As everyone knows the role of a clinical supervisor, there is no need for training in supervision.** True or False?

12. **Name two key features present in clinical supervision that supervisors must know about in order to be effective as a clinical supervisor.**

13. **Clinical supervision can be stressful at times. One factor that can contribute to stress in supervision is**

    (a) organizational needs.

    (b) lack of organizational support for supervision.

    (c) role confusion.

    (d) no training in supervision.

    (e) low level of competence as a supervisor.

    (f) all of the above.

14. **Supervisees, regardless of education and experience, want and need support and acceptance from their supervisors.** True or False?

15. **Two important variables for success as a supervisor are**

    (a) aloofness, and absolute certainty that they are right at all times.

    (b) willingness to give supervisees constant and continuous detailed corrective feedback about what they are doing.

    (c) commitment to the role of clinical supervisor and to supervisees' growth and development.

Answers: 1. True; 2. False; 3. False; 4. a; 5. True; 6. False; 7. f; 8. True; 9. False; 10. e; 11. False; 12. Evaluation (hierarchical nature) and nonvoluntary nature of the relationship (low to no choice); 13. f; 14. True; 15. c

Two

ETHICAL AND LEGAL ISSUES IN SUPERVISION (BY BARBARA HERLIHY)

As was emphasized throughout the introductory chapter, a key goal of supervision is to ensure that clients receive competent, ethical services. A number of ethical issues inevitably arise and must be dealt with in supervision. Some issues that pertain both to the relationship between supervisor and supervisee and the relationship between supervisee and client include securing informed consent, ensuring competence, and maintaining relationship boundaries. A supervisory function that has both legal and ethical implications is gatekeeping for the profession. Legal issues that cause concern among supervisors are vicarious liability and malpractice. These topics are examined in this chapter.

INFORMED CONSENT

Informed Consent for Supervisees

The rationale for informed consent in counseling can be stated in simple terms: Clients have a right to know what they are getting into when they come for counseling (Remley & Herlihy, 2005). This same principle applies equally to the supervisory relationship. Supervisees have a right to be fully informed, at the outset, about what supervision will entail.

The right of supervisees to receive informed consent creates a responsibility on the part of the supervisor to provide supervisees with a great deal of information. No matter how thoroughly supervisees are prepared, supervision will inevitably hold some surprises for them. However, these surprises should be due to the learning process itself and the complexity of human functioning, not due to carelessness or omissions on the part of the supervisor (Bernard & Goodyear, 2004). Information that supervisors should discuss with supervisees during their initial meeting includes the following:

- *Purposes of supervision.* All supervision shares the same general purpose of fostering the professional growth and enhancing the skills of the supervisee while protecting the client from harm. It is not unusual, however, for supervisees to embark on the supervisory process with a kind of tunnel vision that is focused on the end goal of completing a prescribed number of clock hours to fulfill an internship requirement or to obtain a license to practice. When a supervision relationship is undertaken with the intent of having the supervisor sign off on the required hours, there is little chance that supervision will be a growth-producing experience for the supervisee (Remley & Herlihy, 2005). Beginning the supervisory relationship with a discussion of the goals and purposes of supervision helps to establish that professional growth will be the focus of supervision.

- *Information about the supervisor.* Supervisees need to know that their supervisors are qualified by training, experience, and credentials so that they will feel confident that the supervisory relationship will benefit them. Therefore, supervisors need to describe their qualifications. Because there are likely to be differences in perspective that need to be negotiated (particularly when the supervisor and supervisee are from different disciplines within the mental health field), supervisors should explain their theoretical orientations and supervisory styles and discuss any potential problems that could be created by differences that exist.

- *Expectations, roles, and responsibilities.* Just as clients sometimes have very little notion of what to expect in counseling, supervisees may enter a supervisory relationship having given little thought to the specific responsibilities they will be expected to fulfill. The supervisor has a responsibility to explain the nature of the supervisory relationship, how evaluation will be conducted, and how boundaries will be managed. If the supervisor is providing administrative as well as clinical supervision to the supervisee, distinctions between the responsibilities of the two roles should be clarified.

    Supervisors need to make their requirements clear regarding what they expect from their supervisees in terms of taking responsibility for their own learning. Does the supervisor want them to make and review tapes of their counseling sessions? Come to supervision sessions prepared with specific questions? Do outside reading and attend professional development seminars? Present cases for consultation? A crucial question to address is how the supervisee will be evaluated, including processes, procedures, and timing for ongoing and summative evaluation.

Some writers (Bernard & Goodyear, 2004; Remley & Herlihy, 2005) have recommended the use of a written supervision agreement that is reviewed and signed by both parties. This kind of contract can articulate the details of the supervisory relationship and help to avoid later misunderstandings.

- *Logistics of supervision.* A discussion of logistics should lead to an agreement on a myriad of details: frequency of supervision sessions, duration of sessions, fees and payment arrangements (if applicable), forms of documentation that will be required from both the supervisor and supervisee, modalities of supervision that will be used (such as video- or audiotaping, live supervision, case consultation, group and individual supervision), procedures for handling emergency situations, and any contractual obligations of both parties that will need to be fulfilled.

- *Ethical and legal considerations.* It is risky business for supervisors to assume that their supervisees have been taught and know all they need to know about ethical and legal counseling practice. Supervisors are, to some extent, responsible for the acts of their supervisees. Supervisors can protect themselves and safeguard the welfare of their supervisees' clients when they ascertain at the beginning of the supervisory relationship whether there are areas of ethical and legal practice in which the supervisee may need further instruction or clarification (Remley & Herlihy, 2005). When deficits in knowledge or skill are noted, the supervisor would be wise to assume an instructional role and assure that the supervisee acquires the needed competencies.

Rapid Reference 2.1 summarizes the elements of informed consent for supervision. More detailed information and examples can be found in Chapter 6 under documentation of supervision.

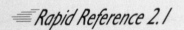

Rapid Reference 2.1

Elements of Informed Consent for Supervisees

- Purposes of supervision
- Information about the supervisor
- Expectations, roles, and responsibilities
- Logistics of supervision
- Ethical and legal considerations

Informed Consent for Clients of Supervisees

The supervisee's clients must be informed that their counselor is under supervision. Sometimes supervisees are tempted to gloss over the fact that they are under supervision, out of a fear that their clients may have less confidence in their abilities to provide competent services. Supervisors should ensure that these fears do not inhibit supervisees from informing clients of their supervision status. If clients seem uneasy about the idea that a supervisor, who is a faceless stranger to them, will be listening to audiotapes of their counseling sessions or watching from behind a one-way mirror, arrangements might be made (if possible) for the client to meet the supervisor to express any concerns and ask questions directly (Remley & Herlihy, 2005).

Clients need to understand how supervision affects their confidentiality. Because supervisors will have access to confidential client information, clients should be informed regarding what information about them will be shared, with whom, and for what purposes. Will the supervisor be reviewing tapes of counseling sessions? Reading clinical case notes? Observing counseling sessions from behind a one-way mirror? If the supervisee is receiving group supervision as well as individual supervision, clients need to know this and also to understand that the supervisee will protect their identities when discussing their cases within the group format.

Sharing client information with a clinical supervisor is ethically acceptable and is not considered a breach of the client's confidentiality. The umbrella of confidentiality is understood to be extended to other professionals (such as supervisors, consultants, or fellow members of a treatment team) with whom a counselor shares client information when the purpose is to improve services to clients (Remley & Herlihy, 2005).

Privileged communication is the legal counterpart to confidentiality. Supervisees need to know whether their relationships with their clients are considered to be privileged under the law in the state where they practice. Generally, the answer depends on whether the supervisor's communications with clients are privileged. Privilege is usually extended to assistants and supervisees of professionals who themselves have privileged communication with their clients (Remley & Herlihy, 2005).

From an ethical perspective, it is important for supervisors to remember that they share the same obligations to client confidentiality as does the supervisee. Supervisors must maintain the confidentiality of any materials in their possession that may contain identifying information about clients, and they need to ensure that tapes of sessions are erased after they have served their purpose.

COMPETENCE

In the past, it was generally assumed that a professional who was a skilled

DON'T FORGET

Clients of supervisees must be informed that their counselor is working under supervision.

practitioner would also make a good supervisor. Today, it is recognized that being a highly competent practitioner of one's profession does not necessarily translate into being a competent supervisor and that supervision requires a specialized knowledge base and unique skills.

Competence in supervision is an elusive concept that can be difficult to define, particularly because competence is not an either-or characteristic. Competence exists on a continuum with maximum professional effectiveness on one end and gross negligence or incompetence at the other extreme. Generally speaking, however, competence as a supervisor is viewed as a quality that can be intentionally acquired through training, credentials, and experience.

To become a competent supervisor, it is necessary to acquire specific training in supervision. Professional organizations of most mental health professions make this obligation explicit to their members. For example, the Association for Counselor Education and Supervision's (ACES) *Ethical Guidelines for Counseling Supervisors* (1993) require that those who undertake a supervisory role receive training in supervision before taking on that role, and the National Association for Social Workers (NASW) *Code of Ethics* (1999) requires social workers to have the knowledge and skills needed to supervise properly. Best-practice standards for competent supervision in counseling, as described in the ACES "Standards for Counseling Supervisors" (1990), include the following knowledge and skill components:

- Effectiveness as a counselor
- Attitudes and traits such as sensitivity to individual differences, motivation and commitment to supervision, and comfort with the authority inherent in the supervisory role
- Knowledge of and skill in applying ethical, legal, and regulatory dimensions of supervision
- Understanding of the professional and personal nature of supervision and the impact of supervision on the supervisee
- Understanding of the methods and techniques of supervision
- Appreciation for the process of counselor development as it unfolds in supervision
- Skill in case conceptualization and case management
- Ability to evaluate performance fairly and accurately and to provide constructive feedback
- Knowledge of oral and written reporting and recording procedures
- Knowledge of the rapidly expanding body of theory and research about supervision

Credentials are another possible means to gauge competence as a supervisor. Although a license or certification is required to practice most mental health professions, there is no standardized credentialing process for supervision. Counselor licensure boards in some states (e.g., California, Louisiana, Ohio, Texas) require those who supervise counselor interns not only to be licensed as counselors but also to hold a separate credential as a board-approved supervisor. The American Association for Marriage and Family Therapy (AAMFT) also offers an approved supervisory credential. The Center for Credentialing and Education (CCE), an affiliate of the NBCC, offers a national supervisory credential, but it is a voluntary credential. As was noted in the introductory chapter, supervisor competence is a vital issue that remains to be addressed on a consistent basis by the mental health professions.

The third criterion for achieving competence is clinical experience. Supervisors are expected to be well experienced in the areas of client services in which they are supervising. It would be impossible for any supervisor to have the breadth and depth of experience that would be needed to be competent to supervise in every specialty area, in every practice setting, and with every type of clientele who might present for services. Therefore, those who intend to provide supervision should be very clear about the kinds of cases they would not supervise (e.g., genetic counseling, child sexual abuse, or gerontological counseling if the supervisor lacks experience with these issues) and the kinds of settings that are outside their range of experience (e.g., inpatient treatment facilities for the chronically mentally ill if the supervisor's experience is limited to the school setting).

In many cases, supervisors do not have the luxury of choosing whom they will supervise. Difficult questions regarding supervisor competence arise when professionals are required to supervise the work of someone from a different discipline than their own or to provide supervision of work with a clientele with whom the supervisor has little training or experience. Supervisors in these situations are vulnerable to accusations of practicing beyond the boundaries of their competence, which would be an ethical violation. Several options are available to professionals who are required by their employers to provide supervision in such instances, although none of the options are particularly appealing. The supervisors can seek additional training to learn about the unfamiliar discipline or clientele, they can state to their employers their objections to being required to provide the supervision and explain the rationale for their objections, or they can themselves seek supervision of their supervision. Having a record of one's objections could help to provide a defense against any future charge of practicing beyond one's competence. Working under supervision of supervision while seeking further training would help to ensure that adequate services are provided while supervisors are stretching their boundaries of competence to encompass the new supervisory responsibilities.

Multicultural Competence

An aspect of supervisor competence that is receiving a great deal of attention in the literature is multicultural competence. In our increasingly diverse society, it is essential that supervisors are multiculturally competent. It is impossible for supervisors to give supervisees knowledge and skills that the supervisors do not themselves possess (Haynes, Corey, & Moulton, 2003). The type of supervision relationship that is most effective in facilitating supervisee growth is a progressive relationship in which the supervisor is at a more advanced level of cultural identity development than the supervisee (Helms & Cook, 1999). Thus, before beginning to supervise, supervisors must gain personal awareness and insight regarding their own multiple cultural identities. These identities have been shaped by experiences of privilege and marginalization based membership in various cultural groups (based on such factors as socioeconomic class, gender, race or ethnicity, sexual orientation, religion, and disability status). Supervisors must first assess their own levels of cultural identity development and then address the cultural identity development of their supervisees. If they neglect to do this, they may inadvertently perpetuate stereotyping, misdiagnosis, and culturally insensitive practice on the part of their supervisees (Hays & Chang, 2003). By contrast, research has shown that addressing cultural identity development makes the supervisory relationship and process more effective (Ladany, Brittan-Powell, & Pannu, 1997; Ladany, Inman, Constantine, & Hofheinz, 1997).

Because it is the supervisor who holds the power in the supervisory relationship, it is the *supervisor's* responsibility to raise the issue of cultural diversity in supervision (Bernard & Goodyear, 2004; Estrada, Frame, & Williams, 2004; Haynes et al., 2003; Ryde, 2000). Many supervisors feel anxious about addressing cultural differences. In a study by Constantine (1997), 40 percent of supervisees reported that their supervisors seemed reluctant to bring up and discuss cultural issues. However, if supervisors remain silent, they will be sending the implicit message to their supervisees that such topics are taboo. The question is not *whether* to bring diversity into the conversation but *how* to do so.

The essential first step is for supervisors to create a climate of honesty and trust in which supervisees will feel safe to speak openly about cultural diversity issues (Estrada et al., 2004; Haynes et al., 2003). Hays and Chang (2003) have suggested that supervisors can create a safe climate through personal self-disclosures, by sharing with their supervisees how their own cultural heritage influences their counseling and supervisory relationships. Once this safe climate has been established, Haynes et al. have suggested that supervisors ask supervisees directly about their cultural identities and how these may affect their practice of counseling. This can be accomplished by including multicultural competencies in the supervision agreement and using them as a vehicle to open the discussion. Estrada et al. have suggested other strategies that could be collaboratively employed by the supervisor and supervisee, including the construction and discussion of cultural genograms, the use of racial identity development inventories as a springboard for discussion of personal and cultural perspectives that may shape the work of the supervisee and the supervisor, and mutually undertaking the task of learning about the cultural contexts of the supervisee's clients.

> **DON'T FORGET**
> ....
> It is the supervisor's responsibility to raise the issue of cultural diversity in supervision.

It is vital that supervisors model cultural sensitivity for their supervisees, promote culturally appropriate interventions, and conduct multicultural case conceptualizations with supervisees. Regardless of cultural differences or similarities within the supervision triad, it is the supervisor's cultural competence and openness that will dictate whether the supervisee learns and grows as a multiculturally competent counselor (Bernard & Goodyear, 2004).

BOUNDARY ISSUES IN SUPERVISION

The codes of ethics of all the major mental health professions caution against entering into a dual relationship whenever a power differential exists between two parties, such as a counselor and client or supervisor and supervisee. Despite this caution, the codes recognize that dual relationships cannot always be avoided nor are they necessarily always harmful. The complexities involved in maintaining appropriate boundaries in counseling and supervision have made dual relationships one of the most controversial of all ethical issues in the helping professions (Herlihy & Corey, 1997).

Boundaries in the Supervisor-Supervisee Relationship

The supervisory role creates some unique boundary issues. It is important to keep in mind that not all forms of dual relating are unethical. The key criteria for determining whether a dual relationship in supervision is ethically problematic are (1) the likelihood that the supervisor's judgment will be impaired and (2) the risk that the supervisee will be exploited. A second point to remember is that dual relationships in supervision really cannot be avoided. Dual and even multiple relationships are inherent in the supervisory position (Borders, 1997) and cannot be regulated out of existence (Peterson, 1993). The question is not how to *avoid* dual or multiple relationships in supervision but, rather, how to best *manage* them.

One of the most difficult questions related to boundaries in the supervisory relationship is how to distinguish between counseling and supervision. Possibly, the confusion stems in part from the terminology used in some of the most popular models of supervision, including Bernard's (1997) discrimination model. In the discrimination model, three supervisor roles that are identified are counselor, teacher, and consultant. Yet ethical guidelines make it clear that the supervisor is not to function as a counselor to the supervisee. The *Ethical Guidelines for Counseling Supervisors* (ACES, 1993) states that supervisors should not establish a psychotherapeutic relationship as a substitute for supervision. In other words, the supervisor must not convert a supervision session into a counseling session when a supervisee's personal issues become the focus of the conversation. Yet the personal growth and professional growth of the supervisee are so inextricably intertwined that it is almost impossible to draw a clear line between them. Supervisors would miss important opportunities to foster supervisee development if they were to refuse to explore how the personhood of supervisees impacts and is impacted by their work as counselors. When personal issues arise for the supervisee, the key is to keep the focus on how these issues affect the supervisee's clients and professional functioning.

If the personal issues of supervisees appear to be having a negative effect on their work with clients, it is the supervisor's responsibility to recommend that they seek counseling to resolve these issues. Recommending to supervisees that they seek counseling infuses an emotion-laden issue into the relationship, as the supervisees may feel that they have been judged to be incompetent. The supervisory relationship might become strained, and supervisees might be less open about discussing their own experiencing within the supervision sessions (Herlihy & Corey, 1997). On the other hand, converting a supervision relationship into a counseling relationship is inappropriate because it shifts the focus away from the welfare of clients. Maintaining this delicate balance when the supervisee's personal

CAUTION

Supervisors must not allow a supervisory relationship to become a counseling relationship.

issues emerge in supervision requires a constant vigilance on the part of the supervisor.

A supervisory relationship boundary that is easier to discern is the line that leads to romantic or sexual involvement. This line cannot be crossed. Sexual intimacies between supervisors and supervisees are forbidden for reasons that are obvious. Because of the power differential, the possibility always exists that the supervisee could be exploited in the relationship. The supervisor's judgment is bound to be impaired, and fair evaluation would be difficult if not impossible. Because it is the supervisor's responsibility to set the boundaries in the supervisory relationship, supervisors who find that they repeatedly feel sexually attracted to supervisees need to examine their own needs. Haynes et al. (2003) have suggested that supervisors ask themselves "What is going on in my own life that may be contributing to this occurrence? How might I be using my professional work as a way to meet my personal needs?" (p. 172). Despite all the caveats, intimate relationships sometimes do evolve in supervision. When this happens, the supervisory relationship should be ended and the supervisee transferred to another supervisor.

Although the *Ethical Guidelines for Counseling Supervisors* (ACES, 1993) states that "supervisors should not engage in any form of social contact or interaction which would compromise the supervisor-supervisee relationship" (p. 3), social relationships between supervisors and supervisees occur quite commonly and may be inevitable. A supervisor and supervisee may be colleagues in the workplace and attend many of the same social gatherings, they may attend professional conferences together, and they may share involvements in the same professional organizations. Although it has been argued that "once a client, always a client," that claim is not made about supervisees. There is likely to be some relaxing of the boundaries as supervisees near the end of their supervision experience (Herlihy & Corey, 1997). As the supervisee matures professionally, supervision becomes more consultative in nature. Supervisees evolve into professional colleagues, and it is unnecessary to be overly concerned about dual relationships that occur "within the positive context of a maturing professional relationship" (Bernard & Goodyear, 2004, p. 60).

Boundaries between Supervisees and Clients

Although supervisors would rest more easily if they could guarantee that their supervisees would always behave ethically, there is really no way to ensure that this will happen. Judging from the amount of literature on the topic, it appears that one of the worst nightmares of supervisors is that a supervisee will become sexually involved with a client. Most writers (e.g., Bridges, 1999; Ladany et al., 1997; Samuel & Gorton, 1998) have recommended that supervisors be proactive in preventing supervisee boundary violations by raising the topic of potential sexual attraction to clients. It is crucial that supervisors create a safe climate in which supervisees feel free to discuss sensitive issues such as feeling a sexual attraction to a client or dealing with a sexually seductive client. Supervisors need to be prepared to help their supervisees grapple with the complexities of boundary issues, consider the cultural and contextual variables that may be involved, and develop their ethical reasoning skills as problematic situations arise.

EVALUATION AND GATEKEEPING

Supervisors are ethically obligated to provide fair, objective, and accurate evaluations of their supervisees. Supervisors and supervisees alike often feel uncomfortable and anxious about evaluation, and supervisors may be tempted to avoid dealing with it when feedback will not be positive. Avoiding the responsibility, however, can have serious consequences. A supervisee could sue a supervisor who provides an inaccurately negative evaluation that prevents the supervisee from obtaining licensure, employment, or a graduate degree (Haynes et al., 2003).

One of the purposes of evaluation is to facilitate the supervisee's skill acquisition and professional growth. To accomplish this goal, evaluation needs to be an ongoing process that occurs throughout the supervisory relationship. When the supervisor assesses the supervisee to be deficient in the acquisition of skills, opportunities must be provided for remediation. The supervisor needs to be prepared to describe clearly to the supervisee the specific competencies that are targeted for improvement, criteria for successful performance, methods of assessment, and the time frame within which the improvement must occur. When the supervisee's deficiencies are limited to discrete skills or identifiable gaps in knowledge, remediation plans have a good chance for success. See Chapter 6 for more material on goal setting and evaluation.

When supervisees fail to meet minimal performance criteria due to impairment, supervisors are faced with some tough decisions. They should first attempt remediation. If the supervisee's impairment is due to issues such as substance abuse or personal problems in the supervisee's life, the supervisor may need to insist that the supervisee take a leave from his or her professional duties and seek treatment or personal counseling. If the impairment stems from a more characterological problem, such as a personality disorder, then remediation efforts may not be effective. In these instances, supervisors may need to fulfill their gatekeeper role and refuse to endorse the supervisee for graduation, licensure, or employment. Supervisors serve as gatekeepers for quality control, and this duty to the public and to the profession takes precedence over

> **DON'T FORGET**
>
> Supervisors serve as gatekeepers to the profession.

all other considerations in final evaluations of supervisees (Pearson & Piazza, 1997).

Before taking the drastic step of dismissing a supervisee from a training program or refusing to endorse a supervisee, supervisors have an ethical and legal responsibility to provide the supervisee with due process. Supervisees' rights to due process mean that they must be given specific and ongoing feedback regarding their deficiencies and must be given opportunities to improve their performance. Supervisors are advised to provide evaluation both orally and in writing, state remediation plans in terms that are as specific and behavioral as possible, establish a timeline for achieving goals, and provide a process for the supervisee to appeal the decision (Forrest, Elman, Gizara, & Vacha-Haase, 1999). Supervisors cannot let their fear of legal reprisal from the supervisee prevent them from exercising their gatekeeping function as a measure of last resort. A strategy that supervisors can use to protect themselves legally is to consult with colleagues and get a second opinion before issuing a negative final evaluation. Chapter 8 contains more information about working with difficult supervisees and the termination of supervisees from supervision.

LEGAL CONCERNS

Two legal issues that are important for supervisors to be aware of are vicarious liability and malpractice. This chapter concludes with an explanation of the concept and application of vicarious liability and some suggestions for risk management (malpractice prevention).

Vicarious Liability

Supervisors often are quite concerned about whether they can be held legally responsible for any mistakes of their supervisees that might cause harm to a client. The legal principle of vicarious liability holds that individuals who have control and authority over others will be held accountable for the negligence of those under their control. According to Remley and Herlihy (2005), the amount of control that an administrative or clinical supervisor has over the supervisee will in large part determine the degree to which the supervisor will be held responsible. Thus, it seems more likely that a supervisee's direct administrative supervisor would be held responsible, while a supervisor who is not employed at the same work site as the supervisee and meets only weekly with the supervisee would be less likely to be held accountable. However, the issue is not that simple. What is equally important is whether the supervisor knew or should have known about the supervisee's negligent acts. Lack of awareness is not an adequate legal defense for a supervisor (Remley & Herlihy, 2005). If the supervisor was aware of the problem but made an incorrect judgment in trying to rectify the problem, the supervisor has a good chance of not being found liable. Yet if the supervisor was unaware and should have been more vigilant, vicarious liability is more likely to be imposed. Close monitoring of supervisee performance is crucial.

Avoiding Malpractice

Although malpractice lawsuits against supervisors are not all that common, they are a source of considerable anxiety for supervisors. Practicing sound risk management strategies is vital for supervisor self-protection, and there are a number of excellent strategies that supervisors can use. As has been noted previously, establishing a trusting and open relationship with the supervisee is essential so that the supervisee is willing to admit and discuss uncertainties and mistakes. Mental health professionals should always carry professional liability insurance that covers their work as supervisors, and they should ensure that their supervisees also have insurance coverage. Rapid Reference 2.2 lists several malpractice prevention strategies.

Many problems can be avoided by practicing within one's boundaries of competence as a supervisor. Carefully documenting one's supervision is extremely important and will be vital if the supervisor should need to provide evidence in court of competent supervisory practice. If a negative final recommendation was made

Rapid Reference 2.2

Malpractice Prevention Strategies

- Establish an open and trusting supervisory relationship
- Maintain professional liability insurance
- Practice within the boundaries of your competence
- Document carefully
- Respect the due process rights of supervisees
- Consult with colleagues
- Keep up to date with evolving ethical standards and legal developments

and the supervisee brings suit, the supervisor must be able to show that problems were identified, a remediation plan was developed, and the supervisee was afforded due process.

Consulting with colleagues and experts when questions and difficult issues arise is an excellent strategy for risk management. Courts apply a standard of care that basically asks whether the professional acted in a way similar to how other similarly trained professionals would have acted in the same situation. If supervisors can demonstrate that they consulted and that the consultants recommended the course of action that the supervisors actually followed, they will have a good defense against malpractice.

In summary, supervision entails significant responsibilities, both ethically and legally. Fortunately, all of these responsibilities can be managed effectively if supervisors are well prepared for their supervisory role, practice supervision conscientiously, and keep up to date with developments in the ethical and legal arenas.

Putting It Into Practice

Case Example

Katherine is in private practice as a marriage and family therapist in a small, rural community and has been asked by the director of a nearby county mental health agency that serves emotionally disturbed adults to supervise Megan, a new counselor who is working at the agency. Megan has recently married and moved to town after graduating with a master's degree in counseling. She now wishes to pursue her professional counselor licensure, but there is no one at the agency who is qualified to supervise her for this license. Even though Katherine has never done supervision, she tells the director she will be glad to do it as a favor. After all, Megan has an on-site supervisor who meets with her regularly to discuss cases, so it shouldn't be very difficult. However, at the first meeting, Megan says she does not have any confidence in the competency of her on-site supervisor and so feels relieved to have another supervisor off-site who is competent and will be able to tell her "the right thing to do with her clients." Katherine is uncomfortable but reassures Megan that she does know what she is doing and so Megan can call her any time she doesn't know how to proceed with one of her clients.

Teaching Point: The first ethical issue is that Katherine has no training in supervision, no credential to qualify her to supervise a post-degree candidate for licensure purposes, and no background or experience with the client population that Megan is serving. Katherine needs to use an informed consent agreement to clarify her role and relationship not only with Megan but also with the agency director and the on-site supervisor.

(continued)

There are also a number of dual relationship issues as well as problems with confidentiality of information that should be considered and discussed. Of particular concern to everyone should be how Katherine is to proceed if she feels concerned about something Megan tells her is happening at the agency that could involve serious risk to clients. It would be unethical and could lead to some serious problems if Katherine, as an off-site supervisor, tries to advise Megan on her client cases, especially those that involve danger and risk, unless she is asked by the site supervisor or administrator. Both ethically and from a liability standpoint, Katherine needs to be able to consult with the on-site supervisor if she has concerns about a client situation and needs to encourage Megan to do the same.

 TEST YOURSELF

1. **Clinical supervisors are ethically required to inform all clients of**
    (a) the supervisory process.
    (b) the impact on their care and confidentiality.
    (c) the status of the supervisee.
    (d) what methods will be used for supervision.
    (e) how to find them if have any concerns or questions.
    (f) all of the above.

2. **Taking time to document clinical supervisory activities in some manner is a good idea for any malpractice prevention plan.** True or False?

3. **Supervisors must maintain the same obligations to client confidentiality as does the supervisee.** True or False?

4. **To be a competent supervisor**
    (a) it is not necessary to get training in supervision.
    (b) it is sufficient to be skilled with clients.
    (c) it is important to get training in supervision.
    (d) it is sufficient to do with your supervisees what your supervisor did with you.

5. **The criterion for competence in supervision is**
    (a) training in supervision.
    (b) credentials in supervision.
    (c) competence in clinical practice with clients.
    (d) all of the above.
    (e) only b and c.

6. **It is important for supervisors to assess their own level of cultural identity development before they can address cultural issues in supervision.** True or False?

7. **To bring diversity into conversations with supervisees**
   (a) create a climate of safety and trust.
   (b) use personal self-disclosure.
   (c) employ cultural genograms.
   (d) talk about issues of diversity as part of practice with clients.
   (e) do all of the above.
   (f) do only a and d.

8. **What is the key criterion in deciding if dual relationships in supervision could be problematic?**
   (a) Risk that supervisee could be exploited
   (b) Likelihood supervisor's judgment will be impaired
   (c) Prior knowledge of the supervisee
   (d) Age, gender, and sexual preference of the supervisee
   (e) Only a and b
   (f) All of the above

9. **Sexual intimacy with supervisees**
   (a) is allowed if the supervisee consents.
   (b) is usually not a good idea.
   (c) is forbidden always.
   (d) can help build rapport and trust.

10. **To avoid becoming a therapist to a supervisee**
    (a) keep exploration focused on clients and professional functioning with clients.
    (b) never bring up the topic of the supervisee's thoughts and feelings about clients.
    (c) move back behind the desk when discussing anything personal.
    (d) dress in a suit and tie.

11. **Boundaries around social relationships with supervisees are less important as supervisees evolve into professional colleagues.** True or False?

12. **Supervisors' only function is to teach and train the next generation of counselors and therapists.** True or False?

13. ***Vicarious liability* is a legal term for supervisors carrying responsibility for actions of their supervisees with clients.** True or False?

(continued)

14. Consultation with other supervisors

    (a) is an excellent risk management strategy.

    (b) is a waste of time.

    (c) is not necessary because the supervisor is an expert.

    (d) is part of standard-of-care criteria used by the courts.

    (e) should only be employed if the supervisor knows he or she has really screwed up.

    (f) a and d.

    (g) none of the above.

15. Name at least two malpractice prevention strategies for supervisors.

Answers: 1. f; 2. True; 3. True; 4. c; 5. d; 6. True; 7. e; 8. a and b; 9. c; 10. a; 11. True; 12. False; 13. True; 14. f; 15. Establish an open and trusting supervisory relationship; maintain professional liability insurance; practice within the boundaries of your competence; document carefully; respect the due process rights of supervisees; consult with colleagues; keep up to date with evolving ethical standards and legal developments.

Three

MODELS OF CLINICAL SUPERVISION

Traditional clinical supervision is based on an apprenticeship-master model. Trainees learned their craft through observing a skilled practitioner work with patients and then practicing under the expert's tutelage. Learning was considered a socialization process. It flowed from supervisor to supervisee, and, as a result, new practitioners not only learned clinical skills but also cultural norms and unwritten rules of the profession (Hawkins & Shohet, 2003). Freud expounded on this apprenticeship-master model by requiring all would-be analysts to be in analysis with an expert psychoanalyst in order to learn the art.

The field of clinical supervision is long on tradition but short on improvements. As an area of specialization within the allied health profession, there has been slow realization of the need for innovation in supervision practice, models, methods, and techniques. New supervisors still proceed based on their own experiences in clinical supervision and rely on traditional approaches rather than seeking out new supervision-specific models.

POPULAR APPROACHES TO CLINICAL SUPERVISION

There are several popular approaches to clinical supervision that beginning supervisors might mistakenly assume are the only viable choices available. Therefore, it is important to discuss these approaches and delineate significant pitfalls and problems that exist with each of them before turning to current supervision research and writing.

The No-Model Model

In this supervision model, clinical supervisors are selected or appointed because they are excellent therapists, clinicians, or counselors, not because they have training in supervision. Supervisors using this model say to themselves, "I am a competent clinician; therefore, I will be a competent supervisor. I will just do with my supervisees what my supervisors did with me." Usually the no-model model represents a reactive, retrospective approach to supervision. The focus is on putting out fires in severe cases and depends heavily on supervisees' ability to identify their problems and willingness to ask for help with them. The following statement embodies this supervision approach: "Let me know if you have any problems. My door is always open."

Numerous problems abound with this model. First, supervisees are not clients, and so supervision requires different skills, methods, and techniques. Second, simply repeating what someone else did in the past may not lead to success in the present. Certainly this approach does not encourage innovation. Last, relying totally on a supervisee's judgment and forthrightness about problems might be a recipe for disaster. With the no-model model, only limited attempts are made to monitor supervisees' activities, and no real planning is engaged in nor serious involvement undertaken in the teaching and training function. As supervisors are ethically and legally responsible for the activities of supervisees in terms of client care, supervisors should be much more active and involved in training and monitoring supervisees. (See Chapter 2 on ethical and legal issues in supervision.)

The Expert Model

The expert model of clinical supervision is the traditional model of supervision found within the medical community. This model proposes that the clinical supervisor is a master and the intern or trainee a blank slate who learns how to do the work by following this expert around, watching and imitating the expert's actions. In this approach, it is assumed the supervisor, as the expert, has all the knowledge and therefore directs the work of supervisees without question. During case consultation supervisees are asked to report what they have done with their patients, and the supervisor critiques these actions and makes corrective suggestions, which gives the process a right and wrong character.

Sometimes the concepts of leadership and authority are mixed into the expert model so that scores of clinical supervisors believe they have to establish their authority over supervisees, which means that to admit they are wrong or to ask supervisees what they think is viewed as a loss of leadership. Another aspect of the expert model that is important to recognize is supervision is regarded as something required for beginners or trainees, but once a certain level of experience is achieved, it is no longer necessary. Therefore, supervision beyond the initial stage of development is seen as a punishment, not an opportunity for growth.

Again, there are several potential problems with this approach. First, supervisees fearful of criticism and negative judgment might edit or be selective in what they discuss in supervision or even might avoid supervision altogether unless it is a dire emergency (Hantoot, 2000). Second, although successful in certain settings and circumstances, especially when practiced with beginning supervisees, this top-down model of authority does not take into account a supervisee's level of competence at more advanced stages of growth and development.

Therefore, while the expert model may have application with beginners, it should not be used as the singular model for delivery of clinical supervision in all cases. Rather, a more collaborative approach may be called for, especially with more experienced supervisees, to build motivation. Supervisees beyond the beginning of training need to take an active part in setting goals and solving problems. This, in turn, may increase trust, alleviate anxiety, and improve the working alliance. Also, current leadership models are stressing a more collaborative approach in order to increase motivation and satisfaction rather than the older emphasis on authority. Whether supervisors agree with this current trend, precious time and energy can be wasted in supervision dickering over this issue.

The One-Size-Fits-All Model

In this approach, clinical supervisors consider themselves in charge and, as a result, direct all activities of supervisees under their care, regardless of their expertise and level of experience. In other words, they treat all supervisees in the same way. Developmental needs, individual differences, and differing levels of competence are not taken into consideration. Nor does the supervisor attempt to experiment with different methods and techniques that may be preferred by supervisees of differing backgrounds and experience. Many times supervisors take this approach because they experience the role of clinical supervisor as a burden. As a result, they are not actively engaged in planning nor do they give supervision the time required. Others follow this approach because they mistakenly believe they have to treat everyone the same in order to be fair.

Regardless, like the expert model, the one-size-fits-all model is another top-down model of authority and leadership that is not recommended. Supervisees do vary in their competency, expertise, education, and experience level and will need these differences addressed in supervision in order to build a successful working relationship and to ensure the supervisee's continued growth and development.

The Supervisee-as-Patient Model

Unknowingly, many clinical supervisors approach supervisees as patients by thinking of them in terms of *DSM-IV-R* diagnostic categories and the five axes, particularly Axis II. When mistakes occur or problems develop, the hunt is on for finding pathology in supervisees, not in relationship factors or the situation (Hawkins & Shohet, 2003). It is important to understand that approaching supervisees through the medical model of personality assessment as used in clinical practice is not transferable to supervision. The first problem with applying this model to supervision is that it is designed to assess and treat mental illness. Hopefully, most supervisees are mentally healthy and not impaired by psychological illness. Second, it is not a model designed to teach or train individuals or to promote teamwork and motivation. Last, rarely do supervisees appreciate interpretations or assessments of their behavior by supervisors that are more appropriate for psychotherapy patients. In most cases, rather than being open to the supervisor's feedback and suggestions, supervisees may become angry or withdraw. Finally, in a handful of employment situations, even if one is asked to supervise a person for whom an Axis II diagnosis is in some way appropriate, clinical supervisors are still left to figure out how to help this person best serve his or her clients. Therefore, supervisors need to seek out models designed for supervision, not psychotherapy. It is important to make a distinction between the two.

> ## CAUTION
> ....
> The medical model of diagnosis and treatment of mental illness is not transferable to clinical supervision. Remember, supervisees are not patients.

CREATING A PERSONAL SUPERVISION MODEL

Because clinical supervision is a different relationship than psychotherapy or counseling and has different qualities and characteristics, there is an obvious need for a model of supervision separate from that utilized with clients. To create such a viable model of supervision, there are a number of factors to consider.

The first is the practitioner's discipline. Within the mental health field there are a number of different viewpoints on the process of change. Each discipline makes different assumptions that guide practice, training, and delivery of service. In general, psychiatry, nursing, and clinical psychology subscribe to a medical model of disease and illness, marriage and family therapy supports a systems viewpoint, counseling follows a relationship and strength-based foundation, social work adheres to a case

CAUTION

Recognize that diverse viewpoints exist in supervision. Be respectful, sensitive, and tolerant of differences.

management model, and substance abuse treatment for the most part subscribes to a support model. These differences among disciplines can have an immense influence on the supervisory process and, if not acknowledged and understood, can contribute to many misunderstandings and difficulties.

The second issue to consider is the theoretical model that forms the underpinning of each supervisor's clinical practice. There are a large number of supervision models based on particular theories, assumptions, and techniques of counseling and psychotherapy (e.g., psychoanalytic, cognitive, rational emotive, family systems, solution-focused, and the narrative approach). However, as most practitioners today subscribe to a technically eclectic or blended model of psychotherapy whereby the philosophical assumptions and techniques of two or more theoretical models are applied, supervisors may wish to do the same in supervision. Rapid Reference 3.1 gives a sample of concepts selected from popular psychotherapy models that have application in supervision.

Although supervisors may wish to apply concepts and techniques from their own discipline and theoretical viewpoint to create a personal model for clinical supervision, it is hoped they will take time to become familiar with the supervision literature. A number of models have been conceptualized specifically for supervision and offer a wealth of ideas. A number of these are highlighted in Rapid Reference 3.2.

Parallel Process Model or Isomorphism

Parallel process and isomorphism might be considered viewpoints rather than actual models of supervision. The term *parallel process* refers to a relationship dynamic found in supervision in which a supervisee's experience with clients will be reflected in the relationship with his or her supervisor (Doehrman, 1976). For example, when a supervisee is feeling overwhelmed and stuck in assisting a particular client, he or she may present him or herself in a similar fashion in supervision.

Isomorphism is the term family systems therapists use to describe a similar relationship phenomenon between systems and structures (Raichelson, Herron,

≡ *Rapid Reference 3.1*

Therapeutic Concepts That Apply to Supervision

Transference and countertransference: Whether one uses these exact terms, supervisors and supervisees are seen to emotionally react to each other in terms of previous experiences with authority.

Distorted thinking: Both supervisors and supervisees may be victims of illogical or irrational thinking, perfectionism, generalizations, mind reading, and so forth.

Behavioral descriptions: This is essential to goal setting, corrective feedback, and evaluation.

Social learning theory: Modeling, demonstration, and role-play are important teaching techniques to promote learning.

Social cognitive theory: This theory stresses the importance of self-efficacy in learning. Self-efficacy is the belief in one's own ability to manage different situations.

Systems change: The premise is that individuals exist in systems and that a change in one person in the system will bring change in others. Concepts such as triangulation, overfunctioning and underfunctioning, and gossip as an indicator of anxiety in the system all could be applied to supervision.

Solution-focused questions: Supervisees are understood to possess strengths and resources to solve their own problems. Questions, such as miracle questions, are designed to facilitate problem solving on the part of supervisees.

Gestalt-humanistic: This approach stresses the importance of awareness in the here and now and the need for flexibility in order to move back and forth between awareness of the moment and awareness of the larger picture.

Narrative stories: This approach stresses the importance of seeing problems from the other person's perspective and allowing the person to tell his or her story.

Primavera, & Ramirez, 1997; Storm et al., 2001). For example, resistance in supervision is viewed as an outgrowth of differences among theoretical models, not individual dynamics. Both concepts of isomorphism and parallel process recognize that relationships on any given level influence those on other levels. As a consequence, Edwards and Chen (1999) proposed a need for interactive transparency in the supervisory relationship that would include clients in the supervision process. Understanding the existence of parallel relationship dynamics in supervision will provide supervisors with a hypothesis to approach relationship difficulties throughout supervision. A more extensive discussion of the application of parallel process can be found in Chapter 8.

≡ Rapid Reference 3.2

Models of Supervision

Parallel Process

Main Assumption: A parallel exists between experience of supervisees with clients and supervisees with supervisor.

Application: Examine relationship problems with supervisees in terms of parallel relationship difficulties with clients.

Isomorphism

Main Assumption: Relationship parallels exist between systems.

Application: Look beyond the individual to understand and resolve difficulties.

Interactional

Main Assumption: Supervision is a reciprocal relationship based on mutuality of needs.

Application: Understand that relationship issues in supervision will impact client care.

Relationship

Main Assumption: The supervisory relationship is the medium through which supervision occurs.

Application: Create an atmosphere of safety and trust. Understand the role of power and authority.

Interpersonal Process Recall (IPR)

Main Assumption: Supervisees experience anxiety when beginning to work with clients.

Application: Provide supervisees with opportunities to explore affective response to clients.

Developmental

Main Assumption: The supervisor, supervisee, and supervision relationship will change in quality over time.

Application: There is a need to customize supervision based on level of development.

Interactional Supervision

Interactional supervision was developed in the field of social work by Lawrence Shulman (1993). The interactional model of supervision will be particularly useful to those who have administrative as well as clinical supervision functions or practice in a case management format.

Interactional supervision takes a systems perspective on supervision, point-

DON'T FORGET

If you want your supervisee to treat the clients with compassion and caring, you have to treat them similarly.

ing out the reciprocal nature of relationships among supervisors, supervisees, clients, and organizational systems. For example, supervisors need supervisees to do the work to serve the clients, whereas supervisees need the support of supervisors and organizational systems to accomplish this goal. This relationship interaction between supervisor, supervisee, and organizational systems will in turn influence client service. Thus, when the supervisory relationship is going well, the clients will receive excellent service. When supervision is not going well and there is anger or dissatisfaction, the client will suffer as a result.

The mutually interactive nature of supervision is also reflected in the concept of the working alliance in supervision. Bordin (1983) coined the term *working alliance* to describe the importance of mutuality of agreement on the goals and tasks for supervision and trust between supervisor and supervisee in a successful supervision experience. More on the working alliance in supervision can be found in Chapter 7. The development of self-efficacy in supervision is another area where the interactional nature of supervision and the importance of mutuality and support are evidenced (Ladany, Ellis, & Friedlander, 1999; Lehrman-Waterman & Ladany, 2001).

In conclusion, interactional supervision stresses the importance of mutuality and respect in the supervisory relationship and the powerful impact of the supervision relationship on client care.

Relationship Models

Relationship models of supervision place relationship considerations central to the supervisory process (Campbell, 2000; Kaiser, 1997; Kaiser & Barretta-Herman, 1999). Proponents of the relationship model view supervision as a complex relationship impacted strongly by issues of safety, trust, the use of power and authority, dual relationships, multicultural differences, and other contextual variables such as organizational climate, guidelines, and resources. Numerous studies demonstrate the importance of support, understanding, and safety by supervisees, regardless of their level of experience (Bischoff, Barton, Thober, & Hawley, 2002; Hart & Nance, 2003; Magnuson et al., 2000). In fact, experienced advanced supervisees view the supervision relationship as the most important aspect of high quality, desirable supervision (Campbell, 2001–2005).

Thus, in order to be effective, supervisors must focus time and attention on developing a positive working relationship with their supervisees. Supervisors need to work to create an atmosphere of safety and trust during supervision, promote shared understanding and agreement about the tasks and goals required, and be fair, respectful, and empathic toward the needs of the supervisee.

A number of factors influence the development of a positive working relationship. Kaiser (1997) has identified four key elements: accountability, personal awareness, trust and power, and the use of authority. These four elements interact with one another and affect the quality of the relationship. Recognition of potential problems, such as dual relationships, multicultural differences, and conflicting roles and expectations as well as how the supervisor plans to limit harm from these factors, is essential to defuse anxiety and improve trust in supervisees.

> **DON'T FORGET**
>
> Supervisors benefit from rejecting the authority model of supervision ("do what I tell you with no arguments") for a relationship-based interactional model. Likewise, forgoing a one-size-fits-all supervision style, which depends primarily on the self-report of supervisees, in favor of a proactive, involved, individualized problem-solving model enhances the supervision experience.

Activities such as a structured orientation, the use of a written informed consent or contract, the inclusion of supervisees in setting goals and in the evaluation process, maintaining an open system of feedback that flows both ways, and challenging assumptions with regard to multicultural differences are all practices of the relationship model.

Interpersonal Process Recall (IPR)

Interpersonal process recall points the supervisor's attention to the profoundly important role of a supervisee's thoughts and feelings on the relationship with clients and provides supervisors a means to approach this topic effectively (Kagan, 1980a; Kagan & Kagan, 1997). Norm Kagan developed IPR while training beginning counselors at Michigan State University. He became aware of the anxiety new counselors experienced in their first sessions with clients. These anxiety responses, such as the fear of being engulfed by a client's needs or the demand to be omnipotent, interfered with building of effective and ethical relationships with clients. However, many times if a supervisor attempted to point out anxiety and its potential causes to supervisees, he or she might be met with defensiveness or be seen as overstepping boundaries and functioning more as a therapist than a clinical supervisor. Thus, the primary goal of IPR is to provide clinical su-

DON'T FORGET

The goal of IPR is to provide clinical supervisors a model for the facilitation of trainees understanding of themselves and client dynamics.

pervisors with a model and method designed to facilitate trainees' understanding of themselves and client dynamics, especially the role of nonverbal behavior, in an ethical manner.

The primary means for this investigation is audio- or videotaping. The supervisee makes a tape of a client session and then sits down with the supervisor to review it. Applying IPR, the supervisor serves as a consultant to the supervisee's self-exploration through the medium of inquiry questions (Kagan & Kagan, 1997). Stopping the tape, the supervisor might inquire "What were you thinking or feeling right then when the client said [or did] that?" "I noticed that when the client began to talk about his anger, you changed the subject." Interpersonal process recall–style questions that focus supervisees' attention on themselves and the relationship process with clients could also be employed in case consultation, live, or group supervision. More material on IPR can be found in Chapter 5.

Developmental Models

Conceivably the largest area of research and writing in supervision is on developmental models. Watkins (1997) called his model the *supervisor complexity model* (SCM); Stoltenberg, McNeil, and Delworth (1998) titled their developmental model the *integrated developmental model* (IDM), and Bernard (1997) chose the name *discrimination model* for hers. The premise of these developmental models is that the supervisor, supervisee, and the supervisory relationship all grow and change over time, which certainly makes intuitive sense. It follows logically that those who wish to practice the developmental perspective need to tailor supervision to specific developmental needs of supervisees. In other words, beginning supervisees would need different things from their supervisor than those at a more advanced stage. Despite wide acceptance and intuitive appeal, there is a paucity of empirical research evidence to support these assumptions beyond the beginning stage of training and development (Gonsalvez et al., 2002; Ladany, Marotta, & Muse-Burke, 2001; Schechtman & Wirzberger, 1999). Regardless, embracing a developmental perspective can be very helpful in terms of goal setting, planning, application of methods and techniques, selection of role and style, and time management concerns. Developmental thinking invites supervisors to individualize supervision plans and to become more flexible and creative in order to increase learning and prevent common relationship difficulties. What's more, developmental models dovetail well with the other supervision models discussed previously.

A Comprehensive Model of Supervision

After reviewing the assumptions and principles of the aforementioned supervision-specific models, it should be easy for those new to supervision to grasp the need for a comprehensive model of supervision that captures the complexity of this role and relationship and serves as an umbrella over all their actions with supervisees and their clients. In order to practice ethically as a clinical supervisor, it is crucial to recognize the multifaceted and interactive nature of the supervisory relationship and the impact of this relationship on clients and, as a result, place the relationship with supervisees at the center of their preferred supervision model. In doing so, supervisors

Putting It Into Practice

Case Example

After Becky became a clinical supervisor, she began to experience problems with her supervisees. Two were openly hostile, and one was very apathetic about supervision. She couldn't understand why she was having so many difficulties. She was a very competent clinician, and she expected the same level of competence in others. Moreover, she was very busy with her own client load. Even so, from the beginning she had told them to come find her if they had any problems.

However, over coffee with a colleague, she discovered that Tom, one of her new supervisees, had been faced with a difficult crisis situation but had not come to her for supervision. In fact, she didn't know anything about it until her colleague mentioned it. Becky was both angry and let down. She said to her colleague "What is wrong with these people? What is wrong with Tom? He knows he is supposed to come to me with any problems. This is just an example of Passive Aggressive Personality Disorder. He should be fired. After all, you know that you can't do anything with that type of person."

Teaching Point: Becky does not have a clear understanding of the purpose and role of clinical supervisors. She is practicing the no-model model of supervision. She believes that because she has expertise with clients, that will translate into effectiveness as a supervisor. She has also fallen into the trap of seeing relationship problems with her supervisees as signs of pathology on their part, not as indicators of problems with her supervision model, style, and methods. When problems occur, she blames the supervisee, pathologizes his behavior, and does not understand how this represents a message to her to do something different as a supervisor. She makes the assumption that people will just find her if they have problems. Her model is reactive, not proactive. She has no plan for supervision and has not thought out her role nor delineated expectations for her supervisees.

recognize the needs of supervisees for safety and support; they understand the reciprocal nature of supervision and the need to promote mutuality of fairness and respect; they are able to take into account the developmental nature of supervision and be flexible and open to customize their role, activities, and style; and last, they recognize the impact of systems variables such as time, organizational climate, budgets, and support on supervision and, in turn, on client care. The following chapters of this book will describe the practices of supervisors who subscribe to the comprehensive model of supervision.

TEST YOURSELF

1. **It is important for supervisors to create a separate model designed specifically for supervision.** True or False?

2. **There is a large body of empirical literature that supports the effectiveness of developmental models with all levels of supervisees and situations.** True or False?

3. **The recommended model of clinical supervision is the expert model.** True or False?

4. **The recommended model of supervision suggests**
   (a) making the relationship with supervisees central.
   (b) understanding the importance of trust and safety.
   (c) providing support and understanding to supervisees.
   (d) understanding the developmental, interactional nature of supervision.
   (e) all of the above.

5. **When problems occur with supervisees, it is best to use language from the *DSM-IV-R* manual to resolve them because both supervisor and supervisee understand these terms.** True or False?

6. **When problems occur with supervisees, it is best to**
   (a) refer to the *DSM-IV-R* manual for assistance.
   (b) let the supervisee know they belong on Axis II.
   (c) examine what is not working and work to make changes.
   (d) tell the supervisee it is "my way or the highway."

7. **One of the best approaches to take as a clinical supervisor is to**
   (a) never admit you make mistakes.
   (b) sit in your office and wait to see if problems occur.
   (c) just do with your supervisee what your supervisor did with you.
   (d) have a clear idea of the goals and purpose of clinical supervision and be actively involved.

8. **The parallel process model is helpful to understanding problems with supervisees.** True or False?

9. **In order to be fair, it is best to do the same things in supervision with all supervisees regardless of their expertise or level of education and training.** True or False?

10. **Give two examples of therapeutic concepts that can apply to supervision.**

11. **The interactional model of supervision stresses**

    (a) the reciprocal nature of the supervisory relationship.

    (b) how systems influence supervision.

    (c) the role of the ego and the id in supervision.

    (d) the fact that supervisees are totally responsible for the success of supervision.

    (e) a and b.

    (f) c and d.

12. **Kaiser (1997) identified four key elements that influence the creation of a positive supervision experience: Which of the following is one of Kaiser's four key elements?**

    (a) Accountability

    (b) Personal awareness

    (c) Trust and power

    (d) Use of authority

    (e) All of the above

    (f) None of the above

13. **Interpersonal process recall (IPR) is only useful with beginners.** True or False?

14. **Developmental models invite supervisors to**

    (a) individualize supervision.

    (b) be flexible.

    (c) apply a variety of methods and techniques.

    (d) think and act like a parent.

    (e) do all of the above.

    (f) do only a, b, and c.

15. **Supervision is primarily**

    (a) a socialization process.

    (b) a means to keep new people out.

    (c) a useless, outdated enterprise.

    (d) a waste of time.

    (e) all of the above.

Answers: 1. True; 2. False; 3. False; 4. e; 5. False; 6. c; 7. d; 8. True; 9. False; 10. For the correct answer, refer to Rapid Reference 3.1; 11. e; 12. e; 13. False; 14. f; 15. a

Four

FORMATS FOR CLINICAL SUPERVISION

Once a model for supervision has been selected, the next step is to select a structure in which to actualize the model. Even though historically the design for delivery of clinical supervision is one where supervisor and supervisee sit down together for an hour and review cases, there are actually a number of other possible formats, such as group, peer, or team supervision. Live observation, cotherapy, videotaping, written exercises, demonstrations and role-play are examples of methods and techniques that could be combined within each of these formats to enrich the supervision experience.

Even the most experienced supervisor would do well to spend significant time pondering all of these possibilities for a number of important reasons. First, the format for delivery of supervision, along with the selection and combination of methods and techniques, will play a significant part in the growth and development of supervisees. Second, the choice of format, methods, and techniques serves a key function in monitoring the activities of supervisees and facilitating a high quality of care for clients. Third, the use of a variety of formats, methods, and techniques will also be an integral piece of ethical clinical supervision practice as they enhance the fair treatment of supervisees, especially in the area of dual relationships, multicultural differences, and evaluation. (See Rapid Reference 4.1.)

When considering all the options for supervision structure, it might be helpful to familiarize oneself with the advantages and disadvantages of each of the formats. It is also important to consider the supervisor's own level of competency in utilizing each of the formats. Other considerations are

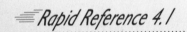

Rapid Reference 4.1

Goal of Supervision Formats, Methods, and Techniques

- Improve knowledge, skills, and self-awareness of supervisees
- Increase objectivity to avoid bias and impaired judgment
- Improve monitoring and control of supervisees activities
- Facilitate independent functioning and decision making

time, money, resources, requirements for supervision, the developmental level of the supervisee, their learning style, the client population, and multicultural differences.

Regardless of the format selected for supervision, knowledgeable supervisors realize that having some

> ### DON'T FORGET
> Whatever supervision format is selected, it will be necessary to orient supervisees to the purpose and goals for each one, to supply some type of structure for the format, and to provide for the supervisee's safety.

elementary structure for the selected format is essential to success. Applying the developmental perspective, the role of structuring belongs primarily with supervisors with beginners, whereas when working with more experienced supervisees this structuring process should be done collaboratively.

INDIVIDUAL SUPERVISION

Since Freud's time, individual face-to-face case consultation has been the primary modality for clinical supervision. Traditionally, supervisees bring in case material about their clients to discuss with the supervisor. This may be done in a formal session, usually once a week for 1 hour, or informally as needed. Today, most graduate programs and state licensure boards require a minimum of 1 hour of individual face-to-face supervision per week for all pre- and post-degree trainees. Sometimes supervisors are allowed to substitute group supervision on an every-other-week basis, but such sessions never entirely replace individual meetings. The supposition is that regular one-on-one individual meeting time with clinical supervisors is necessary both for the growth and development of supervisees as well as for monitoring purposes.

The structure for individual supervision doesn't need to be elaborate, but some modicum of organization will increase the benefit. Rapid Reference 4.2 provides suggestions for structuring individual supervision. Certainly beginning supervisees appreciate supervisors who have a plan for supervision sessions as it helps to reduce their anxiety. Experienced supervisees also appreciate some structure and direction, but they usually want to have more say about what happens in supervision. All supervisors need to think through the purpose and goals for supervision and, at a minimum, create some initial structure for the relationship.

> ### DON'T FORGET
> There will be a need for structure and direction on the part of supervisors in any crisis situation, regardless of the level of expertise of supervisees. In other words, there will always be an interaction between the supervisor, supervisee, and the needs of clients.

≡ *Rapid Reference 4.2*

How to Structure an Individual Supervision Session

1. Think ahead to the purpose and goals for the session.
2. Include the supervisee in planning for the session.
3. Ask the supervisee what they need most from the session.
4. Create a structure for the session: Start with successes, not problems.
5. Create questions to stimulate thinking.
   - "What are your feeling responses to the client?"
   - "How was it for you to sit with this client?" (Irma Rahtjen, workshop participant, Kansas City)
   - "How connected do you feel to this client?" (Michael Winters, workshop participant, Houston, TX)
   - "What is your plan of action [intervention strategy, treatment goal] with this client?"
   - "Can you identify any multicultural issues that may affect your relationship with this client?"
   - "What did the client say or not say was the problem and how might this be important to success?"
   - "What personal issues are you aware of that may affect working with this client?"
   - "Are there any ethical issues present in this client situation?"
6. Whenever possible, combine case consultation with other methods and techniques, such as a written case review sheet, role-play, or a short demonstration.
7. Include some time for a teaching component within each session (more on creating a topical focus for supervision follows).
8. Ask the supervisee at the end of each supervision session about the benefit of supervision that day.
   - "What is one thing you will take away from supervision today?"
   - "How was supervision helpful to you?"
   - "What was missing?"
   - "What do we need to talk about more next time?"
9. Document the session. (See Chapter 6.)

A number of factors can influence the structure of individual supervision such as the purpose of the supervision, identified goals, supervision rules and requirements, level of expertise of supervisees, client needs for monitoring, as well as time, availability, and other organizational concerns. Decisions about how to best use the supervision time could be made weekly by supervisors simply asking "How do you want to use your supervision time today?" or "How can I be most helpful to you today?" Nonetheless, as time progresses, supervisors still need to give consideration to the overall goals for supervision to be sure progress continues in that direction.

Adding a topical learning component to supervision sessions can also enrich the experience. Subjects such as suicide, trauma, abuse, anger and resistance, multicultural differences, termination, or substance abuse might not have been covered in graduate school, or, if they were, application of classroom materials to actual client situations may require considerable effort. There are a number of possibilities for how to do this within individual supervision. (See Rapid Reference 4.3.) For

≋Rapid Reference 4.3

Three Examples of How to Utilize a Topical Approach in Supervision

Supervisor: "As you were talking about your frustration with Mr. Smith, I realized that you have been struggling with several clients who don't say much, and you don't get much of a verbal response to your questions. I know when I started out, I felt the same way you do and so have had to develop different ways of approaching such clients." Three types of supervisor suggestions could follow this introduction:

1. "Let's role-play this situation with Mr. Smith and see what comes up. It may give you new ideas as to how to approach other clients similar to Mr. Smith."

2. "For the next month or so, let's take a closer look at working with clients who are difficult to engage. I think it will be beneficial to spend some time in supervision on that topic. I have one or two articles on suggested approaches that you are welcome to look at. However, I expect that you will want to research the subject yourself to see if you could come up with at least one different approach to try with Mr. Smith. We'll start our next supervision meeting talking about your ideas."

3. "One fruitful area for exploration in supervision is the topic of transference and countertransference with clients. In other words, looking at what a client is doing or not doing that is affecting our relationship with him or her. I know it goes on with me sometimes with my clients, and, of course, there is a lot of literature out there on this topic, so, to my way of thinking, it would be a good idea to spend time in supervision examining our hot buttons with clients. It is a very important part of ethical practice. How does that sound?"

example, a topic such as learning to address client resistance or noncompliance could be inserted into a case review or selected as the focus for a portion of a supervision session or a series of supervision sessions.

There are a multitude of advantages to individual supervision. First, supervisors are able to give each supervisee their complete attention. They can individualize supervision, which will facilitate building trust and a working relationship. The supervisee may feel safer with the supervisor in such a situation and be more willing to take risks and be open. As a result of such trust, both supervisor and supervisee may feel freer to experiment with other modalities beyond traditional case consultation and explore issues more deeply.

There are also disadvantages to relying exclusively on individual case consultation. First is the problem of isolation and the potential for an inaccurate view of the supervisee. By not watching the supervisee interact with others, the supervisor is relying on the supervisee's self-report and may not have a true picture of the supervisee's skills and abilities. Another issue is that individual supervision could be open to bias, impaired judgement, exploitation, and harassment on the supervisor's part. On the other hand, supervisees may withhold information or lie because of worries about criticism or a poor evaluation (Hantoot, 2000). Along with the problems of supervisor bias and supervisee deception, individual supervision can also become repetitive and boring over time. Both supervisor and supervisee would need to continually suggest new ideas and activities to avoid such a quandary.

The greatest drawback to individual supervision, which relies exclusively on the self-report narrative of supervisees about their clients, has to do with monitoring the quality of client care. If not combined with other formats, methods, and techniques that allow supervisors more direct observation of the supervisee's activities, potentially serious liability issues for clinical supervisors could arise.

Putting It Into Practice

Case Example

Sandra, a new and inexperienced counselor, was assigned to work with an African-American couple that had just called the agency for an appointment. The presenting issue was the husband's recent loss of his job and the turmoil created by this fact. Each reported the other partner as "depressed and not doing well." The wife wanted them to move back in with her parents as a temporary solution to their financial problems. She felt this would give them needed time to straighten things out. The husband was adamantly against such a solution. Sandra was bewildered by the level of arguing between the couple during the session and came to the conclusion that the husband was "angry and abusive" because the wife kept saying she wanted to move back in with her family. At the beginning of supervision, her supervisor asked her "What would you like to talk about today?" and Sandra said she wanted help with this couple. Her supervisor asked her what was her assessment of the situation and plan for counseling with them. Sandra launched into her analysis of the problem as being the husband's anger and probable abuse of the wife. In response to this report, the supervisor gave Sandra a series of actions to take to protect the wife and recommended the husband be referred to an anger management group.

Teaching Point: The supervisor made the error of assuming a certain level of conceptualization and assessment skills on the part of this new, inexperienced supervisee. By not following up very broad, open questions with more specific ones, much pertinent information was lost. For example, in order to access more detailed information, the supervisor might have inquired about what the couple was doing that led her to that conclusion. Another important question that should have been asked concerns multicultural differences between the supervisee, Sandra, and the couple. A multiculturally competent supervisor would know that culture has an effect on how people respond to crisis situations. Knowing the cultural aspects of this couple's situation, the supervisor would have made other recommendations. Certainly this points to the potential mistakes that can be made by supervisors relying completely on the self-report of supervisees and not following broad questions up with requests for specific examples of behaviors that support the supervisee's perceptions and conclusions.

GROUP FORMATS FOR SUPERVISION

In addition to individual supervision, there are three other supervision formats that take place in a group: group, team, and peer supervision. There are distinct differences in structure and leadership function among these three formats for supervision. However, overall, they are alike in that supervisors in each format have to address identical issues of managing group dynamics; understanding group process; building group cohesion; establishing structure; setting rules and boundaries; and handling issues of confidentiality as well as decision making and the leadership role. Therefore, this section contains the majority of general material on working with groups in supervision, while the sections on team and peer supervision cover information specific to that format.

Group Supervision

Group supervision is another supervision format that has advantages as well as drawbacks. Group supervision can serve as a complement to individual supervision. When coupled with audio- or videotaping and experiential techniques, it can become an even more efficient learning tool (Ray & Altekruse, 2000). However, much of the time it is selected simply as a means to solve the supervisor's time constraints rather than to increase learning benefits for supervisees. The most common structure selected for group supervision is actually individual supervision in a group setting where each supervisee is given an allotted time to present cases, and most interactions are between the supervisor and this one individual. Depending on the size of the group, this may appear to be a satisfactory solution for overworked supervisors.

However, with more forethought, group supervision can have more far-reaching benefits, such as encouraging team building, promoting risk-taking, diffusing issues of power and authority, addressing multicultural differences, and invigorating bored or burned out supervisees. Haynes et al. (2003) make a strong case for the value of group supervision as providing a heightened learning environment with the use of experiential techniques such as role-play and role reversal. Certainly when supervisees progress much beyond the beginning stage of development, moving out of the traditional model of individually focused group supervision into a more group-focused model will expediently increase the benefits.

Many of the same universal therapeutic factors Yalom (1995) identified for group therapy exist in group supervision and represent the largest part of its benefit. For example, checking out perceptions, trying out new behaviors in a safe environment, seeing that one is not alone, learning to give and receive feedback, engaging in self-exploration, seeing alternative ways to solve problems and intervene with clients, developing tolerance for ambiguity, and appreciating differences in perspectives on problems are all benefits of group supervision.

CAUTION

Groups will be more effective as training vehicles if the leader is not involved in the evaluation process. If the group leader is both the administrator and the clinical supervisor, he or she must disclose the extent to which self-disclosure and participation in the group will be a part of evaluation.

However, creating a cohesive and safe group environment for this type of learning to take place is a complicated balancing act requiring more preparation and skill on the supervisor's part than many realize. In most instances, the supervisor's level of training and experience with group

> ### CAUTION
> Supervisors in group supervision should not mistake supervision sessions for group psychotherapy and should make sure supervisees understand the distinction.

methods will be more important to effective group supervision than the type of supervisee.

Thus, supervisors engaged in group supervision will need to be well versed in group dynamics, understand group development and the role of conflict in groups, as well as be comfortable with confrontation. Additionally, supervisors must be familiar with the difference between group supervision and group therapy and be able to draw a clear line between the two. As those who have a background in groups know, it will be just as important in group supervision as in group counseling and therapy to establish at the onset group goals and expectations and create a structure and some guidelines for behavior in order to increase success.

There are many advantages to group supervision. The greatest benefit is that it expands both the supervisor's and supervisee's perspective of each other and of clients. Using group dynamics and group process can increase involvement and empower supervisees to solve problems, develop tolerance for differences, and build teamwork. Groups provide a wonderful place for experiential techniques, such as role-play, role reversal, and family sculpting, which can enrich and enliven the supervision experience. Through sharing anxieties and life experiences, checking out intuition, and learning to give and receive feedback, most supervisees will increase in their confidence and self-efficacy (Page & Hulse-Killacky, 1999). As supervisees exchange insights and points of view, they develop an appreciation for the value of peer consultation so essential to ethical practice. Group supervision also helps supervisors to see their supervisees in a different light as they interact with others. Furthermore, there is less danger of improper or harmful behavior on the part of supervisors.

Success with group supervision also depends greatly on how it is presented to supervisees (Yalom, 1995). It is possible that some supervisees will have no real background or experience with groups outside the classroom, sports, or social activities. For others, the primary group experience will be a therapy or a support group. Thus, supervisors will need to emphasize the educative purpose of the supervision group as an assured way to help clients. Offering choices in the selection of the group structure and including supervisees as much as possible in goal setting and planning will also help build a positive group experience for members. Another concern that should be tackled is anxiety. Group members, especially beginners, may bring a host of fears, sometimes rational and sometimes not, to the group that if not addressed to some degree, can linger and create barriers to group cohesion and interfere with learning (Fitch & Marshall, 2002).

Just as there are many advantages to utilizing group supervision, there are also many drawbacks. Perhaps the biggest drawback is providing equal time to all supervisees in the group. Overlooking some supervisees can contribute to gaps in monitoring of client care as well as missed opportunities for learning. If the supervisor is not skilled in group dynamics and facilitation, instead of building safety and a sense of trust, the opposite may occur. For example, both supervisors and supervisees could overstep boundaries and fall into the trap of turning group supervision into group therapy. When the clinical supervisor is also the administrator, keeping boundaries clear will take continuing effort. Another important issue is confidentiality. Just as with group therapy, without strict rules and vigilance on everyone's part, information gained in the supervision group can spill out into other arenas and become problematic.

Other disadvantages include using the group as a forum for complaints; scapegoating of members; splitting into subgroups that compete against each other; or, after time, becoming so internally focused on the group dynamics and group process that discussing client cases becomes secondary. All of these possibilities will result in poor monitoring of client care (Munson, 2002).

Stages of Group Development

The first step for supervisors to insure success of group supervision is to have a basic understanding of group dynamics (Linton, 2003). One model of group development that might be helpful to all supervisors is the five-stage developmental model for groups: forming, storming, norming, performing, and adjourning (Tuckman & Jensen, 1977). According to the theory, there is a task component and a relationship component within each stage of development. During the *forming,* or first stage, as groups get organized, the primary task is orientation to group goals and the setting of rules,

> **CAUTION**
> ....
> If using experiential techniques in group supervision, such as role-play, role reversal, Gestalt empty chair, or doubling and soliloquy from psychodrama, be careful to maintain clear boundaries and focus activities on helping clients, not on conducting therapy with supervisees.

structure, and purpose. The relationship component at this stage is characterized by members' needs for safety and dependence on the group leader. Schutz (1977) refers to this stage as the inclusion stage typified by members' concerns such as "Will I be heard and understood?" "Will I be liked?" or "Will I be seen as competent?" Supervisors set the stage for the group by modeling behaviors that increase participation and development of group cohesion.

CAUTION

It is a mistake to assume lack of disagreement is a sign of group cohesion. Instead, this can be symptomatic of group flight from conflict and confrontation and indicate a lack of safety on the part of group members.

As the group progresses over time and people get comfortable, the group accordingly will move to the next stage, *storming*. At this point, members may feel safer to disagree with the group facilitator or other members of the group. Differing viewpoints on client problems and disagreements about intervention suggestions and theory are natural and normal as supervisees become more confident and experience level increases. Certainly with highly experienced clinicians, open discussion of this kind is the heart of the group process. Although some conflict can be healthy, supervisors need to work hard to manage the conflict so as to maintain safety and trust and keep the group focused on the task at hand.

If successful in resolving differences and creating a structure for positive disagreement, the group then moves on to the *norming* stage that is characterized by a collaborative atmosphere, free exchange of ideas, and openness to differing viewpoints that are seen as helpful to the group purpose. On a relationship level, the group begins to form a sense of "we-ness" or positive morale, and members will be eager to attend each session (Kormanski, 1999). Group members act friendly, warm, and supportive of others' suggestions and ideas. Decision making is deemed a shared responsibility

Putting It Into Practice

Example of Noting Parallel Process in Groups

Mary, a supervisee, is presenting a client case in a very monotone voice, with little affect. Sam's (the group supervisor) attention begins to drift off. Recognizing his state, Sam says to Mary, "Mary, as you talk about this client, you have little energy in your voice, it sounds very flat and matter of fact, and, as a result, I find myself becoming bored and my mind drifting. I am wondering if that is similar to how you feel with this client? Are you bored working with him? How involved do you feel?" Mary notes the accuracy of the feedback and begins to talk more directly about her experience with this client.

and seeking consensus an implicit value for the group. Helpful feedback occurs among members as well as from the leader. Members will have more insight about group process and parallels between what is occurring in the group and what is occurring with clients and are able to use such information productively to further aid client care.

Establishment of such group norms propels the group into the *performing* stage whereby the group becomes very task oriented, and much is accomplished during group time. At this stage, the focus will be on client care, and the relationship component of the group will take the shape of member abilities to understand group process and willingness to self-correct when getting off target. For example, in the early stage of group development, as supervisees discuss cases, the leader might jump in with a reflective comment on the group process and invite the group to ponder the existence of parallel process. At this stage, however, supervisees themselves would suggest such a possibility without leader intervention and come up with their own ideas for correction.

The last stage of group development is called the *adjourning* stage, which signals the end of the structured group experience or accomplishment of the identified group purpose. The relationship task for group leaders at this point is to help members end the experience on a positive note. Typically, endings are formalized with rituals and ceremonies that give closure, recognize achievement, and help members say good-bye. With group supervision, the adjourning stage could be for an individual member as the required supervision time comes to a close or for the group itself. In open-ended supervision groups, consideration might be given to the idea of structuring the supervision group to periodically have a beginning and an end in order to force consideration of group structure and dynamics and propel members to new action.

Observation of Group Dynamics

One excellent suggestion to improve group supervision is to appoint a group process observer for one or more meetings at the beginning stage of the group and then follow up with observation of the group at various other times over the life of the group. Supervisors who are interested in the safety of group members and in building a collaborative supervision team would find the addition of group observers very helpful to this end.

The observer could track group member behavior and communication patterns for short time periods and then share his or her observations with the group as a means to encourage self-awareness, improve communication, track stages of group development, and advance the goals for the group (Treadwell, Kumar, Stein, & Prosnick, 1997). The observer may wish to monitor the level and type of participation by various group members or who talks to whom and how often. For example, one supervisee may speak directly to the person he or she thinks is most likely to disagree with his or her ideas, whereas another supervisee may address all remarks to the person perceived to have the most power and influence in the group. Sometimes supervisees may couch all remarks with disclaimers or use generalities and avoid addressing any remarks directly to group members because of concern for safety. The group observer could point out these behaviors as a means to facilitate discussion about safety, power, and influence in the supervision group.

A sociogram is a useful tool to help examine group development (Treadwell et al., 1997). Group theory has suggested that in the early stage of group development, most exchanges will be between the leader and individual members, whereas with more mature groups, the majority of interactions will be group oriented. A map of group interactions done over a period of months could show such changes in development and remind members of the importance of group-directed interactions as a measure of group cohesiveness.

To make a sociogram (see Figure 4.1), circles are drawn to represent individual group members and the group leader. Watching the group interactions for a 15-minute period, the observer would draw a straight line to represent each interaction by a group member. A typical diagram might chart the level of group participation, how many interactions are with the group leader, how many are member to member, and any that would be considered to the group. Group-oriented interactions are any that are addressed to the group as a whole. This includes process comments about what is happening in the group, observations that focus attention on group goals or promote group cohesion, or questions addressed to the group in general.

Behaviors by members that help or hinder open communication, such as plops, interruptions, distractions, and the number of "atta boys" or "atta girls" (encouraging remarks), as well as negative comments made by the group leader could also be charted in 15-minute increments. A *plop* is when a group member makes a suggestion or asks a question and no one responds or the topic is changed. This behavior is very detrimental to group participation and group safety. Interruptions are also damaging to group effectiveness. Too many interruptions represent the fact that the members are not really listening to each other but instead are busy forming their own thoughts on the subject being discussed. The outgrowth of numerous interruptions is that the group appears disorganized, and members will look to the leader to exert more influence to handle the problem. The observer's role is to encourage group members to examine their own behaviors and decide on a self-monitoring strategy to solve the problem.

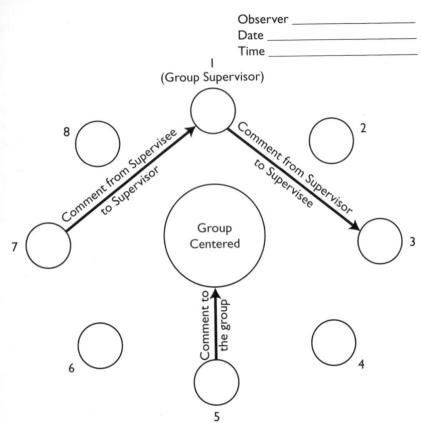

Make a line with an arrow for each comment. Begin at speaker. Point arrow where comment is directed. Chart interactions for 10–15 minutes and then process observations with the supervision group.

Figure 4.1 Group Supervision Observation Form

Another category of remarks that will be essential to feelings of safety in the group are the number of negative or critical remarks versus positive or supportive ones made by the group supervisor and group members. According to group dynamics theory, it takes three or four supportive or encouraging remarks ("atta boys" or "atta girls") to counteract each negative or critical remark. Observers should look to see if there is any pattern to critical remarks. For example, if every time one person says something in the group, the same person immediately follows with some sort of criticism of what they said or a "yes, but," it is a good indicator of conflict and who likes whom. This behavior can also highlight the existence of subgroups, a phenomena that if not addressed by the group can lead to splitting, taking sides, and scapegoating.

Structuring Group Supervision

A number of important issues must be considered in order to build an effective supervision group, such as size of the group; developmental level of the supervisor and supervisees; disparity in education, competence, and experience level of supervisees; dual relationships; use of power and authority; evaluation; self-disclosure of personal material; confidentiality of information; record keeping; multicultural differences; and the impact of differences in theoretical model and professional discipline. According to Enyedy et al. (2003), there are five types of issues that hindered learning in group supervision: conflicts between members, problems with the supervisor, supervisee anxiety, logistical constraints, and poor group time management.

It follows, therefore, that no matter the circumstance or level of expertise of supervisees, supervisors, like any group leaders, need to spend time at the very beginning on the structure and goals of the supervision group. It is natural that supervisees will have anxiety about the coming group experience, and it is up to the supervisor to set the tone for the group and create a safe forum for learning through the establishment of rules and clear boundaries for group interactions (Christensen & Kline, 2001b; Fitch & Marshall, 2002). Characteristically, rules for group supervision would mirror those used in group therapy or support groups: Use "I" statements, own your own opinions, avoid advice giving or telling people what they should do, keep feedback specific to the issue at hand and avoid generalities and personality labeling, be respectful of differences, treat others in the group the way you want to be treated, and keep all information gained from the group confidential.

One rule that may lead to debate is whether supervisees can seek each other out for consultation on client cases outside of the supervision group. Sometimes this activity can drain energy from the group or lead to splitting and subgrouping. On the other hand, depending on the makeup of the group and developmental level of supervisees, such activity may cement learning from the group (Bischoff et al., 2002).

> ## DON'T FORGET
> Before beginning group supervision, address the following:
> - The goals and purpose for the group
> - Expectations and roles of both supervisor and supervisees
> - Safety and set rules
> - Potential areas of conflict
> - How to resolve problems
> - Evaluation

≡ *Rapid Reference 4.5*

Questions for Supervisors to Use for the Initial Contracting Stage of Group Supervision

1. "What would you like to have happen here in this group? What do you hope to get out of being in this group? How can this group meet your needs? What would make this experience truly memorable [or successful]? How do you want to use the time we have? How do you see my role in the group?"

2. "On evaluation, how do you want this to go? Ideas? My role? Yours? What kind of input do you want me to consider? Do you want some way to give written feedback as well as verbal feedback to each other? Should this feedback be included in the evaluation piece?"

3. "How do you want to handle conflict? Members who don't participate or who dominate the discussion? What about discussion of personal problems or conflicts between members? How do you want to handle those situations?"

4. "What actions by group members or by me could be harmful? How do you want to address such behavior? Any dos and don'ts here?"

5. "What about confidentiality? Do we want to set a rule that we will not discuss outside the group any material or personal information learned about each other in the group?"

Other structural considerations for group supervision include the following: How will problems with members, such as domination or withdrawal, be handled? What methods and techniques might be employed to increase the benefit of group time? What multicultural differences exist within the group, and how might these differences be addressed in the group to avoid misunderstandings and unnecessary conflict? How can the supervisor assure the safety of group members as they expose themselves and admit mistakes and deficits? What about confidentiality of information in the group? Last, what rules, regulations, and organizational concerns need to be considered? Rapid Reference 4.5 gives a list of questions supervisors may wish to ask at the beginning of group supervision in order to settle rules and structure.

DON'T FORGET

The safer members feel in the group, the more they will participate. As new supervisees are added to an existing supervision group, return to the initial phase and go over goals, expectations, structure and rules. Insert an inclusion style exercise to help the person feel at home. For example, go around the group and have everyone introduce themselves; discuss their backgrounds, experience, and other pertinent data; and then describe how the group has been beneficial to them. The new supervisee could be invited to do the same.

Supervisors as leaders set the stage from the beginning for the group by modeling behaviors that increase participation, promote safety of group members, and lead to the development of group cohesion. Magnuson et al. (2000) found the supervisor's ability to address supervisees' concerns and provide them an equitable and safe environment is a distinctive attribute of effective group supervision. The supervisor as facilitator needs to draw members into the group through the use of basic rapport-building skills, such as encouragers, cheerleading, empathetic responding, reflecting feelings, clarifying, paraphrasing, and summarizing. Early in the group, members watch the leader to see what the leader does, so the supervisor's actions become more important than what he or she says. For example, if a supervisee brings up a concern, how does the supervisor handle it? Does the supervisor criticize, attack, and blame or respond supportively and encourage reflection? Members may also watch other group members' interactions, who respond to whom, interruptions, plops (questions or suggestions that are ignored), and critical responses by other members before they decide if it is safe to participate.

Another factor that can influence success with group supervision is how competition between supervisees is handled. Competition between supervisees is a normal aspect of all supervision groups as members seek to demonstrate their competence and curry favor from the supervisor. This phenomenon can be witnessed in a number of ways as supervisees attempt to gain the supervisor's attention and praise: interrupting other supervisees when they speak, disagreeing with suggestions, attacking and criticizing others' expertise, and playing the

Putting It Into Practice

Examples of Supervisor Statements to Encourage Group Participation

- "Thanks for speaking up. I appreciate your honesty. I think we will all benefit from your thoughtful feedback."
- "I really appreciate your sharing that with the group. I can see you are really getting more confident and willing to take risks in the group."
- "Mary, [or a particular member] you haven't said much so far. What are your thoughts about what has been going on so far in supervision?"
- "Let's stop and summarize what has been going on these past few minutes to make sure we are all on the same page."
- "Jack, I know you have experience with a client like the one Mary is talking about. Anything you would like to add to my suggestions?"

game of "I have one better." This pattern can be especially noticeable between very experienced and inexperienced supervisees or when new supervisees join an ongoing supervision group. If it occurs, calling participants' attention to this behavior and how it negatively impacts the group is needed.

From the aforementioned information, it should be obvious to all supervisors that it is extremely important to spend time in the beginning of any supervision group establishing the structure and rules for the group, the dos and don'ts for behavior, as well as discussing goals and objectives, expectations, confidentiality issues, and the role of evaluation. If new supervisees are added to the group over time, this same information needs to be reviewed.

Group size.   If everyone in a group is going to get equal time, and the usual guideline is 15 minutes per supervisee, then the ideal size of a supervision group is four to six members with a maximum of seven for an hour and a half group. If including more supervisees were necessary, then the meeting time for the group would need to be expanded accordingly to be fair to all members or another structure chosen.

Selection of members.   Ideally, supervisees in the group would not have too much disparity in level of education and experience or in organizational setting or population served as these situations present unique problems for supervisors to address if the group is to be successful. Some variability with group membership can make things interesting, but, again, if too much disparity exists, it is challenging for supervisors to help members see commonalities and give value to the supervision experience rather than shut down or turn off. For example, beginners and more advanced supervisees need different things in supervision. Beginners need help to simplify and focus their thinking about client problems and want specific techniques to use with each client. Experienced clinicians, on the other hand, may want to explore issues more broadly, examining the pros and cons of different theoretical points of view and intervention strategies. For beginners, involvement in this form of discussion can be overwhelming and confusing and possibly leave them with a decreased sense of competency. Subgrouping may also result as members try to manage their needs. Thus, if both inexperienced and experienced supervisees are in the group, supervisors will have to work hard to strike a balance between the needs of the

CAUTION

Because of liability issues, it would be best to also work individually with supervisees outside of the group in any dangerous or high-risk situations with clients.

two. The same problem of keeping members involved would be true of supervision groups where participants come from diverse organizations that serve different populations and where issues and client problems vary widely.

Therefore, supervisors should seek to have some control over the numbers and makeup of the group and, whenever possible, seek some level of homogeneity of members. Other concerns would be member differences in theoretical models or discipline area. When supervisors and supervisees subscribe to different theoretical models, it can be very confusing if everyone is not well versed in the model being discussed. Again, supervisors would need to be sensitive to how these differences in viewpoints and approaches would be handled in the group in order to ensure feedback and suggestions would be given and received with tolerance and openness.

In situations where there is great disparity in experience level among group members, a plan might be to pair supervisees into teams with the more experienced supervisee taking on the role of mentor. When the novice presents a case in the group, input would come first from the supervisor along with the identified mentor. Then before others join in, the supervisor could check to see if the supervisee can handle any more information at that time.

As the group progresses over time and the skill level of the group increases, the supervisor, as facilitator, would hope to see other members of the group take on greater leadership responsibility. For example, in a mixed group of experienced therapists along with some beginners, in the early stages the facilitator or supervisor might invite those with more knowledge to speak first to model what is expected and then, as time passes, switch and have the less experienced supervisees begin.

Allocation of time in group supervision.   There are many possibilities for structuring group supervision besides having each supervisee in turn receive the same allotted time for presenting cases. One strategy is to start every group by asking members what their needs are for the group that day and whether any members have something urgent they need group input on, then decide who gets time and how much. A variation on this is to follow up this introductory discussion with an exploration of the various needs of members from the aspect of identifying which issues represent core concerns of the group (Hawkins & Shohet, 2003). For example, a group member may ask for supervision time to address a client's lack of commitment to change. This issue may resonate with others in the group so that everyone can share in the learning process and benefit in some way from supervision time spent on that one client. Another idea is to stop periodically as one supervisee is presenting a case and ask others to consider how problems and suggested solutions with this particular client might parallel aspects of work with their own clients: "As you are talking about Mrs. Jones's problems, it probably is a good time to talk about cognitive techniques and their success rate with anxiety versus traditional talk therapies."

Another structural variation is to generate group discussion and more generalized learning through the use of case studies. Each supervisee would be asked to present a case study to focus group member discussion on a particular topic, such as Eating Disorders, trauma, or Borderline Personality Disorder. All of a group session could be used in this manner or just the first or last half of the group session.

Supervisors can also alter their involvement in the group by moving back and forth between the expert role and the teaching function, which may serve to facilitate learning. That is, as supervisees discuss cases and members bring up suggestions, a short period of instruction on how to select different intervention strategies may be inserted.

Giving and receiving feedback.   One agreed-upon advantage with group supervision over individual supervision is providing a place for supervisees to check out perceptions, broaden their perspective, reflect on their behavior and its impact on others, and increase self-confidence as a result of member feedback. It is this process of giving and receiving feedback that propels the success of the supervision group as a learning tool. However, to reap this benefit requires careful attention by supervisors in how they model and train members to give feedback in a positive manner. People vary widely in comfort level with corrective feedback, how open they are to it, and whether such feedback will be received as positive and lead to the development of self-confidence and self-efficacy or whether it will have the reverse effect (Hulse-Killacky & Page, 1994). Yalom (1995) observes that feedback is not a commonplace transaction in our society except in intimate relationships, such as between parent and child or husband and wife. Therefore, setting the stage for the educative purpose of corrective feedback exchange in the super-

DON'T FORGET

- Make clear at the beginning of the group the purpose of corrective feedback is for learning and growth.
- Encourage a discussion with supervisees about their comfort level and previous experiences with feedback.
- Start with positive feedback before giving corrections.
- Keep feedback focused on specific behaviors and away from judgmental statements about a person's character or personality.

vision group, modeling how to do so in a constructive manner, and encouraging a collaborative approach as a group norm all become essential leadership skills to encourage a constructive feedback experience in the group.

A number of factors will influence how safe supervisees feel to give and receive feedback in the group. First, and probably foremost, is the group supervisor's comfort with giving and receiving feedback? If the supervisor is uncomfortable with giving and receiving feedback, it might be questionable whether he or she could model or train group members in how to do so in a positive manner. Second, what are the individual group members' experiences with giving and receiving corrective feedback? Are childhood memories of teacher or parental corrective feedback painful? Third, what are members' attitudes toward the expression of differences of opinion? Is feedback viewed as disagreement or a negative statement toward an individual and hence damaging to interpersonal relationships? And last, is there a cultural component that encourages saying only nice things to people and avoiding saying anything that could be construed as disrespectful or troublemaking (Hulse-Killacky & Page, 1994). Supervisors would do well to ponder their own thoughts and feelings about giving and receiving feedback and encourage the same self-exploration by all supervisees in the group. More in-depth information on how to give corrective feedback can be found in Chapter 8.

Confidentiality in group supervision.   Just as with group counseling and group therapy, maintaining complete confidentiality of group information is impossible. Group supervisors can request that all information about the group and group members' self-disclosure be kept confidential and not discussed with anyone outside of the group, but complete confidentiality of information cannot be guaranteed. The first reason is the supervisor's evaluative role and the fact that the supervisees' behavior in group supervision would be a part of that evaluation. Second, group leaders do not have control over the actions of group members outside of the group itself. Therefore, to be ethical, the issue of confidentiality should be brought up at the very first meeting and a dialogue encouraged about how group members wish to manage confidentiality. It should also be obvious that the evaluation process needs to be discussed in the group before much time passes.

Another confidentiality issue to explore is how to best protect the confidentiality of clients while cases are being discussed in group supervision. As a general rule, it is expected that professionals, when involved in consultation or supervision, will only disclose information about that client that is essential to the consult, and only to other professionals involved in that client's care, and

DON'T FORGET

Before treatment begins, every effort should have been made to clearly communicate with clients through the use of an informed consent document, the supervisory process, and what steps are being taken to protect the confidentiality of their information during supervision.

will practice the highest standards for confidentiality with all client information.

Documentation of group supervision. One concern many group supervisors have is record keeping with group supervision. It would be ethically and legally a sound idea to keep a short written description of each group meeting that contains the names of clients discussed by each supervisee, a brief description of recommendations, and a few sentences about other issues covered in the group. A sample form is given in Rapid Reference 4.6. It is also a good suggestion, from a liability standpoint, to ask all supervisees in the group to individually keep track of which of their clients were discussed and recommendations received. As with other supervision notes, any documentation of group supervision must be kept confidential and should be brief, mostly behavioral,

Rapid Reference 4.6

Sample of a Documentation Form for Group Supervision

Group supervisor's name: _____

Date of group meeting: _____ Length: _____

List of members present along with brief synopsis of client cases discussed and recommendations:

Supervisee 1: _____ (name of supervisee) _____

List of client cases discussed with recommendations:

a. _____

b. _____

Supervisee 2: _____ (name of supervisee) _____

List of client cases discussed with recommendations:

a. _____

b. _____

Other topics discussed (e.g., discussed lethality checklist for suicide and application to a case): _____

_____

without indulging in lengthy discussion of group interactions or subjective opinions about particular supervisees.

From a teaching and training perspective, including a review of what type of note taking is expected from leaders of client groups would also be an essential topic in any supervision group where supervisees are themselves leading groups with clients. For example, how might note taking in support groups for kids in a school setting differ from that required by therapy groups or substance abuse support groups.

Group leadership style.   Leadership style is a critical factor in the outcome of group supervision. Activities of the group supervisor establish a climate of safety and a forum for open feedback and risk taking in the group. A supervisor's flexibility and openness to new ideas and viewpoints and a supervisor's ability to show compassion and empathy and willingness to treat all supervisees with dignity and respect shows supervisees how to interact in the group and what type of climate is desired.

Supervisors also continually model and teach group leadership skills that supervisees can use in their own client groups. For instance, balancing the needs of individual supervisees and the needs of the group is a continual leadership task in any group. Supervisors could choose to stop a lengthy discussion with one supervisee about a case and check back with the group to see where others are at that point. Other times, if it appears members have become sidetracked into personal issues or arguments, the supervisor might say "We seem to have wandered away from our stated goal for this group right now. Is this what you want to be doing with our time?" No matter what intervention is selected, how the supervisor manages the innumerable issues that come up in the supervision group will be an impor-

> ## DON'T FORGET
> ....
> Supervisors need to be constantly monitoring what is happening in the group and have a sizable repertory of skills in order to intervene effectively.

> ## CAUTION
> ....
> With group supervision, be sure to maintain safety. Monitor and control members' responses to each other. Set rules from the beginning: Absolutely do not allow any member of the group to attack, belittle, name call, or threaten any other member in the group. Watch out for interrupting, not responding to members when they speak (plops), and negative or critical responses. Manage domination by one or two members and subgroups.

≡ *Rapid Reference 4.7*

Group Leadership Skills for Supervisors

- Understands stages of group development
- Provides structure for the group
- Creates a safe environment
- Establishes basic ground rules for the group
- Sets boundaries and requests confidentiality
- Maintains order and focus on tasks
- Initiates activities to accomplish group goals
- Uses time effectively: starts and ends the group on time
- Uses leadership skills to promote group cohesion
- Models positive regard for each member
- Encourages participation
- Attends to nonverbal behavior
- Uses active listening skills, such as making process comments, paraphrasing, reflecting feelings, responding empathically, summarizing, clarifying, and asking open-ended questions
- Uses modeling to teach skills desired
- Models appropriate self-disclosure
- Gives periodic feedback to the group and to individuals
- Handles conflict in the group
- Confronts difficult members and counterproductive behavior

tant learning experience for all group members. A list of group leadership skills can be found in Rapid Reference 4.7.

Managing conflict.   It is important for clinical supervisors to maintain order in the supervision group and not allow destructive hostility or negative communication patterns to destroy group cohesion and safety (Marshall, 1999). Supervisors need to strongly emphasize the need for tolerance within the group. The easiest tactic is to model and demonstrate for group members how to challenge and confront in a positive manner. Another powerful means is the use of here-and-now process comments or questions that draw attention to group dynamics and group communication patterns and invite members to self-explore. For example, the supervisor might observe a lack of participation by several members and

≡Rapid Reference 4.8

Examples of Leader Interventions Designed to Moderate Conflict

- "Matt, your feedback sounded a little harsh; could you say it in a different way? I think Jolene would appreciate your feedback, but maybe soften it a bit so she can really hear you."
- "Rather than saying everyone feels this way, could you give an example of what you mean?"
- "Whew, that sounded rather hostile. Is there another way you could say it?"
- "I really value your expertise, but when you come at me so abrasively, I don't get the full benefit. Could we back up? What is it exactly you want me to know?"
- "I hear the anger in your voice and wonder what is happening for you right now? What are you feeling as you say that?"
- "I know that you two do not get along, but I would appreciate it, and I am sure others agree with me, if you two could table the hostilities while you are in our supervision group."
- "How is what is going on right now in group benefiting our clients?"
- "It seems as if we are spending most of our time in supervision today arguing among ourselves about various small issues. Is this how we want to spend our time?"

so note the behavior through a comment about the group energy: "Everyone's pretty quiet today. I don't feel much energy right now in the group." This comment could then be followed up with a group directed question: "What do you see going on in the group?" or "Where is everyone today?" Other examples of leader interventions designed to work with conflict and negative communication patterns are listed in Rapid Reference 4.8.

Addressing multicultural differences in group supervision. It is sometimes easy when working with supervisees, especially those with advanced degrees, to assume that because everyone in a supervision group is a professional, multicultural differences are not an issue. However, many differences can impact group cohesion: gender, gender preference, race, ethnicity, age, physical handicaps, and field of discipline, to name a few. These differences can either enhance the group experience or create divisiveness depending on how they are addressed. Contrary to what many believe, promoting self-awareness in group members concerning multicultural differences can lead to an improvement in both general counseling

CAUTION

Watch scapegoating of group members if there is an imbalance in group membership on race, gender, sexual orientation, age, discipline, theoretical model, or any other significant multicultural difference.

skills and multicultural competence (Torres-Rivera et al., 2001). Rapid Reference 4.9 gives a number of suggestions for how to initiate a discussion about multicultural differences in group supervision.

Team Supervision

Team supervision is another traditional group format for supervision that is made up of a number of variations. In medical settings, the supervisee is part

≡Rapid Reference 4.9

How to Introduce the Topic of Multicultural Differences in Group Supervision

1. Bring up the issue of multicultural differences in the group at the start. "How important do you think race, gender, ethnicity, or other differences are in relationship building with clients?"
2. Ask supervisees to discuss cultural differences when they present each client case in the group.
3. Normalize the existence of differences in the supervision group. Note at the beginning of the group that there will be differences in viewpoint, theoretical model, attitudes, and beliefs among group members and with you, the supervisor. Encourage supervisees to openly explore these differences in the group.
4. Use self-disclosure to highlight the powerful effect of differences on relationships with clients through sharing one or two examples from your own experience. These experiences with clients could be positive as well as negative.
5. After some time passes and supervisees are more comfortable in the group, go back to the topic of differences and how they might effect relationships in the supervision group and with you. "How does the fact I am female and you are male [or that I am considerably older] impact our relationship? Positives? Negatives? How might these same issues be present in our relationship with clients?"
6. Play devil's advocate. If a supervisee seems to be in love with a particular diagnosis or interpretation of client problems or shows bias toward certain cultural groups, suggest when they present a client case that they change the gender or race of the client and then review his or her assessment of the client's strengths and problems.

Putting It Into Practice

Group Supervision Case Example

In group supervision, Helen, a beginning-level supervisee, began discussing one of her client cases that was creating difficulties for her. She said she found herself disliking this client because at their first meeting, he kept questioning her ability to help him because of her youth and lack of experience. Other members of the group who were more experienced jumped in immediately with a number of suggestions for how to handle such a situation. Helen sat silently listening to this feedback. The group supervisor interrupted the discussion with a process question. "Helen, what are you experiencing right now as the members give you this feedback?" In response to this question, Helen stated she felt overwhelmed by all of the suggestions and that the group response left her feeling very inadequate and doubtful of her abilities. The supervisor then asked her if she thought that might be similar to how she felt with her client, to which Helen readily agreed. The group leader then invited her to explore in more depth how she might wish to approach this client and how the group may be helpful to her in that endeavor.

Teaching Point: The supervisor used group process as vehicle to help Helen feel more empowered. By interrupting group feedback, the supervisor prevented the group from feeding Helen's perceived inadequacies and, instead, turned the event into a supportive learning experience.

of a team of mental health professionals from different disciplines, such as a psychiatrist or psychologist along with a social worker, a nurse, and a counselor. They all work together to train the supervisee. A variety of methods and techniques can be employed with this format. Sometimes the entire team is involved in the evaluative component, but in other instances, this role falls to the team leader, who may or may not seek input from others. Obviously, such a format can be a powerful teaching and training model, for it provides for the open exchange of ideas and suggestions among different disciplines. When the team leader includes team members equally in setting the structure and the evaluative component, this model can help defuse dual relationship issues and prevent misuse of power and authority.

Team supervision is also practiced in graduate school programs. A team of supervisors, many of them graduate students in training, will stand behind a mirror and give suggestions or directions to the supervisee by phone or a bug in the ear. Afterward, the entire team will process the session with the therapist in training. Sometimes the team will observe the session from behind the mirror and then reverse positions so that the family and therapist are behind the mirror to observe the teams' discussion of the session. By giving supervision live, and by using a team of supervisors, many problems of traditional one-on-one supervision that is done retrospectively and relies heavily on self-report can be avoided. When videotape is added, it can be even more powerful. Also, having supervisees themselves supervise other trainees increases everyone's confidence, mastery, and trust.

A third model for team supervision is used for internships, postdegree licensure situations, or both. In this model, supervisees are assigned a rotation in a particular area of a hospital unit or clinic for a set period of time. For example in a year-long internship, supervisees might be assigned three rotations. The length of time would vary depending on the requirements of the training program and the organizational context. In many instances, clinical supervisors involved in these rotations will periodically meet to discuss each supervisee's progress and difficulties as well as areas for further training.

Another use of the team supervision format in organizational settings arranges staff members into supervision groups or teams. Such workplace teams, which function more as consultation groups, offer members a safe place to reflect on their clinical work and the organizational pressures that impact it, such as the conflict many counselors and psychotherapists experience between professional ethical standards and organizational ethics. Workplace teams have many other benefits as they have been found to increase job satisfaction and morale and, in many instances, initiate important changes within the organization. More information on supervision teams in the workplace can be found in Chapter 9.

Structuring Team Supervision

As with any type of group, makeup of the team, structure, goals, and evaluation are important factors to be considered. (See the previous section on group supervision for more details on how to structure groups in supervision.) Homogeneity of the team can also be a key issue. A fair amount of homogeneity among team members can lessen friction. On the other hand, some difference in discipline, theory, or approach to clients is the primary benefit of team supervision. Before beginning the supervision process, supervisors need to discuss with supervisees the differences among team members so that they do not get confused or overwhelmed by all of the varying viewpoints. If the makeup of the team involves supervisors and supervisees from a variety of disciplines, organizational settings, or theoretical models, pairing of team members could be built into the group process. In other words, when a social worker presents a case, the first feedback comes from other social workers on the team who share a similar viewpoint. Then, other team members who come from different backgrounds could be in-

vited to share their thoughts and concerns. Such a structure supports the
idea that differences in viewpoint,
theoretical models, and disciplines
exist in the mental health field without team members becoming lost in
arguments about who is right or who
is wrong.

Team leaders will also need to
keep an eye on the group process
and work hard to forge mutual trust
among all of the members. One idea
is to appoint a team observer for each
meeting who will monitor the group
process and the team's ability to work
together, and then, at appointed
times, make comments and suggestions. A review of important factors to consider in planning for team supervision is listed in Rapid Reference 4.10.

> ≡ *Rapid Reference 4.10*
>
> ### Considerations for the Team Supervisor
>
> - Makeup of the team
> - How differences in perspective will be managed
> - Structure and goals for the supervision experience
> - Rules to promote trust
> - Role of supervisees in the team
> - Evaluation procedures
> - The procedure to monitor effectiveness of the team

There are many advantages to team supervision. First and foremost is that
by receiving feedback from different viewpoints, supervisees expand their intervention repertory. Second, team supervision can also promote fairness and
prevent harm that may come from dual relationships. For example, when clinical supervisors are also administrators, and supervisees are employees receiving
supervision for licensure purpose, delegating others to do either all or part of
the clinical supervision piece or organizing a supervision team can solve likely
conflict of interest problems.

Organizationally, team supervision can help to increase staff unity, improve
morale, and lower stress levels. For supervisees, it promotes the importance of
collaboration to solve problems and improve client care. The old adage that two
heads are better than one certainly applies here. Last, when more-experienced
clinicians are included in the training team, they have an opportunity to share
their wisdom with new professionals, which, in turn, can invigorate fading energy, give new meaning to work, and revitalize enthusiasm for training among
all team members.

Nevertheless, just as with other supervision formats, disadvantages to the team
supervision format exist. Perhaps the biggest problem is time. Successful team
supervision requires considerable time for up-front planning and execution. For
example, the team-behind-the-mirror format is labor intensive and requires the

creation of a training room with mirrors in a facility. Last, it may be difficult to coordinate everyone's schedules so they are able to engage in team supervision.

Another issue is one of cooperation and safety. Organizational climate can have a potent impact on the success of team supervision. In situations where there is open conflict and hostility among team supervisors, supervisees may feel caught in the middle and experience considerable anxiety over conflicting suggestions and directions. Even in the best of circumstances, receiving a large number of suggestions from different theoretical models or perspectives can be a bit overwhelming. Along with these problems, supervisees may encounter concerns about confidentiality and the misuse of information on the part of particular supervisors.

Another probable disadvantage is that considerable transference and countertransference (thoughts or feelings that are generated by past experiences in one's family of origin, particularly with authority) can be brought into the su-

Putting It Into Practice

Team Supervision

Cynthia, a graduate intern, was assigned to an inpatient medical setting where she was to lead psychotherapy groups for patients. From the beginning Cynthia was told that she would be supervised by the team staff as a whole but received no additional information about what to expect or how this would be done. She assumed she would receive information about supervision and be oriented at the first team meeting. However, at the first team meeting, Dr. Frank began by asking Cynthia to review what had happened in her first group with patients. As Cynthia began to relay her experiences, Mrs. C, the unit nurse, interrupted several times to give Cynthia information and feedback about several of the patients in the group. When this occurred, Mrs. D., the unit social worker, verbally disagreed with every point the nurse was making. Cynthia became confused and finally stopped talking altogether, waiting for Dr. Frank to moderate the argument and give her directions on how to proceed. However, Dr. Frank turned and scolded her, saying "Well, don't you have anything more to say? Is this all you have to tell us? I expected a higher level of knowledge and competency from a graduate intern from University X. What a disappointment."

Teaching Point: Cynthia did not receive sufficient information concerning team supervision previous to her beginning her internship. The team of supervisors did not have a basic structure or plan in place for supervision and how it would progress. Relationship problems between two members of the team dominated the case review and caught Cynthia in the crossfire. Cynthia mistakenly believed the psychiatrist, as the highest status member, was in charge of the team, so he would be the one to give her directions. This lack of planning and orientation for supervision by the team staff, along with Cynthia's failure to seek more information before the first team meeting, had the result that Cynthia was wrongly attacked and blamed.

pervision team. If monitored and used correctly, transference and countertransference among team members and the leader can make a positive contribution to supervisees' professional development. However, if not recognized and processed by the team, this same family-of-origin material can have a deleterious effect on the team.

Even with these disadvantages, team supervision can be adapted to any circumstance and should be a welcome addition to the traditional individual clinical supervision model. It would make sense for busy clinical supervisors to consider the addition of some type of team supervision to one's supervision plan, even if it only occurs occasionally during the supervision period.

Peer Supervision

Peer supervision occurs when supervisees are organized into some type of structured group experience without the actual clinical supervisor being present. Busy supervisors will find that peer supervision, if structured carefully, can function as a complement to individual supervision. For supervisors who are balancing both administrative and clinical supervision, providing supervisees with opportunities to work together without the supervisor's presence has many advantages, especially in defusing issues related to power and authority. Without doubt, a peer supervision group could also be used for the purpose of providing supervisors with supervision of supervision. (See Chapter 9.)

Structuring a Peer Supervision Group

Offering peer supervision can be a valuable addition to any clinical supervision experience. However, just as with the other types of group supervision, a number of issues need to be addressed to improve success, such as size, structure, rules, allocation of time, and evaluation. Those pondering adding peer supervision should review the section in this chapter on group supervision for more detailed suggestions.

There are a number of issues to address when establishing a peer supervision group. First is the purpose of the group, its format, and structure. Peer supervision groups will be more successful if structured with clear learning objectives and if tight boundaries are set as to appropriate content for the group. Just as in other formats, supervisees need to be involved in the planning process and some modicum of struc-

CAUTION

Peer supervision should never be used as a substitute for actual supervision.

DON'T FORGET

Structure will enhance the value of peer supervision. To improve chances for success, let members of the peer supervision group create the goals, structure, rules, and evaluation component.

ture established before the group begins. Obvious questions to consider are how time will be utilized, whether the group will be leaderless or will the supervisees themselves rotate leadership or appoint a leader, and whether each person will be given time to present a case or just one or two at a time, and so forth. Perhaps the simplest structure is to preselect two or three questions that each supervisee will have to address when presenting cases in the group and to appoint a facilitator or timekeeper to keep everyone on track. This same timekeeper could also serve as the group observer, who will give a few comments on the group process and seek suggestions from the group on how to improve the use of time.

Another issue is the size and makeup of the peer supervision group. To improve the value of the experience, there ought to be some degree of equality among participants, some similarity in client cases discussed, and a fairly high level of training and experience among members so that feedback among members will be accurate (Powell, 1993). The size of the group will also play a part in the group's success, with no more than six supervisees per group recommended in order to easily manage the group and offer everyone time for supervision. Realistically, however, even in small peer supervision groups that last for only 1 hour, just one or two supervisees might get to present at each meeting.

Another important concern is the evaluation component as to how it will be carried out and how feedback will be used. For example, supervisors could ask members of the group to create a short rating scale as a means to give each other feedback and then collect copies to use as part of the formal evaluation. However, if trust is an issue, such as in situations where the clinical supervisor is the administrative supervisor or major professor, it may be decided to keep all feedback exclusively among members of the peer group. Whatever structure is selected, training on the use of any evaluation tools or rating scales will be necessary before the group begins.

CAUTION

Peer supervision is difficult in situations where:

- there is too much disparity in the education and experience level of supervisees
- the organizational system is toxic, and full of blame, and punishment, so that supervisees do not feel safe
- there are situations of upheaval and organizational change

The advantages of peer supervision are numerous. Peer supervision can increase the supervisor's ability to overcome time limitations, defuse problems of power, encourage independence and self-management, foster teamwork, and build group cohesiveness. Peer supervision can also offer help to beleaguered supervisors who are struggling with a difficult supervisee by removing themselves from the scene and allowing for different interactions with the peer group.

Naturally, there are also many disadvantages with peer supervision. First is the loss of control as supervisees may ignore the supervisor's structure and direction, misuse the group to scapegoat or harass a member, or add more conflict to problem situations. Second, to be effective, peer supervision requires planning, teamwork, and openness on the part of the supervisor to solicit feedback from the group. Additionally, as mentioned previously, if the organizational context is problematic and people don't feel generally safe, peer supervision can turn

Putting It Into Practice

Peer Supervision

A large nonprofit agency that served children and families in the community had a sizable training program with master and doctoral level interns, some within degree and some postdegree, from all over the country. The training director believed strongly that giving these interns time to process their experiences would have great benefit. A biweekly peer supervision group for trainees was established and had been functioning effectively for many years. Rachael was a new postdegree intern who had had a really bad experience with supervision at her previous site and was struggling. Her supervisor was upset with Rachael because she seemed so closed and defensive to receive any feedback, and he tried mightily to open Rachael up to no avail. Rachael, in the mean time, had attended several of the peer supervision meetings but felt very isolated because everyone in the group seemed to be so positive about the internship supervision and how much they were learning. This was opposite to her experience. Finally, one member in the peer supervision group confronted Rachael about her lack of participation and seeming indifference. With fear and trepidation, Rachael explained about her previous experience with supervision where she felt scapegoated by her supervisor and her supervision group. The members of the group thanked her for taking the risk to be so forthcoming with them about her bad experiences in supervision. Each member offered her support, and many shared some of their bad previous experiences with supervisors. They also encouraged her to share this same information with her supervisor, who most members felt was an open and caring individual. Rachael felt a huge weight lift off her shoulders.

Teaching Point: A peer supervision group can provide a safe place for supervisees to process their thoughts and feelings and help with the overall supervision experience.

DON'T FORGET

Combining supervision formats can accomplish the following:

- Help to monitor as well as to train and develop
- Help to solve problems and manage difficulties, such as issues of bias, subjectivity, and dual relationships

into a forum for griping and feed everyone's anger and frustration. Also, if supervisees are inexperienced or group members very diverse educationally and in terms of experience, it would be difficult to create a genuine peer supervision group. For example, if members run the gamut from psychologists to paraprofessionals and from people who are inexperienced to practitioners who have been in the organization for 15 years, the resulting interactions would probably not be representative of true, collaborative peer supervision.

In closing, exploring the use of at least one other format for supervision beyond traditional individual supervision has much to offer both supervisors and supervisees from a teaching and learning perspective as well as the monitoring function. Whereas adding something new to a supervision plan, such as group or peer supervision, might require in the beginning some additional time and effort on the part of supervisors, the rewards should outweigh any extra inconvenience.

 TEST YOURSELF

1. **Clinical supervisors should consider expanding their use of formats, methods, and techniques because**
   (a) variety is the spice of life.
   (b) using a variety of formats, methods, and techniques improves learning, expands ability to monitor, and enhances fairness.
   (c) it is not really necessary to go to all that bother.
   (d) switching among methods and techniques keeps supervisees on their toes.

2. **Regardless of format selected, it is important to have some elementary structure for the format to ensure success.** True or False?

3. **There is no reason why busy supervisors cannot substitute group supervision for individual supervision.** True or False?

4. **The best way to start individual supervision with a first-time supervisee is to**

   (a) ask them "What do you want to talk about today?"

   (b) suggest some type of structure and ask for comments and suggestions from them.

   (c) just start out reviewing cases.

   (d) make it clear that you are the expert and in charge, so you will tell them exactly what to do.

5. **The biggest problem with individual supervision is**

   (a) bias and impaired judgment on the part of supervisors.

   (b) improper use of power and authority.

   (c) withholding of information on the part of supervisees.

   (d) finding time to do it.

   (e) all of the above.

6. **Whenever possible, combine case consultation with other methods and techniques, such as a written case review sheet or role-play.** True or False?

7. **Any supervisor that is skilled in group therapy can do group supervision.** True or False?

8. **With group supervision, supervisors need to**

   (a) constantly balance the needs of supervisees with needs of the group.

   (b) make sure there is plenty of diversity in the group to keep it lively.

   (c) be sure to take time to set structure and rules for the group.

   (d) just get started and let the group structure itself as they go along.

   (e) do a and c.

   (f) do none of the above.

   (g) do all of the above.

9. **Everyone who participates in group supervision is completely prepared to give and receive feedback, so supervisors do not have to waste precious supervision time talking about that issue.** True or False?

10. **In toxic environments where people are upset and angry, peer supervision is the best strategy for supervisors to consider to defuse the situation.** True or False?

(continued)

11. Team supervision means

   (a) having a group of supervisors behind a mirror who call in suggestions to supervisees.

   (b) having the team of supervisors come from different disciplines and having everyone work with the supervisee.

   (c) rotating supervisees through a series of supervisors.

   (d) all of the above.

   (e) none of the above.

12. The primary issue for beginning supervisees in any supervision format is

   (a) "Will I be safe?"

   (b) "Will I be seen as competent?"

   (c) "Will I be able to outsmart my supervisor?"

   (d) "Will I be able to get through with the least amount of effort?"

   (e) all of the above.

   (f) only a and b.

   (g) only b and c.

13. Open conflict within group supervision is normal, natural, and healthy, especially if members feel comfortable to say exactly what they think regardless of anyone's feelings. True or False?

14. When there is great diversity in level of education and experience in a supervision group, it is best for group leaders to

   (a) let the more experienced supervisees take over the group because they know what to do.

   (b) limit the amount and kind of feedback to less experienced supervisees so they don't become overwhelmed and shut down.

   (c) initiate open theoretical discussions about ways to approach client cases so that beginners will get a grasp of the complexity in the work.

   (d) excuse the more experienced supervisees from the group because it will be a waste of their time.

15. Including topics in supervision is an easy way to increase learning in supervision. True or False?

Answers: 1. b; 2. True; 3. False; 4. b; 5. e; 6. True; 7. False; 8. e; 9. False; 10. False; 11. d; 12. f; 13. False; 14. b; 15. True

Five

METHODS AND TECHNIQUES FOR CLINICAL SUPERVISION

A variety of methods and techniques could be selected to use with the various supervision formats described in the previous chapter. For example, methods such as case consultation, written activities, audio- and videotaping, live supervision, and cotherapy can be utilized within individual, group, team, or peer supervision. Then techniques such as modeling, demonstration, role-play and role reversal, Gestalt empty chair, and psychodrama could be employed with each format or method. In other words, formats, methods, and techniques can be combined in a vast array of combinations to increase the effectiveness of supervision.

Regardless of the format selected—individual, group, team, or peer—it is important to determine what method or technique might work best to help each supervisee learn and grow (Campbell, 2000; Storm et al., 2001). This task first requires supervisors to be familiar with the methods and techniques available to them. (See Rapid Reference 5.1.) It also requires a familiarity with each supervisee's strengths, deficits, and preferred style of learning as well as a willingness to adapt to those needs.

For example, case consultation is the most common method of supervision employed with supervisees at all levels of experience, yet it is totally a verbal and auditory learning approach that requires a vast repertory of skill and knowledge by supervisees about any number of subjects and the capacity for abstract thinking, such as the ability to identify and select important information out of a myriad of details, as well as verbal fluidity in order for it to be done successfully. It may not be the most effective learning strategy for supervisees who are concrete in their thinking and less able to handle cognitive complexity, visual or kinesthetic learners, or people for whom English is a second language. Instead, the addition of written assignments, such as a case review sheet or written questions, to the standard verbal form of case presentation will increase learning for many supervisees.

Another reason to use a variety of methods and techniques in supervision is

≡Rapid Reference 5.1

Sample of Supervision Methods and Techniques

Case Consultation
- Structured questions
- Thematic topical selection of cases for training purpose

Written Activities
- Journaling
- Activity log
- Review of written documentation
- Process recording/Verbatims
- Structured case review sheet
- Simulated case scenarios
- Actual case vignettes

Live Observation
- Sit in the room during a client session
- Stand behind a mirror and observe

Interactive Live Supervision
- Individual or team behind the mirror with phones or bug in the ear
- Watch part of session and then participate
- Cotherapy

Modeling and Demonstration
- Model intervention strategy
- Demonstrate skill, supervisees rehearse it, and then role-play

Audiotaping and Videotaping
- Use of IPR
- Review a tape and give written feedback
- Structured process commentary

Experiential Methods
- Role-play
- Role reversal
- Psychodrama
- Gestalt empty chair
- Family sculpting
- Art therapy
- Genograms

it not only improves the clinical supervisor's training function, but it also assists in the critical role of monitoring by providing the supervisor a much broader picture of what is occurring with supervisees and their clients. For example, by adding written assignments, role-play with role reversal to individual case consultation, or videotaping and cotherapy to group supervision, it provides supervisors with a more complete picture of supervisees' skills and ability to work competently with clients. Hence, it is essential for clinical supervisors to expand their repertory within each format to include a variety of methods and techniques and be able to combine them for maximum learning and monitoring benefit. The purpose of this chapter is to familiarize readers with the advantages and disadvantages of the most common supervision methods and techniques and discuss their application in supervision.

CASE CONSULTATION

Case consultation is perhaps the most popular and best-known method of supervision and is core to traditional supervision dating back to the time of Freud. It is the basis of supervision activity in all formats from individual to group, team, or peer. Typically, supervisees bring in their client cases and present them to the supervisor, reviewing their assessment of the client's problems and their plan of action. Supervisors ask questions, make suggestions, and discuss various options available in each situation. Timing and content may vary, especially with new supervisees or in times of crisis, but normally case consultation is entirely a verbal self-report of a supervisee's cases. With large numbers of clients to serve and limited time and resources with which to help them, this method is considered to be the most effective for monitoring purposes.

In the early stages of supervision, supervisors may wish to structure case consultation, whereas more advanced supervisees should be the ones to suggest the focus and content for the consultation. For example, supervisors could decide they want a quick overview of most of the supervisees' cases, or they may want specific detailed information about particular ones. Some supervisors concentrate exclusively on problem clients while others want to hear about supervisees' successes as well as difficulties. Supervisees themselves may want to detail a spe-

CAUTION

To maximize the benefit of case consultation, it is necessary to create a structure, identify goals and purpose, and tie it to learning objectives. No matter what, it is best to create two or three provocative questions to use in case consultation to stimulate thinking and increase learning on the part of the supervisee.

cific problem with a client, or they may seek more extensive assistance from the supervisor with an entire client situation. At issue for all supervisors is how to maximize the use of time in case consultation to the greatest benefit to clients. As experienced supervisors know, having a focus for each case consultation session will help improve the profit gained from the time spent. Another suggestion is to include some kind of thought-provoking questions as supervisees discuss their cases. More information about the use of questions in case consultation follows in the next section.

A strong argument can be made for the number of benefits accrued from using the case consultation method. This method helps supervisees organize information; conceptualize problems; make assessments; decide intervention strategies; consider the larger context of a problem, such as the role of cross-cultural issues or ethical dilemmas; develop a theoretical model of change; integrate theoretical understanding with practice; process relationship issues, such as parallel process or transference; promote self-awareness on the part of supervisees; and encourage independence (McCollum & Wetchler, 1995; Noelle, 2002). Rapid Reference 5.2 summarizes the benefits that can be gained from case consultation.

═ *Rapid Reference 5.2*

Benefits from Case Consultation

Case consultation can be used to do the following:

- Protect clients and promote development
- Explore assessment and diagnostic skills
- Teach case conceptualization
- Apply techniques and theory
- Process relationship issues
- Promote self-awareness, especially the impact of personal feelings on client care
- Teach ethics
- Explore the impact of multicultural issues on clients and client care
- Promote development of self-efficacy in supervisees

However, there are also a number of important drawbacks to relying exclusively on case consultation as the only supervision method. First, case consultation is a self-report method and therefore can be subject to deception, especially when supervisees are fearful of criticism or making mistakes (Noelle, 2002; Webb & Wheeler, 1998). In the article "Lying in Psychotherapy Supervision: Why Residents Say One Thing and Do Another," Hantoot (2000) reported psychiatry residents frequently left out information or misrepresented facts in order to avoid conflict, criticism, or poor evaluations from supervisors. Second, the success of self-report methods depends on the observational and conceptual abilities of the supervisee and is, in itself, a skill honed by years

of practice. Expecting novice supervisees to be able to identify and select
potential problem situations; to know
what the supervisor needs to know;
and to be willing to bring mistakes,
difficulties, and vulnerabilities into
case consultation might be unrealistic. If self-report is the only method
of supervision, not only does it make

DON'T FORGET

For those supervisees where English
is a second language, do not rely exclusively on verbal case review. Add
written case review sheets and/or
structured written assignments, taping or live observation, and role-play.

the supervisor vulnerable to missing potential problems but it also limits the supervisor's effectiveness as a teacher and trainer.

To avoid such difficulties, especially in the beginning of the supervisory relationship, it is recommended that supervisors include at least one more direct
method of gaining information about supervisees' interactions with clients, such
as the use of taping, live observation, or review of some or all of the written documentation for clients (Saccuzzo, 2002). Additionally, including a case review
sheet or written assignment along with self-report might help focus supervision
sessions and add benefit from both a teaching and monitoring perspective.

Use of Questions in Case Consultation

One device experienced supervisors use to make case consultation more meaningful as a teaching and training tool is to develop a repertory of thought-
provoking questions to use during case review (see Rapid Reference 5.3). Rather

≡Rapid Reference 5.3

Thought-Provoking Questions for Case Consultation

- "As you are talking about this particular family, are there any ethical issues of
  concern to you?"
- "What subject are you avoiding talking about with this client?"
- "Where are you with this client?"
- "How connected do you feel to this client?"
- "Are there any multicultural issues that may be a factor in your view of [or
  your relationship with] this client?"
- "I hear your assessment of the situation with this client, but I am curious; is
  there another way to conceptualize what is going here? Any other possibili-
  ties to consider?"

≡ *Rapid Reference 5.4*

Examples of Specific Questions to Ask in Case Consultation

- "Tell me one thing you have thought of to try with this client."
- "You said that the client is very depressed and suffers from anxiety. What things did the client say or do that led you to this diagnosis?" or "What indicators did you use to arrive at this assessment?"
- "You perceive this client as fragile and so have shied away from talking with about her coming late to her appointments or not calling to cancel. How might confrontation about her behavior be helpful to this client?"
- "What discrepancies have you noticed between what Mr. Smith says and what he does?"

than allowing supervisees to talk straight through the hour, supervisors interrupt, make observations, and then ask general open-style questions to stimulate thinking. Granello (2000) suggested supervisors tailor questions to the developmental level of supervisees such that in the beginning, questions about client cases would target specific information about the client case and connect it to coursework material, whereas with more advanced supervisees, questions would be designed to capture a more complex synthesis of information. For example, with beginners the supervisor might ask, "Remembering what you learned about the harm to clients from dual relationships, do you see any potential dual relationship issues present in your relationship with this client?" With the more advanced level of supervisees, this statement could be rephrased to "Any ethical issues of concern to you with this client?"

If general open-ended questions do not bring the desired information forth or supervisees seem bewildered, supervisors will need to back up and be more specific (Munson, 2002). Probing-style questions, such as "Can you give me an example of what you mean by that statement?" or a focused-style question, such as "What were you thinking right then?" may also help elicit more detail or give direction to case consultation.

Rapid Reference 5.4 presents some examples of specific probing-style questions to use in case consultation.

WRITTEN TECHNIQUES

There are a number of written techniques for supervision: activity logs, journaling, verbatims, process recording, case review forms, handouts, journal articles, and other reading assignments. Written techniques can be combined with case consultation, review of tapes, and live supervision in any of the supervision formats. Most supervisees are required to maintain a daily log of activities as part of their responsibilities. Supervisors might suggest a particular structure for this log and periodically review it to monitor time management issues, efficiency, and positive or negative behavioral patterns.

DON'T FORGET
....
Part of the supervisor's role is to promote professional growth and lifelong learning. Consequently it is essential that supervisors have an up-to-date collection of articles, handouts, books, and suggested readings to include as a part of supervision.

Additionally, asking supervisees to keep a journal to process their thoughts and feelings while in supervision can encourage self-exploration. This supervision strategy is especially popular for graduate students and beginning counselors. Supervisees could be given a series of structured exercises and self-awareness questions to process in the journal. The focus of a supervision journal is to heighten the supervisee's awareness of any personal thoughts, feelings, beliefs, or values that might impact client care, not for reasons of personal growth or psychotherapy. Therefore, the supervisor would not necessarily have to read any of the journal entries but instead prompt the supervisee to relate material to current client cases. For example the supervisor might ask "Did anything come up for you—thoughts or feelings—that you see might be important in your work with your clients [or this particular client]?" More material on how to use self-awareness exercises in supervision can be found in Chapter 9.

Process recording and verbatims are also popular techniques used in the early stages of supervision. With process recording, supervisees are asked to write up a client session on one side of a page and then process their thoughts and feelings on the other side. Verbatims involve supervisees recreating on paper an entire client session or part of a session that can then be reviewed in supervision.

Perhaps the most effective and easiest written technique for both training and monitoring purposes is to use a standard case review form. This form could be used with beginners in order to assist them in organizing their thinking or with those at a more advanced level to verify expertise. The case review form can be structured to focus attention on the conceptualization of client problems, assessment and diagnosis, selection of intervention strategies, ethical concerns, multicultural issues, or to increase self-awareness about personal responses to clients. Supervisors may wish to create their own case review form to fit their particular circumstances or use the one provided in Rapid Reference 5.5. In addition, there are a number of other case consultation forms available in the literature

≡ *Rapid Reference 5.5*

Sample Case Review Form

Name of the supervisee: _____

Date: _____   Session number: _____

Identifying data about the client: _____

Presenting problem: _____

Short summary of the session: _____

_____

Important history or environmental factors (especially multicultural issues or substance abuse): _____

Tentative assessment or problem conceptualization (diagnosis): _____

_____

Plan of action and goals for therapy (treatment plan, case management): _____

_____

Intervention strategies: _____

_____

Concerns or problems surrounding this case (ethical concerns, relationship issues, etc.): _____

_____

on supervision (Bernard and Goodyear, 2004; Bradley & Ladany, 2001; Falvey, Caldwell, & Cohen, 2002; Haber, 1996; Munson, 2002; Powell, 1993).

There is another important area of writing to focus attention on in clinical supervision: the obligatory client documentation in the mental health field, such as record keeping, charting, intake forms, process notes, and other paperwork required by third-party payers and accrediting bodies. Supervisees often struggle to learn correct documentation procedures and to do them in a timely fashion; consequently, clinical supervisors find themselves spending large amounts of time assisting their supervisees in this critical but complex area of practice. One commonsense suggestion to facilitate this learning process is for agencies and organizations to provide all clinical supervisors with a number of excellent examples of proper documentation and forms. Clinical supervisors could then use these examples for teaching and training purposes. Fill-in-the-blank forms or structured outlines that walk supervisees step by step through the thought process considered necessary to complete the paperwork may also offer additional assistance to those supervisees who struggle with writing.

Reviewing a part or all of a supervisee's documentation is a necessary addition to any supervision plan for monitoring purposes. Depending on the circumstances, job task, and the level of training and responsibility, this review of documentation might start out being inclusive, covering intakes, diagnosis or case conceptualization, progress notes, charts, and treatment plans or protocols. As skill

CAUTION

From both an ethical and legal standpoint, clinical supervisors need to increase their activity and attempts to monitor client safety and the quality of services provided to clients by supervisees. Review of supervisees' written documentation is one highly recommended strategy.

increases, the review might become more random. However, reviewing all diagnosis and treatment plans for doctoral or postdoctoral level psychologists, especially in private practice settings, is suggested by Saccuzzo (2002) because of liability issues.

LIVE SUPERVISION

Live supervision is another popular training technique. There are several ways to do live supervision: observational, interactive, or a combination of both. Each method has several benefits for both supervisor and supervisee. Observational techniques include sitting in the room, standing behind a mirror, and using video or telecommunication. Observation can be used in the early stages of supervision to assess competence and assist in the development of a supervision plan. In later stages, observation can be used as a means for evaluation. Observation and interactive techniques can be combined to provide training opportunities along with the monitoring functioning. While live supervision methods can be seen as intrusive and create a negative response from clients, several studies seem to indicate this is not the case if clients perceive the method employed as being helpful to them and if supervisees are comfortable with the supervisor and the situation (Locke & McCollum, 2001; Moorhouse & Carr, 2001).

Interactive techniques include cotherapy, use of a mirror with phones or a bug in the ear (a tiny microphone placed in the ear of the supervisee through which the supervisor can communicate during a therapy session), modeling, and demonstration. With interactive live supervision, the supervisor takes a more active role. A number of possibilities exist when the supervisor is actually in the room with the supervisee and the client: The supervisor may interrupt periodically to make suggestions, stop the session and take over to model a particular technique and then ask the supervisee to continue, or stop after

> ### DON'T FORGET
> ....
> Seek cooperation and collabora-
> tion from all concerned before any
> live supervision session. Spend time
> educating clients as to the purpose
> and value of live supervision for them
> and their care. Be sure supervisees
> also understand the benefits of the
> live supervision and feel comfortable
> with the supervisor.

half the session and process what has occurred to that point with the supervisee while the client is still in the room. In this instance, to clarify roles and boundaries and prevent confusion, Haber (1996) recommended that a chair be set aside in the room for the supervisor to move to whenever commenting or giving corrective feedback to the supervisee. Limiting comments and interruptions to a small number is also recommended in order to avoid the impression of the supervisor taking over the session.

Cotherapy is another time-efficient method of interactive live supervision that can easily be used with either individual or group supervision and would be an excellent adjunct to traditional case consultation (McGee & Burton, 1998). Supervisors can explain and model techniques at the same time as they learn about the supervisee's needs and style. For some supervisees, it can also help reduce anxiety and encourage risk-taking. However, for others the opposite may be true. Hence, supervisors will have to discuss with their supervisee their needs as a cotherapist and then, as things progress, check on how the cotherapy relationship is proceeding. Another common issue facing some supervisors is managing the dance of power with the supervisee. There are times when supervisors will want to exercise power and direct the client session but other times when they will need to take a secondary role in order to promote the supervisee's independence.

To maximize the benefit of live supervision, a few activities are recommended. First, the supervisor needs to be oriented to the particular client case selected for live observation—the background, the goals for the session, and the planned approach. The supervisee could submit this information in writing before the session to save time. Next, decide whether to observe the entire meeting with the client or just a part of one. Most important, allow 10 or more minutes for supervisor-supervisee feedback immediately following the actual session while thoughts are fresh. Even overwhelmed practitioners, if convinced of the value of live supervision, can negotiate this at least once during a supervision experience. Rapid Reference 5.6 outlines a number of hints to maximize the value of live supervision.

≡ Rapid Reference 5.6

Hints for Providing Effective Live Supervision

To reduce anxiety and promote comfort before beginning the session, do the following:

- Explain clearly to supervisee and clients the purpose of observation. "I am going to be sitting in on your session. Most of my attention will be on your therapist [or case manager], and afterward the two of us will be sitting down together to discuss ideas and options for your care. I am just going to watch, not participate. I really simply want to see how things are going. I see myself here in a supportive function to you both."

- Gain permission from client to observe session. "Are you comfortable with my sitting in? Do you have any questions or concerns?"

- Orient observation process. "I am just going to sit and observe, not participate. You may notice that I am taking some notes during the session. This will be used for discussion in my next supervision session with your therapist [or case manager] and then destroyed."

- Ask supervisee and client for assistance in selecting a viewpoint out of direct view line. "Where would you like me to sit that will be least distracting to you?"

- If the purpose of the visit is strictly observation, make no comments during the actual session.

- If a problem occurs that requires your intervention, be sure to ask permission from both supervisee and client to interrupt and become interactive.

- Plan time (5 to 10 minutes) to process observations immediately following the session.

- Use structured questions or checklists to guide observations and feedback.

- Limit critical remarks. Focus on strengths and progress.

- If possible, observe more than one session as the supervisee's anxiety can sometimes impact the session.

- Add audio- or videotaping along with the observation to increase learning potential.

MODELING AND DEMONSTRATION

Modeling and demonstration are powerful clinical supervision tools. Whether conscious of it, supervisors are continually modeling for supervisees how to be effective mental health professionals. However, traditional case consultation with the emphasis on verbal reporting tends to preclude more action during supervision. Supervisees often complain that they have never actually seen their

DON'T FORGET

Explain to supervisees the purpose of the demonstration. Point out what specifics you would like supervisees to note in the demonstration. Be sure to reserve a few minutes directly following any demonstration to process learning. When possible, follow up any demonstration immediately with a practice session.

supervisor work with clients. Many are starved for just such experience. Modeling and demonstration can be used in a variety of supervision formats, including group supervision, and combined with other methods and techniques, such as reviewing tapes or case consultation. Supervisees can gain extensive benefits from a combination of demonstration, modeling, and role-play practice. For example, with group supervision, supervisors could insert a demonstration into a discussion of a client situation and then invite the supervisee to immediately practice the suggested technique through role-play with the supervisor. "Let me show you quickly how I might go about that. You be the client, and I will be you. Then we will switch roles."

Additionally, modeling and demonstration can be combined with live observation by having supervisees observe the supervisor working with one of his or her clients and then process the experience. This is a highly recommended strategy to apply in order to train novice supervisees how to handle crisis situations.

There is another valuable way to use modeling and demonstration in supervision with a number of possible benefits. Invite several practitioners who have particular expertise in handling difficult situations, such as defusing angry clients, handling traumatic incidents, or reporting abuse to child protective services, to either do a live demonstration for supervisees or create a video for training purposes. This suggestion can have secondary return as a means to counteract burnout and low motivation among experienced long-time clinicians, stretch small training budgets, as well as provide additional support for busy supervisors.

To highlight differences between disciplines in approach to clients or differences in theoretical models, several people could demonstrate how they would work with the same client.

RECORDING CLIENT SESSIONS FOR SUPERVISION

Although research has demonstrated the effectiveness of audio- and videotaping in clinical supervision, it is not widely used outside academic settings (Ellis, Krengel, & Beck, 2002; Wetchler, Piercy, & Sprenkle, 1989). Many times recording sessions using audio, video, or digital technology is not used in supervision outside of academic settings because of anxiety that it will have adverse impact on clients or the idea of recording client sessions in an agency, school, hospital, or private setting appears overwhelming and troublesome. Another dominant fear is that somehow any recording will have an adverse impact on a malpractice lawsuit. However, experience shows that the majority of anticipated problems with recording client sessions rarely occur. If the value of recording sessions as a supervision method is presented correctly so that both supervisees and their clients see the value, most initial anxiety evaporates. And if correct procedures are followed for protecting the confidentiality of clients when using technology, recording client sessions can become an ally of supervisors in many troublesome situations.

Each method of recording has merits and drawbacks. Audiotaping is technically easy, more readily available, and less expensive than using videotaping or digital cameras. It is also less invasive. However, videorecordings can provide a richer source of information. With expanding new technologies, such as digital cameras and camcorders, recording of client sessions is even more accessible as a means for supervision. For example, with a digital camera, the session can be recorded onto a compact disc (CD) to view on a computer or used for a videoconference or teleconference (more on technology in supervision in next section). The same technology could be used to record workshops and seminars as well as demonstrations of intervention strategies by experts. Certainly, building a video and CD library is a relatively inexpensive way to expand professional training in any organization.

Recording client sessions as a supervision method, regardless of the technology utilized, has many rewards as it can be used for both training and monitoring purposes. Recordings of client sessions can serve as an adjunct to any format for supervision: individual, group, team, or peer. Audio- and videotapes or CDs can be reviewed as a many times as desired for different purposes and with various structures. Written questions or assignments can be added to enrich the experience. However, the greatest benefit of using recordings of client sessions for supervision is that through the process of reviewing the session with supervisors, supervisees increase their self-awareness and learn how to supervise themselves.

As with other methods, to reap

CAUTION

Supervisors must take time to prepare both supervisees and clients for recording sessions. They need to discuss the purpose, the benefits, the structure, and how confidentiality will be protected. Additionally, there should be ample opportunity for both supervisee and clients to give supervisors feedback about their concerns.

maximum benefit from recordings in supervision, supervisors will need to think through their goals for its use, have some structure in mind for reviewing the recording with supervisees, prepare both the supervisee and the client involved, and use release forms to protect confidentiality. It is also important for supervisors to believe in the value of this method and have experience with the medium employed.

How to Prepare for Recording Client Sessions

The first area to address is the availability of good quality equipment to use for the recording. If one's agency or organization does not own this equipment, find out how to borrow or rent it. Inexpensive digital camcorders with excellent sound and picture quality are now readily available and many now own them. Next, the technical aspects of using any recording equipment should be covered. Supervisees need to be familiar with all equipment and make at least one practice run at the chosen location to assure success. Nothing is more frustrating than attempting to listen to a tape or watch a video with no sound or the picture is of the floor or ceiling, not the people.

There are a number of aspects to consider that will vastly improve the quality of any recorded session. Use decent equipment and high quality tapes or discs that give better quality recordings. Make sure about the volume and clarity of sound. In most instances, even with the finest equipment, it is best to use separate clip-on microphones to improve sound clarity and ensure that what is discussed will be understood. Clip-on microphones are inexpensive and easy to obtain and use. Choose a quiet, private place both to protect confidentiality and to improve recording quality. Do not use an open space, an office with windows facing the street, or any place that is subject to interruptions. Loud air-conditioning fans, ringing phones and pagers, street noise, and office conversations all disrupt the quality of any recording. Without doubt, have everyone involved in the recorded session turn off his or her pager or cell phone and make sure any outside disruptions are stopped.

When using a video camera or camcorder, be sure to use a tripod to stabilize the picture. To reduce anxiety, place equipment out of direct view if at all possible. For example, place a tape recorder on a side table

DON'T FORGET

Before beginning to record any client session, have the supervisee make a short practice tape to check volume and picture quality, background noise level in the selected site, placement of chairs, and camera angles. Only when satisfied should the actual taping session begin.

between the counselor and client so that it is out of immediate view but within reach. With a video camera, place it at an angle so it is not directly facing the client. Check the picture to be sure it is of the desired subjects. If there is a TV monitor in the room that projects what is being filmed onto a visible screen, turn it off to avoid distractions.

After the equipment and room for the recording is set up, take steps to prepare clients for the session. Make sure clients receive information about the proposed recording at least one session before proceeding. A signed release form should be employed that outlines the purpose of the recording, the limits of confidentiality, the identity of those who will review the tape, and what procedures are in place to protect the confidentiality of client information, such as an assurance of erasure of tape or CD afterward (Campbell, 2000). A checklist to serve as a guide for recording a client session is included in Rapid Reference 5.7.

Occasionally, clients may express anxiety about having their session recorded for supervision purposes. It is normally sufficient to reassure them that they can turn off the tape player or camera at any point if they are really uncomfortable. This option is rarely used because usually after the first few minutes of the session, both client and therapist forget about the recording. However, if after explaining the purpose for the recording and answering any questions the cli-

---

≋Rapid Reference 5.7

Confidentiality and Taping

- Obtain a signed release form from clients before recorded session.
- Fully inform clients about how the recording will be used in supervision and who will see or hear it. If the recorded session will be used in group supervision or a staffing seminar, the client should be informed of that fact.
- Choose a private, controlled space for any recording.
- Protect tapes and discs; keep them in a locked cabinet; don't include identifying data on the outside of the tape or CD holder.
- Fully erase the recorded session when supervision is ended. With audio and video, do not merely tape over the previous session. Instead, rewind the tape and push the record button to completely erase the tape before reusing. If the session has been recorded on a CD, be sure to select the type of disc that can be erased and follow the instructions for complete erasure of material.
- If the recorded session will be used for teleconferencing or on the Internet, additional safeguards, such as encoding and use of a secure site, will have to be considered to guarantee complete confidentiality of client information.

DON'T FORGET

Be sure to cover the use of recordings for supervision in the written informed consent agreement signed by clients at intake. When clients understand how the recording will benefit them, most will assent.

DON'T FORGET

The more passionate supervisors are about the value of recording both as a training and monitoring tool, the more likely supervisees will be enthused and the more comfortable the client will be.

ent may have he or she continues to be reluctant and uncomfortable with the idea, a decision has to be made as to the appropriateness of using this method of supervision with this particular client.

As well as addressing the concerns of clients about the recording, supervisors need to do the same with supervisees. Supervisees may be anxious about the technical aspects of the process, including equipment and room availability. They may also be concerned about confidentiality and the impact of the recording on the client relationship. A further area for supervisee anxiety is worry about the supervisor's critical evaluation of his or her performance. Naturally, taking time to talk about these issues with supervisees would be a prudent strategy. Another suggestion to ease anxiety is to solicit the supervisee's feedback and observations about any recorded session before the supervisor comments.

Reviewing Recorded Sessions with Supervisees

The main value of recording sessions, whether by audiotaping, videotaping, or using digital technology, is that it provides supervisors and supervisees the luxury of reviewing sessions as many times as desired and employing a number of different approaches while at the same time processing any number of different issues. The supervisor may choose to review the recording alone before the supervision session and give verbal or written feedback to the supervisee, use voice-over to critique the session on the recording itself, or review the tape or disc with the supervisee during the supervision session. Written assignments are frequently added to supplement the review and increase learning. For example, supervisors could request a written summary of the client session along the lines suggested in Rapid Reference 5.8.

As tapes and discs can be reviewed numerous times or stopped and rewound and then replayed, there are numerous possibilities for supervision, such as examining relationship issues, processing thoughts and feelings, identifying non-

Rapid Reference 5.8

Topics That Might Be Included in a Written Summary of a Recorded Session

- "What was the plan of action for the session?"
- "What were the treatment goals? Planned intervention strategies?"
- "What did the client say or not say was the problem, and how might this be important to progress? Do you have any hunches about this client?"
- "Were there any multicultural issues that affected the session?"
- "Were there any ethical concerns? Boundary setting problems? Suspected trauma? Substance abuse?"
- "What are your feeling responses to the client?"
- "What personal issues are you aware of that may affect working with this client?"
- "How do you see the review of this recording improving your work with the client? Can you give an example?"
- "If you could redo this recorded session, what would you do differently? Can you name one thing that would improve the session?"

Putting It Into Practice

Using IPR to Review Recorded Sessions in Supervision

After reviewing a short section of the tape or the disc, the supervisor might stop the recording and ask any of the following process questions (adapted from Kagan, 1980b). It is a good idea to have these questions printed on a separate sheet to assist with the review. Offer the same list of printed questions to supervisees.

- "As you look at that segment, what are you most aware of?"
- "How are you feeling about the session at this point?"
- "What were you feeling right then when the client said (did) that?"
- "Where did you want to go with that comment (question)?"
- "What do you wish you had said or done right then?"
- "How was it for you when the client said that? Anything you are in touch with?"
- "I noticed when the client began to talk about their anger, you changed the subject? Any thoughts on that?"
- "What did you notice going on right then?"
- "I wonder, if you had said . . . , what do you think the client might have felt? (thought? done?)"
- "Where were you going when you asked . . . ? What were your hopes?"
- "Anything you wish you had done differently?"

verbal behaviors, and trying out new responses or intervention ideas. Familiarity with IPR would be immensely helpful as a tool to use with any review of recorded material in supervision. Employing IPR, both supervisor and supervisee sit down together to review the client session. In the beginning, the supervisor serves in the role of consultant to the supervisee's self-awareness by asking a series of structured questions to help the supervisee process relationship dynamics with the client. As skill with the method progresses, supervisees will take over the process by asking the same questions of themselves. A discussion of the IPR model is presented in Chapter 3.

In order to improve skill in the use of various recording devices, particularly videotaping or digital technology, supervisors may wish to make several record-

Putting It Into Practice

Case Example

Monica was an intern in a counseling center at the local university. All sessions with clients were videotaped and used in supervision. Her supervisor asked her each week to select certain sections of her client tapes for review and discussion. He gave her instructions and questions to guide selection for each week. After several weeks, she was asked to bring in a video of the client that she felt the least rapport with and select a section of the tape that best represented this problem. During supervision, Monica played the selected portion of the tape with her supervisor who asked her "As you look at this segment, what are you most aware of?" Monica realized her main feeling was one of frustration because this client always seemed to be complaining about everyone else and never taking responsibility for her actions. Then the supervisor rewound the selected section for replay. After the client spoke, her supervisor stopped the tape and asked "What were you feeling right then when Mrs. B. said that? Anything come to you now that you wish you had said at that point? How do you think Mrs. B would have responded?" As Monica processed her thoughts and feelings, she quickly recognized what the client said that irritated her so much and why she felt timid to call this to the client's attention. Then Monica's supervisor quizzed her as to the cost or benefit of not giving the client feedback. "If you protect this client from feedback that she doesn't like, what is the possible outcome? Positives? Negatives? Can you think of way to say what you want to say so the client will be more receptive?" At that point, Monica was aware of the fact that she had never seen anyone do so and asked if her supervisor might show her what he recommended and then let her practice it with him in supervision.

Teaching Point: This case example points attention to the value of recordings in supervision, especially as a training tool for inexperienced supervisees. By viewing only a piece of a recording and asking a few judicious questions, supervisors can increase self-awareness and ownership of supervision.

ings of their own client sessions and then practice reviewing each recording using a few of the suggestions given in the Putting It into Practice box on IPR. Reviewing one of these recordings with supervisees can have merit as a means to demonstrate the value of recording and reviewing of client sessions for supervision while reducing supervisees' anxiety. Rapid Reference 5.9 lists a number of suggestions for the review of recordings in supervision.

DON'T FORGET

In order to improve the value of recording as a method, supervisors must be completely comfortable and proficient with the medium. It is recommended that supervisors make at least one recording of themselves working with a client and practice several means to review the tape or disc before employing the method with supervisees.

≡Rapid Reference 5.9

How to Review Recordings of Client Sessions with Supervisees

1. Set the goals and structure for the review of the recorded session.
   - Keep goals limited in scope.
   - Don't overwhelm the supervisee with critical comments.
2. Respect confidentiality.
   - Do not play any recording of a client session at work or home where others can hear or see it.
   - Keep in locked file cabinet.
   - Avoid giving full identifying data on the front of tape or disc.
3. Have the supervisee prepare for review of the tape or disc.
   - Select section for viewing.
   - Rewind tape to the part considered for review in supervision or mark the section of the disc.
   - Prepare to discuss why this section was chosen.
4. Reduce supervisee anxiety.
   - Check level of supervisee satisfaction with the session before beginning the review. Ask the supervisee to summarize their feelings about the session.
   - Ask the supervisee to start the session review by stating one or two things they did well with this client (or they liked), and then discuss one to two areas for improvement or change.

(continued)

5. Emphasize the training aspect of the review.
   - Ask the supervisee what they would like to get out of reviewing the tape or disc with you. Ask how they see it as a benefit to them.
6. Stop the tape or disc at regular intervals to optimize learning.
   - The attention span for reviewing a tape is approximately 4 minutes (Whiffen, 1982).
   - If desired, longer segments of a tape or disc can be reviewed during supervision, but the goal for that experience needs to be clearly stated before doing so to increase learning.
   - Make sure both the supervisor and supervisee can stop the recording as needed.
   - Have the supervisee comment first whenever one stops the recording.
7. Make an effort to moderate the number of critical responses.
   - Do not stop the recording constantly to give corrective feedback.
   - Keep the feedback specific to whatever the goals were for the client session. For example, if the stated goal was to explore how the supervisee sets boundaries with clients, then restrain critical commentary to that purpose.
   - Offer other general comments and overall suggestions for improvement at end of the session.
8. Act as a consultant to the supervisee.
   - Use IPR questions to facilitate self-exploration.
   - See the Putting It into Practice box covering IPR style questions.
9. If reviewing a number of recorded client sessions with a supervisee, vary the structure of the review to prevent boredom.
   - Request that supervisees change focus in each recording.
   - Have them highlight a part of the session where they demonstrated use of particular skills.
   - Examine relationship dynamics, application of particular theory, multicultural differences, or ethical concerns.
10. Address resistance.
    - If the supervisee seems to be struggling with hearing feedback from the supervisor concerning the recorded session, ask the supervisee to imagine that he or she was the supervisor and then describe what suggestions he or she would make.
11. Return to the goal for the review of the recording at the end of the session.
    - Take time to ask the supervisee what they gained from the time spent on the review of the recorded session.
    - Ask the supervisee how learning could be improved.

Source: Campbell (2000).

COMPUTER TECHNOLOGY IN SUPERVISION

There is increasing interest in the application of new technology to supervision. Several studies have explored the use computer technology for supervision, and results have indicated a positive value for the use of e-mail and online consultation as a supplement to traditional face-to-face supervision (Clingerman & Bernard, 2004; Kanz, 2001; Rosenfield, 2002). For rural and isolated areas such as found in Alaska, the use of online supervision and consultation can help mental health practitioners better meet the needs of these communities in several ways (Kanz, 2001). For example, counselors in rural communities are frequently asked to see clients with specialized needs that may go far beyond their level of competency. The Internet can be used to gather information about the problem and then for supervision or consultation of the actual client case.

There is another burgeoning technology, desktop video conferencing, with application for supervision. While still primarily employed in universities because of the high cost of the technology, there is hope of it becoming more economically feasible in the near future. This technology is thought to have the most promise for long-distance supervision because it includes "real-time communication as well as audio and video information" (Kanz, 2001, p. 416).

There are a number of issues that have to be addressed with the use of e-mail and the Internet for supervision. First and foremost is confidentiality and protection of client data. Clients must be fully informed about the use of the Internet for supervision—the pros and cons—and give their permission. Encryption should be employed at all times. Even so, caution should be used as to the amount of personal data given. For example, instead of saying, "I work for the We Help Counseling Center in Missoula, Montana, and I have a client, Mr. N. Trouble. He is an adult white male who works for the city parks department and is presenting a substance abuse problem along with Axis II diagnosis." The counselor could say "I have a male adult client with a substance abuse problem along with depression [dual diagnosis is a possibility]."

Another issue when using e-mail for supervision is the possibility of misunderstandings when nonverbal cues are missing. Without such information, both supervisees and supervisors will have to work hard to keep communication channels open. On the other hand, many people, especially those who are shy and introverted, find writing e-mail an easier and safer means to open up and express themselves. A study by Clingerman and Bernard (2004) found that novice supervisees felt more relaxed and able to self-disclose their feelings when e-mailing supervisors.

A third area of ethical concern is the problem of licensure and interstate

CAUTION

Use e-mail, phones, and the Internet as a supplement to face-to-face supervision, not a complete replacement.

boundaries. Supervisors considering online supervision, especially for licensure purpose, should contact their licensure board for advice and direction.

Another area where computer technology can help busy supervisors is for the compilation of important information for training and supervision. Documentation, crisis intervention, policies and procedures, standardized intervention strategies, and group supervision techniques represent a smattering of topics that could be included on a CD for training purposes. For example, a CD could be made that covered the ethical codes and standards, laws, regulations, and organizational guidelines along with scenarios to demonstrate their application with clients. A more elaborate suggestion is to create a CD-ROM that includes both video and document material as a training tool (Manzanares et al., 2004).

EXPERIENTIAL TECHNIQUES

Experiential techniques can be very helpful to clinical supervisors in numerous ways. They can increase the level of understanding and empathy on the part of both supervisor and supervisee; bring to the surface underlying dynamics and facilitate supervisee awareness; enliven case consultation; prevent boredom; provide the supervisor with direct information about the supervisee's skills and abilities; provide new perspectives on a situation; support and encourage the use of new methods, techniques, and responses to clients; and suggest new means to get unstuck with difficult clients. Techniques such as role-play and role reversal can easily be inserted into traditional case consultation and do not require much time or in-depth skill. Including experiential techniques such as role-play or psychodrama is also a good learning strategy for kinesthetic learners, those who learn best by doing something, not reading or talking about it.

Many experiential techniques can be adapted for supervision: role-play, psychodrama, Gestalt empty chair, family sculpting, expressive art or movement therapy, relaxation, and visualization. For example, Helmeke and Prouty (2001) devised an innovative exercise to use in an introductory marriage and family therapy

DON'T FORGET

Supervisors are encouraged to add experiential techniques to case consultation formats or group supervision.

course where mock sessions were created in which the clients spoke a language that could not be understood by the therapists. This served the purposes of highlighting various aspects of communication and understanding. Naturally, supervisors should be trained and proficient in the use of any experiential technique before using them in supervision. Supervisors should also understand that experiential techniques can be very powerful and thus provide supervisees with adequate support and encouragement during the process as well as ample time for discussion afterward. Rapid Reference 5.10 gives a summary of a number of popular experiential techniques for supervision.

Rapid Reference 5.10

Experiential Techniques

Role-play: Role-play is an especially helpful technique in supervision. The essence of role-playing is to switch from talking about problems with clients to experiencing them in the here and now. By doing so, both supervisee and supervisor increase in understanding of complex and difficult situations. For example, as a supervisee is talking about a particular client situation and what they plan to do, the supervisor might say, "Demonstrate to me how you plan to confront this client. What will you say and how will you say it?"

Role reversal: Role reversal, whereby the supervisee exchanges roles with the client, can be employed for any number of situations, such as helping the supervisee become unstuck with a client, trying out new behaviors in a safe environment, and increasing empathy and understanding. "You seem to be stuck with this client. Can you switch roles for a minute and imagine you were this person? What might you be feeling? Thinking? Let's try it out now; you be this client and I will be you, and we'll see what comes up."

Psychodrama: Psychodrama can increase the supervisee's awareness of the impact of family-of-origin issues on the helper-client relationship. The most popular psychodrama techniques to use in supervision are *doubling* or the *soliloquy*, whereby the supervisor speaks the supervisee's unspoken thoughts. These techniques will help supervisors understand better the supervisee's internal experience.

Gestalt empty chair: Gestalt empty chair is a technique popularized by Fritz Perls (1969) and is also a wonderful means to explore emotionally charged situations and help supervisees get unstuck with difficult clients by exploring projections and blocks to understanding (Haber, 1996). The empty chair technique requires trainees to play both parts, client and helper, and switch back and forth between them. Asking them as they play the part of the client to exaggerate or do more of whatever they are doing creates what Perls described as an "ah ha" experience (Perls, 1969).

(continued)

Family sculpting: Family sculpting is especially helpful as a means to help supervisees visualize relationship dynamics with clients. It is typically employed with group supervision as it requires a number of people to play the different parts of the family. The supervisee, whose client family is being sculpted, asks other supervisees in the group to play the family members. He or she would then place the various family members in physical relationship to each other and in postures that represent their relationships, creating a visual and spatial picture of family dynamics.

Art therapy: Art therapy includes a broad range of techniques such as employing pictures, drawings, collages, colors, or symbols to represent thoughts and feelings. Art therapy can be used to enhance a supervisee's self-awareness of his or her thoughts or feeling responses to clients or to supervision and can be utilized in individual, group, team, or peer supervision or combined with other methods, such as case consultation or written case review sheets.

Relaxation techniques and guided visualization: Relaxation techniques and guided visualization can increase understanding and free up the supervisee's thinking about clients as well as help reduce anxiety. Teaching supervisees relaxation techniques could also be a part of professional self-care and stress management.

COMBINING METHODS AND TECHNIQUES TO MAXIMIZE BENEFIT IN SUPERVISION

One question busy clinical supervisors need to be continually asking themselves is "How can I use my supervision time most efficiently? Are there ways to increase my ability to monitor the activities of my supervisee and help them to become better practitioners?" Combining methods and techniques is one answer to this important question. Whereas using supervision time to sit and talk about client cases with supervisees is still the means most supervisors use, it should be evident at this point that a better use of supervision time can be brought into being with a little forethought and creativity. Many suggestions require a small modicum of time and skill. The snapshot technique as outlined in Rapid Reference 5.11 and the application of a variety of methods and techniques to build competence in crisis situations in Rapid Reference 5.12 give two examples of how to combine methods and techniques in supervision.

☰ Rapid Reference 5.11

The Snapshot Technique

Goal

The goal of the snapshot technique is threefold: to improve supervisor involvement, knowledge, and understanding of a supervisee's abilities and shortcomings; to help design a training plan; and to improve monitoring.

Method

A snapshot is built through the application of a variety of methods and techniques with a number of a supervisee's clients. The structure and focus of the snapshot will vary by setting, level of experience, and the purpose of the work in that setting. The following example is designed for counseling or psychotherapy. If the supervisee were paraprofessional and involved in task management, education, home services, or a social work case management situation, the snapshot would take on a different character.

Building the Snapshot

1. Select four or five methods and techniques from the list given in this chapter (case consultation, written case review sheets, live observation, role-play, or audiotaping are good for this purpose). Attach thought-provoking questions to boost value.

2. Ask the supervisee to use a different client for each piece of the snapshot (i.e., the application of each method or technique). For example, have the supervisee select a client and role-play some aspect of the relationship in supervision, or use the case review form (Rapid Reference 5.4) to write up another one.

3. Make the snapshot during the first month of supervision.

4. Decide on a reasonable length of time for the supervisee to make the snapshot, that is, 1 week, 2 weeks, and so on.

5. Repeat the exercise later on in supervision to measure growth.

═Rapid Reference 5.12

Combining Methods and Techniques to Build Competence in Crisis Situations

1. Increase Knowledge about Crisis

- Assign reading.
- Give handouts.
- Provide manual or instructions from your organization.
- Review ethical and legal codes and regulations.
- Highlight areas that are commonly of most concern in your organization.
- Provide supervisees a written step-by-step crisis plan that includes what you want them to do and gives the rationale.
- Write up sample crisis vignettes (case scenarios) commonly occurring in your setting and give to supervisees with a list of questions to answer.

2. Expand Crisis Skills

- Demonstrate for supervisee what you want them to do and how to do it right.
- Model desired behaviors and then invite them to role-play those behaviors with you.
- Have the supervisee sit in and watch you or someone else handle a crisis.
- Provide the supervisee with a tape demonstrating key risk management skills.
- Have supervisee walk through a typical crisis case scenario for your setting and explain what they would do.
- Use "what ifs" to change facts in a case scenario and have the supervisee respond to those changes.
- Make the client in the scenario a different race or gender, change parts of the case—such as historical or situational factors that will make the situation far worse—and add in ethical issues to consider.
- Ask to sit in and watch the supervisee handle a crisis.

3. Enlarge Personal Self-Awareness

- Bring up normal types of anxiety that might interfere with ethical practice in a crisis situation, such as anxiety about the impact of breaking confidentiality on the client relationship.
- Explore typical kinds of distorted thoughts such as the need to be needed or the need to be liked that preclude action in crisis.
- Check with supervisees concerning thoughts and feelings after a crisis situation with a client.
- Ask thought-provoking or IPR-style questions during a review of the crisis situation to stimulate self-awareness.
- Give self-awareness exercises or use journaling to promote self-exploration.

Putting It Into Practice

Case Example

Vicky was a new caseworker in a state agency. During supervision, Vicky expressed hesitancy to confront one of her clients about the discrepancy between what he said he wanted to change and his actions. Her supervisor, Mitch, asked if there was anything the client had said or done that led her to shy away from pointing this out to him. Vicky responded immediately that he was unhappy with his previous caseworker because he stated "She was a bitch, always nagging me about what I didn't do right. She didn't care about me. I was just a number to her." Vicky then said "I don't want him to see me that way." In response to that statement, Mitch stated that this is something comes up a lot with clients, and he had a similar experience when starting out at the agency. Then Mitch suggested it might be helpful for Vicky to watch him demonstrate how he had learned to approach this particular situation with clients. But before that, he was curious to hear from Vicky how she would have responded to this client if she had felt comfortable? What exactly would she say and do? As Vicky pondered this question, she recognized she was uncomfortable with any type of conflict or confrontation and shared that with Mitch who reassured her that again, this was normal for beginners and something that was a good supervision topic. He invited Vicky, in order to get in touch with the client's feelings, to reverse roles and be the client while he played the caseworker. Afterwards, Mitch asked her to switch back and become herself and try out something new to say and do in this particular situation. He then suggested she sit in with him on one of his interviews with a similar-type client the following afternoon. Vicky left supervision feeling reassured and supported by Mitch and more competent to confront her clients about discrepancies in behavior.

Teaching Point: Mitch's approach to Vicky demonstrated the use of support and reassurance in supervision along with the application of several supervision methods and techniques in order to move Vicky quickly from feeling incompetent to competent to handle a problem with her clients. Rather than assuming Vicky was impaired in such a way she could not change her behavior, he believed in her ability to learn if given the chance to try new behaviors in a safe environment.

TEST YOURSELF

1. **To use methods and techniques effectively, supervisors need to be**
   (a) familiar with the methods and techniques available to them.
   (b) familiar with the strengths and weaknesses of each supervisee.
   (c) willing to adapt to the needs of supervisees.
   (d) all of the above.

2. **Employing a variety of methods and techniques in supervision**
   (a) improves the clinical supervisor's training function.
   (b) assists in monitoring the activities of supervisees.
   (c) supports both supervisor's and supervisee's ethical practice.
   (d) is only important when working with beginners.
   (e) does a, b, and c.
   (f) does all of the above.

3. **The best way to conduct case consultation is to let supervisees talk without any interruptions.** True or False?

4. **Advantages of case consultation far outweigh any disadvantages, and so supervisors can rely on this tried and true method of supervision with no concern.** True or False?

5. **Reviewing a part or all of a supervisee's documentation is a necessary addition to any supervision plan for monitoring purposes.** True or False?

6. **Live supervision means the supervisor**
   (a) stands behind a mirror and watches the supervisee work with a client.
   (b) sits in the room with the supervisee and client.
   (c) is alive during supervision.
   (d) watches part of the supervisee's session with the client and then becomes active in the session.
   (e) acts as a cotherapist.
   (f) does all of the above.

7. **Many times taping is not used in supervision outside of academic settings because**
   (a) supervisors lack training in using tapes for supervision.
   (b) of fear that it will have adverse impact on clients.
   (c) the idea of taping client sessions seems overwhelming and troublesome.
   (d) of fear that tapes will have an adverse impact on any malpractice lawsuits.
   (e) supervisees won't have time to put on makeup and fresh clothes before the taped session.
   (f) of all of the above.
   (g) a, b, c, and d.

8. **Which of the following is a reward of taping as a supervision method?**

   (a) Taping can be used for training and as a monitoring tool.

   (b) Taping a session can increase objectivity of the supervisor.

   (c) Young and attractive supervisees can gain brownie points with their supervisors.

   (d) Supervisees can be weeded out based on how they look on camera.

   (e) a and b.

   (f) b, c and d.

   (g) All of the above.

9. **It is not necessary to obtain a written release form from all clients before taping of any client session.** True or False?

10. **It is recommended that supervisors get at least one tape of a client session from each supervisee or observe one session live in order to increase objectivity.** True or False?

11. **Experiential techniques**

    (a) can be easily adapted for supervision.

    (b) can be very powerful.

    (c) require ample time for preparation and discussion afterward.

    (d) have no place in supervision and should be avoided at all costs.

    (e) should only be used in Marin County, California.

    (f) a, b, and c.

    (g) b and d.

    (h) are all of the above.

12. **One way for supervisors to be more effective in their use of time is to**

    (a) combine methods and techniques.

    (b) use case consultation exclusively.

    (c) accept only well-trained and experienced supervisees.

    (d) do their paperwork during supervision.

    (e) do all of the above.

13. **Thought-provoking questions can make case consultation more meaningful as a teaching and training tool.** True or False?

14. **A combination of demonstration, modeling, and role-play practice is one of the best teaching plans for supervision.** True or False?

15. **Research has shown without a shadow of doubt that individual case consultation is the most effective way to perform clinical supervision.** True or False?

Answers: 1. d; 2. e; 3. False; 4. False; 5. True; 6. f; 7. g; 8. e; 9. False; 10. True; 11. f; 12. a; 13. True; 14. True; 15. False

Six

PREPARING FOR SUPERVISION

Before beginning to supervise, there are a number of issues to address and a number of questions that need to be answered in order to increase effectiveness as a supervisor: goals and objectives, plans and structure, methods and techniques, evaluation procedures, monitoring concerns, and administrative tasks and paperwork. Supervisors also need to consider the needs of their setting, their discipline, their model of supervision, and their personal style in setting goals and planning for supervision.

Rapid Reference 6.1 lists a series of questions that all supervisors should be able to answer before beginning to supervise. The answers to these questions will serve as the building blocks for the ethical practice of supervision, reduce stress, and assist in the creation of a successful supervision experience for everyone involved. Many difficulties that supervisors face could be avoided by taking time to better prepare.

CAUTION

Don't just jump in and start reviewing cases with supervisees. Take time to set the stage for supervision.

CAUTION

Make goals something to strive for, not just a to-do list. Don't set goals in stone. Stay flexible. Revisit supervision goals on a regular basis throughout the supervision experience (Roman, 2000).

SETTING GOALS FOR SUPERVISION

The first building block of a successful supervision experience is the task of identifying the goals for supervision. Supervision goals serve as signposts along the road to ethical best practice and facilitate the supervision process. Both supervisors and supervisees need to know where they are going in order to plan how to get there.

Taking time to set goals increases the opportunity for success and helps

≡ *Rapid Reference 6.1*
. . . .

Important Questions for Supervisors to Ask before Beginning to Supervise

1. "What is my main goal for supervision? What do I hope my supervisees get out of supervision with me?"
   - "What do I expect?"
   - "What do they expect from me?"
2. "What do I think a competent professional in my field needs to know and be able to demonstrate?"
   - "Do my supervisees agree? What would they put on the list?"
3. "Do my supervisees have different levels of training, education, and experience or come from different disciplines?"
   - "If so, how will this impact my goals, plans, and objectives for supervision?"
4. "How can I best use my supervision time?"
   - "What are the resources accessible to me and to my supervisee for training?"
   - "What are my clinical supervisory responsibilities?"
   - "What are my supervisees' responsibilities?"
5. "Where should I focus my time and energy?"
   - "Are there critical areas that need close supervision and monitoring?"
   - "Are there requirements that need to be met?"
   - "Do some of my supervisees need more supervision and support than others?"
   - "Are there parts of training that could be standardized? Put on CDs?"
   - "Could others be brought in to help with teaching and training? Monitoring?"
6. "Do I have the skills and training to be a competent supervisor?"
   - "In what areas do I need more training as a supervisor?"
   - "What could I do to increase my knowledge and skill as a supervisor?"

with motivation. Setting goals and making a plan for supervision also minimize the potential for misunderstanding and conflict in supervision (Cobia & Boes, 2000). The clearer the goals are, the easier it is for supervisees to understand what is required and to be successful (Lehrman-Waterman & Ladany, 2001). Goals also serve as the means to structure feedback and evaluation and measure progress (Hensley, Smith, & Thompson, 2003).

Naturally, supervisees should be included in the goal-setting process to the fullest extent possible. The more supervisees are involved in setting goals and making decisions about what will happen in supervision, the more likely they are

≡ Rapid Reference 6.2

Sample Goal Setting Questions that Supervisors Could Ask Supervisees in Order to Increase Participation in Supervision

- "What would you like to get out of supervision with me?"
- "Are there areas of practice or topics about which you would like to learn more or improve your skill in?"
- "Do you have thoughts about what your clients' needs are and how supervision might help you meet those needs?"
- "What would need to happen in supervision to make it worth the time?"
- "What is one thing you would most like to take away from this experience?"
- "What are some ideas you have from your other supervision experiences that might help improve supervision with me?"
- "How can I be of most help to you as you work with your clients?"

to care about the goals and be motivated to achieve them. It is hard to encourage people to work on goals they don't value.

If both supervisors and supervisees understand the importance of goal setting, it will become a cooperative task. Rapid Reference 6.2 gives a series of goal-setting questions that will increase involvement on the part of supervisees in setting the goals for supervision.

In order to begin the process of goal setting, supervisors need to think about the purpose and context for supervision. For example, the goals for clinical supervision with paraprofessionals or those who work in a case management format would be different than for counselors and psychotherapists. Another element to consider would be any guidelines or requirements for completion of supervision such as would be found with graduate school internships or postdegree licensure or certification.

The next consideration in designing goals would be the supervisee's level of competency and developmental level. The supervisee's background and experience as well as educational level should influence the goals for supervision. Therefore, before beginning to supervise, time should be spent collecting this infor-

DON'T FORGET

When experiencing problems with a supervisee, such as not coming to supervision, not participating in it, or not following through on suggestions, one solution is to back up to goals for supervision and the supervisee's needs. Explore what would have to happen in supervision to get them excited to participate or make it more meaningful for them.

mation. (See the section in Chapter 7 on orientation for more material on this topic.)

Along with a consideration of the supervisee's level of development and competence, it is also important for supervisors to address the same questions to themselves. A supervisor's background and experience with clients as well as his or her experience as a supervisor would be very important to planning and the goal-setting process. It would be difficult to develop a supervisee's competence in areas in which the supervisor is lacking. Another important issue for supervisors to address at this point would be their preferred style and how flexible and open they are to a collaborative supervision process.

Entwined within all these considerations are the ethical, legal, and regulatory codes for the profession. The context for supervision and the supervisor's and supervisee's responsibilities in regard to client care should be of great concern when setting goals and making plans. Another key matter would be how to address multicultural differences and dual relationships in supervision.

CHOOSING TOPICS FOR SUPERVISION

As supervisors envision their goals for supervision, it naturally draws attention to the teaching aspect of the role. The large majority of activity in supervision is spent on helping supervisees develop or improve skills and expertise in a variety of content areas necessary to ethical practice with clients. These content areas or topics for supervision may vary within each discipline and setting and on the supervisee's level of training and education. Sometimes supervisors are given lists through their organization or by graduate schools or licensing boards. However, many times supervisors are left on their own to decide what to do in supervision.

A number of authors have suggested important content areas to include in any supervision plan (Bernard & Goodyear, 2004; Borders & Brown, 2005; Campbell, 2000; Powell, 1993; Shechtman & Wirzberger, 1999; Stinchfield, 2004; Stoltenberg et al., 1998; Storm et al., 2001). Suggested topics include developing self-awareness, mastering intervention techniques, becoming skilled in the use of assessment and diagnostic methods, developing the ability to work with cultural differences, learning proper written documentation, developing a theoretical basis for practice, knowing one's limitations and being willing to seek consultation, setting appropriate boundaries, and practicing ethically. Other suggestions include development of a professional demeanor, the ability to use referrals and resources of the community, and knowledge of and effective use of systems. As can be seen, the list of potential topics for supervision can be sizable.

DON'T FORGET

Regardless of context, each supervisor still needs to ask this key question: "What does a competent [and ethical] professional in my field need to know and be able to demonstrate?" (Magnuson & Wilcoxon, 1998).

It also should be obvious that many topic areas are quite broad and subject to varying opinions about what they would include.

Once goals and content areas have been identified, each needs to be put into behavioral descriptive terms to the fullest extent possible. Supervisors cannot assist a supervisee's growth and development in a particular area (nor evaluate success) if they cannot describe what it is they expect and want from that supervisee. To make supervision goals as understandable and objective as possible, they also should be written down so everyone is clear on them. This need not be complicated or fancy; a simple list will do. However, it will be better if more time and effort is spent fleshing out these goals and using goal sheets as active vehicles to plan supervision and as the basis for evaluation. In our ethical best-practice model, goal setting is a critical component as it is always connected to supervision plans and activities and to evaluation.

For example, one area of particular importance to most clinical supervisors is good boundary setting on the part of supervisees with their clients. Descriptions of good boundary setting may vary depending on one's field and context. Therefore, to assure understanding, each supervisor would need to give their supervisees a detailed description of what good boundary setting looks like to him or her and include plenty of examples so everyone understands the concept of good boundary setting. These examples and descriptions would then form the basis for evaluation of a supervisee's competence in this area. Naturally, asking supervisees their definition of good boundary setting would be part of this discussion.

DON'T FORGET

Make goals specific and achievable. To avoid conflict and misunderstandings, include specific descriptors of successful accomplishment of each goal. Consider individual differences when designing a supervision plan. Include supervisees' thoughts and desires. Make a time line or tentative schedule for accomplishing goals.

It logically follows that after a discussion of the importance of boundary setting in ethical practice, considerable attention should be paid to this topic as supervision progresses. A number of methods and techniques could be selected to assure supervisees acquire full competence in this area. For example, thought-provoking questions could be asked during case consultation to focus supervisees' attention on boundary setting as a concern with a particular client. Inclusion of case vignettes or case scenarios that involve boundary setting problems, a demonstration on how to respond to a difficult boundary setting situation coupled with a role-play, or live observation and taping would also facilitate learning in this key area.

PLANNING FOR SUPERVISION

After supervisors and supervisees identify the essential content areas that make up the goals for supervision, the next step is to decide how to structure the supervision process to accomplish these stated goals. A number of authors have suggested that supervisors break down each content area into components and, like teachers, place them in an organized supervision curriculum. One good idea is to divide all the content areas of supervision into three components: knowledge and theory, practice and skill, and personal self-awareness (Gould & Bradley, 2001; NBCC, 1999). In theory, each content area of supervision, such as ethical practice, boundary setting, multicultural competence, diagnosis, assessment, treatment planning, crisis intervention, and documentation, may be seen to have three parts: a body of literature that underpins each of these content areas; skills for application of this knowledge with clients; and personal attitudes, beliefs, and values that promote or block effectiveness in each area. For example, to address multicultural competency, supervisees can read books and articles on this topic, learn strategies to respond to multicultural differences with clients, and reflect on their attitudes and beliefs about multicultural differences. An example of the application of the three content areas in supervision—knowledge, practice, and personal—is provided in Rapid Reference 6.3. Rapid Reference 5.12 also employed the same three content areas to show how to combine methods and techniques to develop competence in crisis situations.

Supervisors may want to emphasize one of the three components more strongly at different points over the course of the supervisory relationship. With beginners, the focus might be on information and theory, whereas with more advanced supervisees, the focus would be on intervention strategies and personal self-awareness. Certainly when problems develop, deficits could be present in all three areas, not just one, so it might be more fruitful for supervisors to take a holistic viewpoint than to attempt to categorize deficits as belonging to just one particular area, such as knowledge or skill.

The first component, *knowledge and theory,* refers to theoretical and conceptual knowledge of theory and research that underpins the discipline. The knowledge component includes evaluation of the supervisee's knowledge of theory, ethics,

≡ Rapid Reference 6.3

Application of Three Component Model

Boundary Setting with Clients

Topic Area	Knowledge	Practice	Personal
Methods and techniques	Read ethical codes Use case scenarios Use handouts View video	Apply to cases Ask questions: "What ifs" Demonstrate Role-play	Explore concerns Assign genogram Ask questions Process feelings

law, intervention strategies, multicultural issues, and agency policies. Reading and attending lectures, seminars, and continuing education (CEU) courses are common strategies. The supervisor may want to give short didactic presentations, use handouts, or assign reading to impart information. In addition, the supervisor should encourage supervisees to become involved in professional organizations; attend local, state, and national conferences; and engage in other activities that promote growth and foster a sense of professional identity. Regardless of the method, supervisors should encourage supervisees to continue learning throughout their career.

The second component, *practice and skill,* examines the supervisee's skills and abilities to apply knowledge to client care in an ethical manner. Supervisors can use a variety of techniques and methods, such as live observation, taping, cotherapy, staffings, and training workshops, to contribute to developing the practice component. See Chapter 5 for information on methods and techniques.

The final component, *personal self-awareness,* refers to the importance of supervisees' personal characteristics on their work with clients and the supervisory relationship. Per-

CAUTION

Ethical counselors and therapists must continually update their knowledge base.

DON'T FORGET

Supervisors model enthusiasm for learning and personal growth. Pay attention to how you demonstrate this with your supervisees.

sonal functioning is a critical part of clinical supervision. The personal component includes background, values, beliefs, biases, thoughts, and feelings. Although critical to ethical judgement and decision making, the importance of this component in a supervision plan will vary depending on the role and function of the supervisee. For example, it might be much less important to stress personal self-awareness with paraprofessionals who are involved in education-focused work than for those involved in counseling or psychotherapy.

Although it would be unethical for supervisors *not* to explore the role of personal self-awareness in client care, particularly when attitudes and behaviors could be harmful to clients, the possibility for a dual relationship also exists wherein the supervisor acts as the supervisee's therapist. Developing personal self-awareness in clinical supervision while avoiding ethical pitfalls is tricky. However, with some thoughtful discussion and preplanning with supervisees, even this obstacle can be overcome. For example, good boundary setting is a skill, but it also involves the supervisee's personal beliefs, values, past experiences, worries, and concerns, which make it easy or difficult to achieve. Understanding this fact and discussing typical concerns beginners might have when they start to work with clients would be an excellent addition to any training plan. Further discussion about working with personal self-awareness can be found in Chapter 7.

Another way to approach supervision is to take a systems perspective. Haber (1996) used the metaphor of a house to illustrate the systems relationship between components. Each floor of the house represents some aspect of the supervisory relationship, such as personal self-development, organizational context, and culture and ethics, and all are interdependent in the supervision "house." Supervisees may have deficits in all floors or just in one, and these deficits may interact with each other. Therefore, taking a systems viewpoint and looking at the whole house, not just individual floors, is encouraged when setting goals for supervision.

IDM is another possibility to consider when planning for supervision (Stoltenberg et al., 1998). In the first stage, supervisees depend on supervisors for what to do. In the second stage, the focus is more on clients and trying out new things. Supervisees will go up and down at this point in their dependence on supervisors. At the third stage of development, the focus in supervision is on developing self-awareness and competency along with the ability to use theory with clients. The model shows the interaction of the needs of the supervisee, the environment, and supervision and suggests activities for supervisors at various stages of supervision. It is a particularly helpful model for supervisors working in academic settings.

In summary, supervisors need to remember their role as teacher and trainer. Creating a learning curriculum by dividing the content into three components will assist in organizing supervision and encourage supervisors as well as supervisees to take a personal and professional growth perspective on supervision. It also encourages supervisors to provide a variety of learning opportunities for supervisees that goes far beyond traditional case consultation. This is important not only to improve the skill development and learning by supervisees but also to provide supervisors with a means to respond to multicultural differences. The three components can be integrated into a developmental perspective and used to guide planning, the use of methods and techniques, and evaluation. All in all, adopting a more structured approach to supervision increases interest and improves the value of the experience.

The steps involved in preparing for supervision are summarized in Rapid Reference 6.4.

≡Rapid Reference 6.4

Ten Steps for Goal Setting and Planning

1. Establish goals. Decide what competencies to focus on in supervision.
2. Include your supervisee in selecting goals and in planning.
3. Customize your plan. Consider the developmental level of the supervisee, their needs and desires, as well as the needs of the system and population served.
4. Write out goals.
5. Make goals as specific, clear, objective, realistic, and obtainable as possible.
6. Create a hierarchy of objectives. Recognize that some goals and competencies need to be addressed first while others can be addressed later in time.
7. Divide goals into competency areas:
   - Knowledge and theory
   - Practice and skill
   - Personal self-awareness
8. Select methods and techniques to best accomplish goals. Expand repertory.
9. Tie goals to evaluation. Come up with one or two indicators of successful completion in each goal area.
10. Revisit and review goals periodically. Update and make changes as necessary.

Putting It Into Practice

Case Example

After three years working at an agency, Eileen has just been promoted to supervisor of her unit. Eileen loved her own past experiences in supervision and felt that talking openly about client problems with her supervisors greatly improved her confidence and competence. Because clinical supervision was required of all the staff on the unit regardless of experience or license and everyone has been there for a number of years, Eileen didn't anticipate any problems. She naturally assumed everyone was as enthusiastic as she. However, when she met with John, a former colleague who had been with the organization for 15 years, to begin review of his cases, he stated emphatically that everything was fine and he had no problems to discuss. When Eileen attempted to get John to talk more about his client cases, he got angry and said he didn't need supervision and that he knows what he is doing.

Teaching Point: Eileen made the mistake of not taking time at the beginning of supervision to prepare the ground for the supervisory relationship. She did not recognize John's needs or his thoughts and feelings about supervision. She made the assumption that he had her same viewpoint, and, hence, things would flow smoothly. She did not at the beginning discuss with John his goals for supervision or how supervision time could be best structured to meet both their needs.

DOCUMENTING SUPERVISION

Administrative tasks, such as documenting supervision, are an essential part of any ethical practice model. However, it is often a problem for busy and overburdened supervisors to find the time to do an adequate job of documenting supervisory practices. Even so, it is absolutely necessary that some attention be given to this important area. Giving thought to exactly what type of records should be kept and how to do so in an efficient manner encourages a higher level of involvement by

DON'T FORGET

- Documentation promotes ethical practice as well as prevent malpractice success.
- Documentation should be part of ethical practice as it supports increased planning and participation in supervision.
- Documentation of supervision also serves as a cornerstone of any malpractice prevention plan.
- Create a paper trail to boost credibility and demonstrate involvement in supervision.
- Treat all supervision information with the utmost confidentiality.

supervisors in supervision as well as offering assistance to them in managing stress. Maintaining some documentation of supervision is also emphasized as a key factor in malpractice prevention as it is through the paper trail that supervisors can demonstrate their work with supervisees.

This section provides suggestions about what type of documentation and information might be needed, but each supervisor must customize this to fit his or her particular situation. For example, documentation forms and key information might be different for a graduate intern than for a paraprofessional. There also may be federal or state laws and regulations as well as organizational or professional standards for this important area. Rapid Reference 6.5 provides a generic list of suggested materials that may be sought and kept for supervision.

≡ Rapid Reference 6.5

Suggested Materials for a Supervision File

- Plans and objectives
- Evaluation summary
  - —Dates for evaluation
  - —Methods
  - —Procedures
  - —Evaluation forms
- Supervision log
- Supervision journal (optional)
- Supervision informed consent agreement
- Supervision contract
- Copy of ethical codes, licensure, or graduate program requirements if pertinent
- Copy of the supervisor's resume
- Supervisee's job description
- Copy of supervisee's malpractice insurance (if required)
- Supervisee's vita and background experience
- Sample of supervisee's record keeping or progress notes
- Feedback from clients about the supervisee

Other Material to Have on Hand

- Client release forms for taping
- Structured forms for training purposes
- Articles, reading lists, and web sites pertinent to supervision goals
- Summary of supervisor's background, training, and experience as a clinical supervisor to give to supervisees
- Copies of ethical codes and standards for supervisors apropos to the supervisors and supervisees licensure and professional discipline

Organizing the Supervision File

There are numerous ideas on how to organize paperwork for supervision. One of the easiest suggestions is to put together a supervision file that will contain all forms, handouts, and other supervision information, and then create a folder for each supervisee that will hold specific material pertinent to that individual. This file could be created on a computer or the old-fashioned way, on paper. At a minimum, the following items should

> ### CAUTION
>
> Because of the threat of vicarious liability, described in Chapter 2, it is recommended that in situations with graduate or postdegree interns where supervisees are providing counseling or psychotherapy services, both supervisor and supervisee carry personal malpractice insurance over and above any insurance provided by their institution. Be sure to check if the malpractice policy covers clinical supervision as some do not. A separate rider is often required.

be included in each supervisee's file: goals and objectives for supervision, a written summary of evaluation procedures along with any copies of evaluation forms, a supervision log, and a copy of the informed consent or contract for supervision.

Goals and Objectives for Supervision

A short written summary or outline of the goals, tasks, and objectives for supervision should be included in each supervisee's file. Information and suggestions on how to set goals and objectives and make plans for supervision can be found at the beginning of this chapter.

Evaluation Summary

Each supervisee's file should also include a written description of the evaluation process, including an explanation of evaluation procedures, timing, methods, techniques, examples of paper and pencil instruments, as well as a list of people involved in the evaluation process. More material on evaluation follows in the next section of this chapter.

Supervision Log

Maintaining a log of supervision is absolutely necessary in the ethical practice model for supervision as well as any malpractice plan. The recommended minimum is to keep track of supervision dates, time, length of supervision session, and modality (individual, group, tape, live observation, case consultation) for each supervisee. This running record of supervision would then create a picture of the supervisor's and supervisee's participation in supervision. Frequently, in large organizations, agencies, and hospitals, clinical supervisors do not keep such a log. Rather, they keep track of supervision activity, recommendations, and follow up directly on client files or charts, which is acceptable. However, should problems occur that require legal action, the log provides an easier means to support the supervisor's competency, level of involvement, and attempts to monitor the supervisee's activities with clients.

Additionally, there may be a need for an expanded supervision log form that contains information about what cases and topics were discussed in supervision and also serves as a reminder to supervisors to follow up with certain clients. This type of documentation is especially important when working with interns or prelicensed supervisees who are seeing clients for psychotherapy or in situations where tracking of supervisees and monitoring is difficult.

The supervision log can also serve another important purpose: Because no one can remember everything, a supervision log documents the supervisor's thought processes about supervisees and serves as a foundation for the supervisor's opinions and judgment about a supervisee's actions (Gottlieb, 2004). From an ethical perspective, keeping such a log is an ally. When done correctly, this should serve as the foundation for corrective feedback as well as to make a note of supervisees' achievement and success. Moreover, if difficulties with supervisees require more serious action, having a detailed description covering how often, how much, and when these problems with a supervisee occurred, along with a description of the supervisor's attempts to rectify the situation, becomes essential. Accordingly, it is considered good practice for supervisors to write down their observations about supervisees over the course of the supervisory relationship to illustrate the reasons for their actions. Just use caution to be sure these observations cover the supervisee's behaviors, especially making note of how often they occur, and not the supervisor's subjective interpretations of such behaviors.

Whatever the choice, be sure to document succinctly and accurately, in legible handwriting or typing, and avoid abbreviations or codes that can-

DON'T FORGET

Keep records to help you do a better job as a clinical supervisor, not to meet some legal requirement. Remember, legal standards do not ask supervisors to be perfect or clairvoyant or even to be able to prevent all mistakes, just that they made their best attempts to handle situations ethically and used some thought (Gottlieb, 2004).

CAUTION

When tracking the supervisory process in the supervision log, leave out emotions and stick to behavioral descriptors and quantifiers such as how often, when, how much, and where. Leave the following out of the supervision file:

- Subjective opinions about a supervisee's lifestyle or personality traits
- Subjective analysis of a supervisee's state of mental health
- Topics outside the provenance of supervision, such as ongoing conflicts with other mental health professionals

not be deciphered at some later date. Even though supervision notes and the supervision log are not considered part of the medical record, it is still best to follow similar guidelines as to content and the protection of privacy of information. A number of suggested formats are available for the supervision log. See Rapid References 6.6 and 6.7 for examples.

≡ Rapid Reference 6.6

Material to Include in a Basic Supervision Activity Log

- Date, time, length of session (including canceled or missed sessions)
- Modality: individual, group, video, live, and so on

Example:

Supervisee's name: _____

Supervision meeting date and time		Duration	Modality
8/15/04	2:00–2:50 P.M.	1 hour	Individual
8/19/04	4:00–5:30 P.M.	1 1/2 hour	Group supervision

≡ Rapid Reference 6.7

Additions for an Expanded Supervision Activity Log

- Cases reviewed (use case numbers or client names)
- Treatment plans, problems, recommendations, and follow-up
- Tracking of dangerous and difficult clients (use asterisk or colored magic marker)
- Significant communications about clients: e-mail, phone, letters
- Specific troubles or successes experienced with supervisees: Observations, recommendations (use behavioral descriptors)

Example:

Supervisee's name: _____

Date and time	Modality	Cases reviewed	Actions
3/25/02	I/CC	John Doe	Refer psychiatrist
2–2:50 P.M.		Mary Smith*	Check suicidal ideation, see ASAP
		The Gross family	Terminated

Made gains in ability to identify serious client problems and act in crisis situation. Came up with own recommendations on how to proceed.

Asterisk denotes client in crisis.

Note: See Falvey et al. (2002) for more samples of log forms for supervision.

Informed Consent and Contracts for Supervision

In order to practice ethically, supervisees, just as clients, need to be informed of the purpose, methods, and expectations for supervision before the supervision process begins. The use of an informed consent agreement and a supervision contract can smooth the way and reduce the risk of conflicts (Cobia & Boes, 2000; Remley & Herlihy, 2005; Sutter, McPherson, & Geeseman, 2002). The main purpose of an informed consent agreement and contract in supervision is to orient supervisees to supervision, create a shared understanding about the ethical standards of practice for supervision, and explain the tasks and requirements of supervision. Informed consent agreements and contracts can also help to maintain boundaries, prevent exploitation, and promote a sense of openness and safety in the relationship. In organizational settings where considerable confusion might occur between clinical and administrative supervision or when working with paraprofessionals or others not covered by professional ethic standards for practice, adding a written supervision informed consent agreement that explains the purpose and parameters for clinical supervision would be very useful.

The informed consent agreement and supervision contract may be separate documents or a combination of the two, depending on the supervisory situation. Each has a different aim and purpose. The informed consent agreement in supervision is based on ethical codes and guidelines for the various mental health disciplines, whereas contracts express the implied legal aspects of the supervisory relationship. When proffered at the beginning of supervision, it gives supervisees an opportunity to ask any questions they may have regarding supervision and create a shared understanding about what the ethical standards are for supervision. Both the informed consent form and supervision contract might be used to open discussion with potential or new supervisees as to the nature of the supervisory relationship. They can be used to explore best fit and orient supervisees to supervision.

As such, these documents, especially the informed consent, should be works in progress and not presented as already set in stone. Instead, the informed consent agreement may be revisited over the course of supervision and help create a dialogue between supervisors and supervisees concerning ethical issues and concerns. Supervisors need to encourage

DON'T FORGET

The informed consent agreement in supervision plays a key part in ethical practice. It is a dynamic instrument that informs and shapes the supervisory relationship, not another piece of paper to fill out and put in a file drawer. As issues arise throughout supervision, revisit the informed consent agreement and utilize it as a means to improve and update the supervisory relationship.

an open discussion about the contents of each document and be open to the possibility of changes in each one.

Informed Consent Agreement for Supervision

The content and structure of an informed consent agreement may vary across disciplines and circumstances. However, incorporating some of the following information is suggested. First, supervisors should want to include a short paragraph or two about their background, training, credentials, approach to supervision, and model of practice. Next, in order to ensure a common understanding about the supervisory process, include a statement about the ethical guidelines for supervision along with a description of the structure, goals, tasks, responsibilities, and evaluation procedures. Issues such as dual relationships, multicultural differences, and means available to resolve disagreements could also be covered. Finally, a summary statement of agreement to follow ethical guidelines and standards for practice should be signed and dated by both supervisor and supervisee. A suggested list of content areas to cover in an informed consent agreement for supervision can be found in Rapid Reference 6.8. A sample copy of an informed consent form for postdegree supervision appears in Rapid Reference 6.9.

≡Rapid Reference 6.8

Content of the Supervision Informed Consent Agreement

Professional disclosure: Include a description of your background, licensure, areas of professional competency, supervision training, and experience.

Practical issues: Include when you will meet, where, and payment (if applicable) as well as how to contact you in case of emergency.

Supervision process: Include the purpose of supervision, your model of supervision, and methods and techniques for supervision.

Administrative tasks: Include record keeping, logs, evaluation methods, and means for feedback.

Ethical and legal issues: Include limits to supervision (i.e., explanation of supervision is not therapy), dual relationship issues, limits to confidentiality of information, procedures for handling difficulties should they arise, a statement concerning the importance of seeking help if personal issues impair judgement or the ability to serve clients in ethical manner.

Evaluation procedures: Include a description of methods, timing, and protection of confidentiality of information.

Means to resolve difficulties: Include a statement of how disagreement will be resolved and what options are available to the supervisee.

(continued)

Statement of agreement: Include an agreement to follow the ethical codes and standards for the profession.

Signatures and date of the agreement: Include here an agreement for supervisees to follow the ethical codes and standards for their discipline and especially not to engage in any kind of a harmful dual relationship with clients. Supervisees should also be honest and open with mistakes and seek help if personal difficulties impair their ability to practice ethically with clients.

Sources: McCarthy et al. (1995); Remley and Herlihy (2005); Todd and Storm (1997).

DON'T FORGET

The informed consent form is an ethical statement of your practice as supervisor. It should be open to discussion, clarification, and change. While not required, it can prevent misunderstandings and future problems.

 *Rapid Reference 6.9*

Sample Informed Consent Agreement for Postdegree Supervision

Purpose

The purpose of this form is to provide you with essential information about supervision and give structure to your experience in order to ensure a common understanding about the supervision process. More about these guidelines will be discussed at our introductory meeting, and I welcome your comments and questions.

Professional disclosure

I earned my doctorate in counseling psychology from the University of Houston and a master's degree from Portland State University. I am licensed as a psychologist in the state of Texas, and I am a clinical member of AAMFT as well as an NBCC-approved clinical supervisor. I have been in the field of mental health for over 35 years and have worked in a variety of settings. The primary focus of my private practice work was women, couples, life transitions, and grief. I now practice a blended, technically, eclectic model that combines Rogerian, humanistic, and strength-based philosophy with systems and cognitive thinking. I have been a clinical supervisor for over 15 years, providing individual and group supervision to both doctoral- and masters-level interns as well as postdegree licensure candidates. I have taught the mandatory 40-hour course in clinical supervision in the state of Texas and am still involved in a supervision-of-supervision group to continue my growth and training. I am the author of *Becoming an Effective Supervisor: A Workbook for Counselors and Psychotherapists* (2000), which will be used extensively in our supervision time together.

Practical issues

In order to fulfill the supervision requirements for _____ , we will meet for 1 hour, once a week, on _____ in my office. If a circumstance arises that makes it impossible for you to attend a scheduled session, contact me as soon as you know that you will miss the session in order to reschedule. If you need to speak to me between sessions, please call my office or my cell phone in case of an emergency.

Supervision process

My primary role is to help you master the skills necessary to become independent ethical practitioners and obtain the highest level of competence possible. At the same time, I have the ethical and legal responsibility for all your actions with clients while you are in supervision with me. Therefore, the success of supervision will depend on the development of a trusting, working relationship between us based on a mutual understanding of the goals and purpose of supervision and a willingness on your part to be open to review your work with clients and hear corrective feedback from me about that work in order to learn and improve. On my part, I will take responsibility to create a supportive environment, give timely and helpful feedback, and be available as needed. As a supervisee, you will be expected to be an active participant in the supervision process; be open to feedback; be truthful and share mistakes; take responsibility for correcting any deficits that could harm clients; be prepared and on time for each session; keep proper client documentation, including a log of your supervision; and complete all other work in a timely manner.

It is understood that occasionally as supervision continues, there may be some times of tension in our supervisory relationship, particularly discomfort generated by feedback or disagreement over suggested strategies and interventions. Hopefully, any relationship problems can be solved in a professional manner through open discussion. If not, an outside consultation may be sought. More details about settling problems and grievances are included in the attached supervision contract.

Administrative tasks and evaluation

As your supervisor, I will be providing you with both formal and informal evaluative feedback throughout supervision. At the same time, I also will be seeking your evaluative feedback about supervision and ideas for improvement. A formal evaluation will be conducted quarterly, and at the end of your _____ hours there will be a final evaluation. Evaluation will be based on the goals established at the beginning of supervision and will include oral case presentations, written case notes, live observation, taping, and any other material that you may wish to include.

Legal or ethical issues

It is important that you agree to act in an ethical manner as outlined by the _____ codes and standards for your profession, not engage in harmful dual relationships with clients, follow laws of confidentiality, and, at all costs, avoid acting in any way injurious to clients. It is understood that as your supervisor, I agree to follow the ethical codes and standards for my profession and treat you with dignity and respect.

(continued)

It is also important that you understand that supervision is not intended to provide you with personal counseling or therapy. If personal issues or concerns arise that interfere with or negatively impact client care, you hereby agree to seek counseling or other means to immediately resolve these problems as outlined by your professional ethical code.

The content of our sessions and evaluations will be confidential, except for the following: (1) the return of the final evaluation form to _____; (2) any instance where treatment of a client violates the legal or ethical standards set forth by professional associations and government agencies; (3) any situation when problems between us do not seem resolvable and an outside consultation would be ethically necessary; and (4) situations where termination of supervision is being considered.

Statement of agreement

I have read and understand the information contained in this document and agree to participate in supervision according to these guidelines.

_____   _____
Supervisee signature   Date   Supervisor signature   Date

Supervision and the Informed Consent Agreement for Clients

Ethically, and now under the Health Insurance Portability and Accountability Act (HIPAA), supervisors are required to inform all clients of a supervisee's status and the potential impact of this fact on the client's care and confidentiality of client information. Clients should be informed about the purpose of supervision, how confidentiality of information will be maintained, and how supervision will be carried out. With graduate interns and prelicensed postdegree supervisees, it is especially important to clearly identify this fact to avoid misunderstandings. Information about supervision could be included as a part of the written informed consent agreement given to clients at intake or could be posted separately on an office wall. Rapid Reference 6.10 covers the type of information that should be covered about supervision in the written informed consent form given to clients, especially in situations where precredentialed or prelicensed supervisees are employed while receiving their training.

Under HIPAA, once supervision is explained to clients and the client signs the informed consent agreement for service, clinical supervisors are free to engage in supervision, keep documentation of supervision, and consult with other professionals concerning client care without continually returning to clients for a written release.

One exception to the preceding should be noted. If taping of client

CAUTION

When seeking consultation, limit the amount of personal information given about the client to factors essential to the consultation.

≈*Rapid Reference 6.10*

Information to Include about Supervision in the Informed Consent Agreement Given to Clients

1. Describe the status of supervisees (nonlicensed but employee, graduate intern, postdegree intern seeking licensure status) and what this means for the client and his or her care.
2. Explain how supervisees will be observed: live, audio- or videotape. If all sessions are recorded as a matter of course for supervision, this fact should be indicated to clients.
3. Detail who will be involved in supervision: group/individual/team/staff consultation.
4. Discuss the impact of supervision on client confidentiality and how this will be handled.
5. Tell client directly how supervision will benefit them.
6. In situations when interns and prelicensed counselors, therapists, and psychologists are employed, and especially in private practice, make sure to include contact information for the supervisor.
7. Suggest that if a problem develops with the supervisee, he or she can discuss the problem with the supervisor.
8. Reassure clients at intake that if they are uncomfortable about working with an intern or prelicensed supervisee, their needs will be noted and, if possible, a referral made to another practitioner. Be clear in the informed consent agreement with clients whether this is the policy. In certain circumstances, such as a university clinic where students in training provide all services, this may not be the case.

sessions is used in supervision, then a separate release form is required. See Rapid Reference 6.11 for a sample of a release form to use when taping for supervision.

The Supervision Contract

Supervision contracts are always a good idea. Most graduate internship programs and a number of states now require a written supervision contract before supervision can begin. While not a binding legal agreement such as that used to buy a car, a supervision contract is very useful in delineating roles, relationships, and requirements for supervision (Sutter et al., 2002). If supervision is time limited, offered for a fee, given off-site, or to meet requirements for graduate programs, licensure, or certification, preparing a contract outlining the parameters of this relationship can help to avoid misunderstandings. Contracts, as well as informed consent agreements for supervision, could also have wide application in any organizational system to the same end.

☰Rapid Reference 6.11

Sample Release Form for Permission to Tape Client Sessions

I, _____, give my psychotherapist, _____ permission to tape this therapy session. I understand the purpose of the taping is to improve the skills of my therapist and to increase the effectiveness of my care. I also understand the tape will only be viewed by

• my therapist and his or her supervisor.

• my therapist, his or her supervisor, and members of his or her supervision group of other therapists in training.

• another mental health professional for consultation purposes.

• _____.

All care will be taken to protect my confidentiality. I understand the tape will be completely erased following the supervision session.

Any changes to this plan will be discussed with me, and I will be given an opportunity to change this release form or deny release.

Client _____ Date _____

Counselor _____ Date _____

This release form becomes null and void on _____.

A generic contract form should include a statement of intent; an outline of responsibilities and requirements, such as length, time, and fees; and a description of the format for supervision. Many experienced supervisors also require their supervisees to read the appropriate legal and ethical codes and attach a signed statement of understanding and agreement to practice ethically and adhere to these guidelines along with the supervision contract before beginning the supervision process. Another popular addition to contracts with postdegree supervisees is a disclaimer that participation in supervision does not guarantee their success in obtaining a license.

A list of topics that might be covered in a supervision contract can be found in Rapid Reference 6.12. A sample generic supervision contract follows in Rapid Reference 6.13.

CAUTION

When the clinical supervisor is off-site, it is important to clarify in writing the exact terms of the relationship and responsibilities. Detail procedures with the on-site supervisor for how to handle any circumstance when unethical or harmful behavior on the part of the supervisee is uncovered in supervision with you, if the on-site supervisor has concerns about what you are covering in supervision, and in crisis situations.

≡Rapid Reference 6.12

Possible Topics for the Supervision Contract

- Logistics of supervision: how often to meet, where, when, cost, cancellations
- Clarification of responsibilities
- Outline of dual relationship issues and measures to protect supervisee from harm
- Description of
  —Goals and expectations
  —Requirements
  —Methods, models, and techniques of supervision
  —Evaluation procedures
- Gatekeeping responsibilies
- Procedures for feedback and evaluation of supervisor
- Actions and procedures to resolve grievances and terminate the relationship if unsatisfactory
- Delineate ethical code and standards and impact on supervision

Note: See Remley and Herlihy (2005); Sutter et al. (2002).

Putting It Into Practice

Case Example

Linda is a busy psychotherapist in an agency who has been asked by her director to take on the task of supervising an intern from a nearby graduate school. The director assures her that this will not require much of her time and will provide the agency with free help. However, at the first meeting with the intern, John, he hands her a packet of information from the graduate school outlining the requirements for the internship, including a list of responsibilities and a stack of forms to fill out. Linda is surprised by the demands and responds angrily to the intern, stating she doesn't have time to do this, and he can take his program and shove it. The intern is shocked and unsure what to do next. Linda storms out to see the director and give him a piece of her mind.

Teaching Point: Everyone in this scenario was misinformed about how to begin supervision. The graduate program erred by not giving the field site full information about requirements. The director was mistaken in the supposition that interns are free help and require little supervision. Linda did not seek out more information about the internship before meeting with the intern for the first session. It should be clear that the use of an informed consent agreement and a supervision contract might have cleared the air and gotten everybody on the same page.

Rapid Reference 6.13

Sample Supervision Contract

Supervisor: _____

Address: _____

Telephone: _____ e-mail: _____

Supervisee: _____

Address: _____

Telephone: _____ e-mail: _____

Supervisee's employer (or graduate school): _____

Address: _____

Telephone: _____

Contact person: _____

I agree to provide clinical supervision to _____(name of supervisee)_____ for ____ hour(s) per week of face-to-face supervision and ____ hour(s) per week of group supervision, if applicable, for a minimum of ____ semesters/years as required by _____ graduate school or _____ licensing board. I will complete evaluation/reference forms necessary to verify this supervision and will report on the supervisee's performance during this period of time to the appropriate graduate school or licensing board as required. The above named supervisee, _____, understands that being in clinical supervision does not guarantee success in obtaining licensure, certification, or graduate degree. _____(supervisee's name)_____ agrees to take supervision seriously, to come to supervision on time and be prepared, to complete all client documentation in timely manner, to keep a log of supervision activities, and to act at all times in an ethical manner with clients as outlined in the ___(name of ethical codes and discipline)___. If problems develop in the supervisory relationship, both supervisor and supervisee agree to the use of an outside consultant to help resolve difficulties. It is also understood that either the supervisor or supervisee may terminate this agreement with 30-days written notice.

Supervisor: _____ Date: _____

Supervisor: _____ Date: _____

Clause to add in situations of postdegree licensure when the supervisor is off-site:

The purpose of this supervision is to enable _____ to satisfy the clinical supervision requirements of _____ license. As the independent clinical supervisor, I am not responsible for the supervisee's job performance or for the number or types of cases assigned to him/her or any other aspects of his/her job duties or employment agreement with _____(employer)_____. It is also understood that if ethical concerns arise, I have the right to converse with his or her on-site supervisor about those concerns. ___(supervisee's___

_____ name)_____ agrees to act in an ethical manner in supervision and with clients as outlined by the _____ professional ethical codes while in supervision with me and to take responsibility to quickly address any problems that may cause harm to clients.

Period of time: from _____ to _____

Location: _____

Fee for service: _____ Payment method: _____

Supervisors in situations with graduate interns or postdegree supervisees for licensure or certification should check with the appropriate governing bodies to see if a standard contract form is already available. If not, gather the exact requirements and include them in the contract form.

EVALUATION

Evaluation is a key component of clinical supervision, a cornerstone of ethical and fair practice, and the one factor that sets supervision apart from counseling, psychotherapy, and consultation. In fact, how evaluation and feedback are handled is core to a positive and satisfactory supervision experience (Lehrman-Waterman & Ladany, 2001). It is also the element of supervision that can create the majority of relationship problems because of its powerful impact on control, safety, and trust. With internships, licensure, or certification, the results of the final evaluation are extremely important. Without careful planning, supervisors could unwittingly be guilty of mistreatment, bias, impaired objectivity, prejudice, and favoritism.

Fair Evaluation

All supervisees have an ethical and legal right to receive fair evaluation (Forrest & Elman, 1999; Hensley et al., 2003; Remley & Herlihy, 2005). This fact should become the overriding consideration for all clinical as well as administrative supervisors. What does this mean? It means that every supervisee should be informed about the evaluation process before supervision begins. They should know how they are being evaluated, the methods and techniques for evaluation, and who will be involved in the evaluation process. Evaluative feedback must also be unmistakably related to the stated goals for supervision. Depending on their developmental level, supervisees should be asked to participate in the evaluative process with the ultimate goal of self-evaluation for advanced supervisees. Rapid Reference 6.14 outlines the criteria for fair evaluation.

≡ Rapid Reference 6.14

Definition of Fair Evaluation

Supervisees are given the following:
- Information, from the beginning, as to what is expected of them
- Information as to who will receive the evaluative feedback
- The criteria on which they will be judged and copies of any evaluation forms
- Several examples of what is desired with goals tied to specific behaviors
- Ongoing feedback as to how they are progressing on stated goals
- Plenty of opportunities to be successful and helpful suggestions for improvement

Because the purpose of evaluation in clinical supervision is to mark progress toward the successful accomplishment of supervision goals, evaluation should be tied to goal setting, planning, and selection of methods and techniques. From the beginning of supervision, the goals, content, tasks, and desired outcomes for supervision should be fully described along with plenty of examples of the criteria for judgment, and then any evaluative feedback must be related to those stated goals.

For example if good boundary setting with clients is an important goal, then supervisees should understand fully what this statement means. For example, a supervisor might define setting good boundaries with clients as when a supervisee starts and ends sessions on time, does not give out his or her home phone number to clients, wears professional clothes to work, and never engages in any type of dual relationship, especially a sexual one, with clients.

The evaluative feedback process is considered an integral part of any supervision plan. In clinical supervision, evaluation needs to be a continuous process of both formal and informal feedback whose overall

DON'T FORGET

To be effective, feedback needs to be all of the following:
- Clearly stated with specifics
- Balanced between positives and negatives
- Timely

DON'T FORGET

The stated goals for supervision must be the basis for any evaluative feedback. It is both unethical and unfair to evaluate supervisees' competence in areas not covered in supervision.

purpose is to stimulate learning, encourage exploration, and facilitate the mastery of skills and competencies.

The process of evaluation is a four-step process. The first, and probably most important step, is the establishment of the goals for supervision at the beginning of the experience. The next step involves supervisors giving supervisees ongoing feedback as cases are reviewed within each supervision session. This type of continuous feedback is meant to shape the supervisee's learning as well as to take note of a supervisee's progress toward the goals for supervision. When successful, it helps advance the supervisee's exploration of various options as well as encourages the supervisee to try out new behaviors with clients. This could be informal, with supervisors spontaneously commenting on the supervisee's progress with a specific client or client problem, or, periodically, to promote self-evaluation, supervisors could ask supervisees "How do you think you are doing so far with this client?" or "How successful do you feel at the moment on your goal to be more assertive with clients?" Inserting a scaling question would also be a useful feedback tool for such spontaneous inquiry. For example, "On a scale of one to ten, how successful do you feel with this client?" or "How successful do you think you were applying that particular intervention with this client?"

Rapid Reference 6.15 suggests how to connect goals with evaluative feedback.

The third step, which involves taking time for more formal feedback by supervisors on the supervisee's progress toward goals, should be a natural progression from the time spent on informal feedback during each supervision session. This formal evaluation could be done at set intervals, such as quarterly, with a paper and pencil instrument, a written review of a case along with a verbal presentation, an audio- or videotape, or even a live observation. In this way, if a supervisee is really experiencing problems or significant impairment or deficits are uncovered that interfere with success, these can be addressed in a timely fashion.

The fourth and last step for evaluation would be a final evaluation of the supervisee's successful completion of all supervision goals at the end of a supervision experience. This particularly would be the case with interns and postdegree licensure candidates or anyone for whom supervision is a time-limited experience. In employment settings, this summative evaluation is part of a performance appraisal and occurs yearly. If the other three steps are followed, this final, or summative

DON'T FORGET

Include times for supervisees to give you feedback about how supervision is going for them and if any changes need to be made along the way.

≡Rapid Reference 6.15

Example of Connecting Goals with Evaluation

Set a clear goal for the client session and keep feedback specific to that goal.

Beginning Stage Supervisees

Goal: Ask them to increase a particular skill, such as reflecting feelings, remaining quiet after asking a question, using a reframe, or responding paradoxically when a client seems defensive.

Evaluative feedback: Review a tape of the client session focusing on the use of the specified skill, or focus case consultation on specific examples of supervisees' use of the skills. Have them demonstrate the use of skill in a role-play in supervision.

Intermediate Stage Supervisees

Goal: Ask supervisees to select a focus or goal for session

Evaluative feedback: Ask supervisees to comment before review of the client session on the use of specified skill and level of success in doing it with the client. Have them give specific examples.

Advanced Stage Supervisees

Goal: Have supervisees set a goal for what they want to do differently in the session with the client. Ask them to self-observe and self-correct during the client session and then process how things went in supervision.

CAUTION

Watch global and subjective evaluation criteria. Use behavioral descriptors.

Wrong: I have serious problems with John; I don't think he is competent to practice ethically.

Right: I am concerned about John's ability to practice ethically. These are my concerns. (1) With Jane Doe, he failed to identify her suicidal ideation even though I have gone over this with him in supervision and gave him a printed list of indicators and questions to ask any seriously depressed client. (2) He overstepped boundaries with one of our female clients by offering to meet her outside the office. This is not ethical behavior. Over the past 3 months, we certainly have talked extensively about dual relationships and boundary setting and how it is unethical to form relationships with clients outside of his role as counselor. (3) He refused to follow established guidelines for working with substance abuse in our setting because he disagreed with them, and (4) his documentation of client sessions in more than half of his cases is incomplete.

evaluation, should be an effortless procedure. In other words, the ultimate goal of fair evaluation is no surprises.

A number of variables can influence the role of evaluation in the supervisory relationship: systems variables, the organizational context, the power of the clinical supervisor, the purpose of supervision, its importance to the supervisee, and the image supervisees have of themselves and their competence. The evaluative component may be very significant as in postdegree supervision for licensure or very small as when supervising licensed independent professionals. If the clinical supervisor is also the administrative supervisor, then the evaluative component will frequently be an overriding variable in the success of establishing a working relationship with supervisees. Certainly the emphasis on evaluation will vary depending on the purpose of supervision and the supervisee's developmental level. Evaluation will be more highly stressed with beginning supervisees and those seeking graduate degrees or licensure than with those at a more advanced stage.

When there is substantial importance vested in the final evaluation (a graduate degree or license to practice), it becomes even more critical that the evaluative component is well thought out. Supervisors need to be vigilant about how the final evaluative judgement will come about, what factors will be used, and how information will be gathered and by whom. In circumstances where the clinical supervisor of an intern or postdegree supervisee is also the administrator or the major professor, caution is recommended. Supervisors in this scenario, to avoid charges of bias or impaired judgment, should employ (1) structured criteria to evaluate success, (2) multiple ways to rate a supervisee's competence, and (3) evaluative information about the supervisee from other sources.

Multicultural differences can also play a sizable role in evaluative judgement. Many years of research about the role of gender, race, and cross-cultural differences points attention to the fact that these variables are powerful in supervisors' perception of and behavior with their supervisees (Hays & Chang, 2003; Granello, 2003; Ladany et al., 1997).

Hence, clinical supervisors need to increase self-awareness concerning their perceptions and judgements about cultural differences and create methods and means to respond to these differences in a fair and ethical manner when it comes to evaluation.

CAUTION

In situations where the supervisor has both clinical and administrative responsibilities, supervisors need to openly discuss evaluation procedures and include supervisees as well as others in planning and decision making in this arena in order to increase trust and sense of safety.

Planning for Evaluation

CAUTION

The more importance is attached to the supervision experience (i.e., graduate degree or license), the more active supervisors should be to be fair with evaluation and protect supervisees from the possibility of subjectivity and bias in judgment of abilities. Include others in the evaluative process. Use a multiplicity of methods and techniques and seek feedback about the supervisee from other sources. It is always best if feedback is based on some form of direct observation, such as live observation or a recorded session, and not exclusively on what is reported during case reviews.

Although evaluation is a crucial component of any ethical practice model, it is also the most overlooked component of supervision because of the anxiety it generates as well as a lack of skill and training among supervisors in how do it effectively. Nevertheless, as evaluation affects all aspects of the supervisory relationship, it cannot be ignored.

The evaluative role can be the most problematic for beginning supervisors. Counselors, therapists, and others in social service roles by nature and by training may be uncomfortable with the concepts of hierarchy, approval, and power so core to clinical supervision. To resolve this difficulty, beginning supervisors may seek to ignore evaluation altogether or minimize its function by indicating to supervisees that evaluation is not really important. However, most supervisees are acutely aware of the unspoken evaluative function of supervisors. Deciding not to address the issue directly from the beginning may negatively influence the quality of the working alliance and create unnecessary stress and anxiety for all concerned. Apprehension about evaluation can be the cause of many relationship difficulties between supervisor and supervisee (Ellis, 2001; Ladany, Lehrman-Waterman, Molinaro, & Wolgast, 1999). The steps necessary to prepare for evaluation in supervision are listed in Rapid Reference 6.16.

Evaluation raises in both supervisors and supervisees issues of trust and safety in the working alliance. As a consequence, supervisors need to strive to create an environment where the evaluative function creates positive motivation in supervisees. Normalizing the experience of making mistakes can be critical to encouraging openness to corrective feedback and evaluation. With fore-

DON'T FORGET

- It is never possible to overlook the evaluative component of supervision.
- Supervisees have an ethical and legal right to fair evaluation.
- Supervisees must be informed at the beginning about the evaluative component, including who and what will be involved.

≡*Rapid Reference 6.16*

Steps for Supervisors to Take to Prepare for Evaluation

- Examine one's own past experiences with evaluation in supervision. Identify personal thoughts and feelings that may facilitate or block effectiveness.
- Be clear from the beginning of supervision about the evaluation process, timing, and methods.
- Combine formats, methods, and techniques to insure success and to be fair.
- Be multiculturally responsive. Recognize assumptions, attitudes, and mindsets that may be harmful to supervisees, and actively work to prevent such an outcome.
- Remember that goals and evaluation are tied together, so be sure goals for supervision are well defined.
- Describe in behavioral terms, using examples, what the supervisee is going to be judged on in the evaluation.
- Focus on behaviors, not personality.
- Be fair and realistic. Don't overwhelm supervisees with excessive demands for perfection. Make room for mistakes.
- Apply the developmental perspective: Be able to describe what comprises competency in each area at different levels of experience.
- Share thinking with supervisees and involve them from the beginning in the evaluative process.
- Set aside specific times for evaluation, and include it in the supervision schedule.
- Provide supervisees with opportunities to give you both formal and informal evaluative feedback.
- Include feedback from other sources to assure fairness.

thought and planning, evaluation can change from a fearfully avoided activity to a more positive experience. For example, self-disclosure; the use of vocabulary words, such as *mastery, obstacles, options, improvement,* and *risk-taking;* along with an open discussion with all supervisees about the real purpose of evaluative feedback can go a long way in establishing trust and decreasing anxiety. Peace and Sprinthall (1998) found that in a school training program where supervisors focused on the aspects of development and mas-

DON'T FORGET

The more evaluation experience focuses on mastery and improvement rather than on blame and punishment, the more open and honest supervisees may be in owning mistakes and responding to suggestions for improvement.

tery rather than on right or wrong, it led to a significant increase in skill development among all supervisees.

Central to the evaluation process itself are the supervisor's and supervisee's personal thoughts, feelings, and experiences associated with this task. It is easy for experienced practitioners to forget how it feels to be exposed and vulnerable while one's work with clients is continually open to critical evaluation. Therefore, one rich area for all supervisors to explore with supervisees would be their previous evaluation experiences in clinical supervision as well as other arenas. It usually follows that the more unpleasant and unfavorable these experiences were, the more uncomfortable supervisees might be with the evaluative function. Obviously, all supervisors should do this same type of self-exploration before venturing into the area of evaluation in supervision.

When one supervisor is the sole evaluator of a supervisee's competence, it is absolutely essential to use a combination of methods and techniques for evaluation and seek out independent sources for evaluative feedback in order to avoid problems of subjectivity and impaired judgment that not only might harm supervisees but also clients in turn. For example, liking a particular supervisee can just as often produce a poorly thought out evaluation than disliking. Asking another experienced supervisor to review samples of a supervisee's written work, such as progress notes or client intakes, or review a tape of a supervisee's client session could go a long way toward solving such problems.

Ideally, feedback should be consistent, objective, and based on behavioral descriptions that can be easily understood by supervisees. Behavioral rating scales can help supervisors to accomplish this task and avoid subjectivity in their evaluative feedback. A sample of this type of rating scale for supervisee evaluation is included Rapid Reference 6.17. Other examples of paper-and-pencil instruments, rating scales, and behavioral checklists for evaluation abound in numerous resources, including Bernard and Goodyear (2004), Bradley and Ladany (2001), Campbell (2000), and Storm and Todd (1997). Searching the Internet is another means available to locate forms specific to a particular discipline or setting.

Most problems related to evaluation in supervision concern the area of personal development (Hensley et al., 2003). Supervisors err and get into trouble when thinking about a supervisee's personal suitability to be a mental health practitioner, usually because of ill-defined criteria or descriptors for this area. To solve that problem, it is necessary for supervisors (and graduate programs and organizations) to record key personal characteristics that are essential for competency in clinical practice. This list of personal criteria might include the following: being open, flexible, positive, and cooperative; willing to use and accept feedback; being aware of one's impact on others; being able to deal effectively with conflict; accepting personal responsibility; and being able to express feelings effectively and

Example of a Generic Evaluation Rating Scale to Use with Psychotherapists and Counselors

Competencies	Poor	Below average	Average	Above average	Excellent
Knowledge					
Knowledge of theory and intervention strategies					
Knowledge of DSM diagnostic manual					
Knowledge of role of multicultural differences					
Knowledge of resources in community					
Knowledge of current ethical guidelines and legal issues					
Practice					
Ability to apply intervention strategies					
Timely and thorough documentation					
Ability to develop rapport					
Ability to assess and diagnose					
Ability to respond to multicultural differences					
Ability to formulate treatment goals					

(continued)

Competencies	Poor	Below average	Average	Above average	Excellent
Personal					
Awareness of biases that may interfere with client care					
Demonstrates use of ethical judgment					
Ability to identify thoughts and feelings that interfere with client care					
Ability to identify own strengths and weaknesses					
Ability to accept and learn from feedback					
Seeks consultation to maintain objectivity					

appropriately (Frame & Stevens-Smith, 1995). Impairment or deficits would subsequently be represented by the opposite: lack of demonstrated empathy, inability to work closely with others, inability to handle stress, poor ethical judgment, and intolerance for any deviancy in clients from the supervisee's standards or values (Baldo et al., 1997).

CAUTION

Along with the use of such a rating scale, supervisors would also need to identify what behaviors represent "Excellent" or "Poor" for each category.

With advanced supervisees, evaluation ought to entirely take on a very different form. Rather than relying on a standardized paper-and-pencil instrument, supervisees at this level should be invited to create their own evaluative tools. Asking supervisees to answer the question "What competencies are required to be an ethical practitioner?" and then collecting several examples for each one of the suggested areas will easily do the job. From this discussion, it should be a short step to create a behavioral checklist to be used for evaluation. Be assured, practitioners at this stage of development should not only be able to create their own evaluative tools but also be able to engage in self-evaluation utilizing these measures. Rapid Reference 6.18 gives an example of an evaluation form that could be used with post-degree supervisees who are seeking licensure. It was created from a number of discussions with supervisors about the behaviors that make up an ethical practitioner (Campbell, 2001–2005).

≡Rapid Reference 6.18

Example of Behavioral Indicators for an Ethical Practitioner

- Recognizes ethical issues as they appear in client cases
- Follows ethical guidelines when taking actions with clients
- Is able to articulate his or her approach to solving ethical dilemmas
- Is able to identify what he or she doesn't know and can seek help from supervisors
- Avoids dual relationships with clients
- Follows rules for confidentiality
- Has knowledge and expertise in his or her area of practice
- Has repertory of skills to help clients solve problems
- Has sensitivity to multicultural differences and acts accordingly
- Understands the importance of self-awareness and engages in activities to maintain clearness and objectivity and prevent personal issues and problems having a negative impact on clients

Putting It Into Practice

Case Example

Mary is a clinical supervisor in an agency that provides marital and family counseling. She has been Susan's supervisor for 3 months. Susan just graduated with a master's degree in marriage and family therapy. It is now time for the first evaluation feedback session. Mary's agency has a standard rating scale form that is used for this purpose. Reviewing the form, Mary notes that overall Susan is doing very well. She has great clinical skills, is able to establish rapport with clients, is at ease in situations with angry clients, is able to come up with excellent interventions strategies on her own to use with the majority of her clients, and seems open to supervision and corrective feedback. However, she is struggling with her paperwork and getting it done correctly and turned in on time. Mary arranged to meet with Susan for her first evaluation session, and, after reviewing Susan's positives and noting her strengths, it was time to move to the area of difficulty. Mary began this part of the feedback by noting how difficult the paperwork is for many new counselors and therapists and sharing her own difficulties mastering this same problem. She then asked Susan what her perspective was on the issue and where she thought her problems lie. Susan admitted that she really did not know exactly how to fill out the client forms and document her client sessions, and that was the central focus for her of all of her difficulties. Mary felt this was an area in which she could be helpful. She made a number of suggestions and asked Susan to select the one that sounded best.

Teaching Point: Mary spent time preparing for the evaluative feedback session. She first gave Susan positive and specific feedback about the things she was really doing well. Then when coming to the problem area, she began feedback showing understanding and acceptance. She also narrowed her feedback to two specific problems, and then asked Susan to select the area of most difficulty from her perspective. She also listed several ideas for solutions but again asked Susan to select the one that sounded best to her. This strategy tends to facilitate ownership of problems and solutions by supervisees and reduces defensiveness and lack of cooperation.

Evaluative Feedback for Supervisors

It is also necessary in an ethical and best-practice model to provide supervisees with the means to give evaluative feedback to their supervisors and to register any complaints about supervision in a safe manner. Solicitation of feedback from supervisees can be done informally and formally throughout the supervisory experience. In most instances, simply inquiring how supervision is going and whether any changes are needed is sufficient to solicit feedback from the majority of supervisees. For example, questions such as "How are things going for you? Are you getting what you need and want from supervision?" draw attention to the supervision process and indicate the supervisor's openness to feedback and change.

Adding to that, as a part of the formal evaluation of supervisees, including a supervisor rating scale is a straightforward suggestion. A sample of such a form is included in Rapid Reference 6.19.

Another type of supervision rating form may be used to capture the effectiveness of a particular supervision model and training program. For example, to evaluate the success of a supervision training program for school counselors in Israel, an evaluation form was created based on the discrimination model of Bernard and Goodyear (Shechtman & Wirzberger, 1999). Following the discrimination model, this evaluation form has four sections: counseling, teaching, consultation, and process. Questions on the form vary from asking if the supervisor made them feel comfortable expressing opinions, questions, and concerns (counseling) to whether the supervisor helped them with new counseling strategies they could use with their clients (teaching), helped them set counseling objectives (consultation), or provided useful feedback (process).

Another employment of a supervisor rating scale might be to assess interns'

Putting It Into Practice

Case Example

George is a psychologist in private practice. At a local professional luncheon he is approached by a professional acquaintance, Tom. George knows Tom superficially as another private practitioner in the community. They have talked briefly at various professional lunches and conferences in the past. Tom says he has decided to get certified in another professional specialty area and then asks George if he would be willing to supervise him for that purpose. Tom adds, "not much time would be required" as he is already licensed as a psychologist and has considerable past experience in this particular area. Therefore, he just needs "someone on paper to act as his supervisor for this credential and sign off at the end on the required form." He offers to pay George a substantial sum for this service. What should George say and do? What are the ethical issues here? What role does evaluation play?

Teaching Point: Under the conditions described by Tom for supervision service, George should say no. It would be unethical to proceed with supervision without holding actual formal supervision sessions to review Tom's expertise with clients in this area of specialization and to have established criteria for full competency for the credential involved. Additionally, George himself would need competency in the desired specialty area to qualify as the supervisor. Because supervisors carry responsibility for supervisee's actions with clients when in supervision, such a haphazard plan is risky for George. Not taking the evaluative aspect of the relationship seriously can lead to potential problems should George discover Tom's lack of skill or competency in this arena. Experience in one field does not automatically mean competency in another.

Rapid Reference 6.19

Example of Evaluation Rating Scale for Supervisors to Give to Supervisees

Date: _____ Supervisee: _____

Supervisor: _____

Methods and techniques used in supervision: Videotape _____ Audiotape _____ Direct observation _____

Case presentation _____ Experiential techniques _____ Written _____

Review of case notes and client documentation _____

	Not observed	Not effective	Effective	Very effective
Structures supervisory session				
Provides useful feedback				
Encourages active involvement				
Uses variety of methods and techniques				
Maintains focus in supervision session				
Is available and accessible				
Encourages questions				
Acts supportive				

	Not observed	Not effective	Effective	Very effective
Challenges you to grow				
Promotes self-evaluation				
Focuses on behavior, not person				
Provides helpful suggestions				
Is flexible and open				
Helps you achieve goals for supervision				
Is fair and respectful				
Addresses ethical issues and promotes ethical decision making				
Is multiculturally responsive				

Overall rating of supervisor's competence: Excellent _____   Good _____   Needs improvement _____

Comments: _____

_____

_____

_____ Date _____

Signature of supervisee

_____ Date _____

Signature of supervisor

satisfaction with their field sites. Ladany et al. (1996) came up with a short questionnaire that could be used for exactly this purpose. Using a Likert-type scale, supervisees were asked to rate the quality of the supervision at the site, the amount of time given to supervision, and the extent to which the supervision matched their needs. One revealing question on the questionnaire even asked the supervisee if they would return again themselves for supervision with this same person!

In closing, it should be apparent that time spent on the evaluation component in supervision is not suggested; it is absolutely necessary for ethical practitioners and will garner rich rewards for everyone involved.

SUPERVISION STYLE

One important issue to consider when beginning supervising is personal style. Every supervisor has a style. It includes personality characteristics, leadership style, work values, and learning style. The term supervisor style not only captures the supervisor's approach to supervision but also the way that supervisor will typically respond to his or her supervisees (Friedlander & Ward, 1984).

There are a number of factors to consider when examining the issue of supervisor style. For example, one's need for control versus the ability to delegate and let go of responsibility will make a significant difference in the supervisor's approach to the role. Other factors affecting a supervisor's style are tolerance for ambiguity and flexibility versus a need for a clearly defined supervision structure and guidelines as well as the desire for autonomy and independence versus the need to belong to a secure group or team. Other variables are a supervisor's level of comfort with conflict and confrontation, work values, and preferred learning style. Rapid Reference 6.20 lists a range of influences on supervision style.

The various roles supervisors need to assume during the supervision experience also influence supervisory style. Clinical supervisors combine many roles: teacher, mentor, model, monitor, consultant, counselor, and evaluator. Sometimes supervisors need to lead, and other times they need to follow. Oftentimes supervisors will feel like generals as they seek to lead supervisees into the battle for quality service for clients with meager resources and unmanageable expectations. In other instances, they may believe it necessary to be a team parent.

Because supervisors are constantly balancing the needs of supervisees along with those of clients, role flexibility is considered essential to effective supervision (Hart & Nance, 2003; Ladany et al., 2001). Supervisors must be willing to adjust their role and style to meet each supervisee's learning needs and developmental level. At the start of supervision with novice supervisees, supervisors should be perceptive of their supervisees' need for support at that point in

≣*Rapid Reference 6.20*

Influences on Supervision Style

1. Personality characteristics.
   - Myers-Briggs type preferences
   - Field dependent or independent
2. Leadership style.
   - Autocratic, democratic, or consultative
3. Work values.
   - Autonomy, creativity, teamwork
4. Learning style.
   - Visual, auditory, kinesthetic
5. Environmental factors.
   - Job role, policies, and budget
6. Client population, setting, and safety needs.
7. Developmental level.
8. Training needs/requirements of supervisees.
9. Professional and ethical guidelines.

time and so respond in a warm and friendly manner. But beginners also need direction, structure, information, and monitoring as well as some old-fashioned hand-holding, which means supervisors have to do more than be welcoming and reassuring. Subsequently, as time progresses, supervisors may find themselves within the context of a supervision session needing to change roles and functions, moving between nurturer and supporter to challenger and taskmaster and from counselor to teacher to consultant.

Also, different environments and populations will require a different emphasis. For example, supervisors in inpatient facilities working with severely emotionally disturbed individuals will be required to be very directive and involved in close monitoring of supervisees' actions with clients, whereas those in school settings or in situations where paraprofessionals provide home services will of necessity need to be able to support independent functioning and a loose structure of monitoring. Naturally, all supervisors in crisis situations are expected both ethically and legally to take a more directive approach to supervision, even if supervisees are highly experienced.

DON'T FORGET

Supervisors should try to achieve a balance between their own preferences and those of the supervisee.

Personality Characteristics

Personality characteristics are always a part of supervisory style and, if understood, help increase the effectiveness of the supervision relationship. One excellent strategy to raise the role of personality in supervision style in a relaxed and positive manner is to employ the Myers-Briggs Type Indicator (MBTI). This well-known instrument, based on the work of Carl Jung, was designed to identify people's personality preferences, how they take in and process information, how they make decisions, and their overall lifestyle choices (Myers et al., 1998). It is not a measure of abnormality or mental illness. Although some argument exists about the validity of this instrument and some of its uses (Barbuto, 1997), the MBTI can still be a striking vehicle to open a constructive dialogue between supervisors and supervisees concerning similarities or differences in learning style, communication patterns, and approaches to work. Rapid Reference 6.21 summarizes some of the material from the MBTI that has application to supervision.

Rapid Reference 6.21

Applying the Myers-Briggs to Supervision

Understanding the four dimensions of the MBTI

The MBTI measures a person's preferences on four dimensions that Jung described in his theory of personality type: extroversion/introversion; sensing/intuition; thinking/feeling; judging/perception.

1. The first dimension relates to how people are energized, or what turns them on. *Extroverts* are energized by contact with people, while, on the contrary, *introverts* need more quiet.
2. The second dimension describes what people pay attention to. *Sensors* focus on facts and what they can see, hear, or touch, whereas *intuitive* types rely on a sixth sense.
3. The third dimension describes how the person prefers to make decisions: *Thinkers* tend to use reason and logic, while *feelers* are more subjective, using values and feelings to reach decisions.
4. The last dimension describes a person's overall approach to life. *Judgers* prefer to be planned and organized, whereas *perceivers* prefer spontaneity and flexibility.

Questions to ask in order to explore personal type

1. "How am I energized? Is it with people, or do I need to be by myself?"
2. "What do I pay attention to? Do I like to focus on facts and the details of a situation or do I like to see the big picture and get a sense of something?"
3. "How do I make decisions? Do I like to look at the facts and think about a problem on my own to come up with the answer, or do I prefer to process

my feelings with others in order to find a solution? Do I usually say 'I feel' or do I usually say 'I think?'"

4. "As a supervisor, do I sometimes wish supervisees would just go back into their office and solve situations instead of taking up precious time talking in supervision about all their feelings?" (introverted/thinking vs. extroverted/feeling)

5. "How do I like to live and work? Do I prefer to have a plan or would I rather be more spontaneous? Do I like to be decisive and organized and set goals, plan my career, and plan my life, or am I just the opposite? Do I abhor letting plans run my life? Instead, I like to adapt and be open and flexible about possibilities."

Self-awareness exercises to identify differences in personality preferences

1. One fun self-awareness exercise that will help draw out differences in personal preferences is to ask, "How do I go about planning for vacations? Do I prepare carefully in advance, collecting all of the information and details about destinations and laying out a complete travel plan? Or do I do just the opposite, preferring to get in the car and just go see what happens?"

2. Another revealing question to explore differences in preferences is to examine one's response to test taking. Ask yourself, "Is my favorite expression *it depends,* and, as a result, do I have trouble answering true and false or multiple-choice questions? Or do I love questions that ask for certainty and hate the ones that say 'all of the above' on a multiple-choice test?"

3. Goal setting is another area where differences in personality preferences will surface, sometimes dramatically, in supervision. Ask yourself, "Do I like the words *goal* and *goal setting,* or do I dislike the sound of these terms? Do I like to establish goals and before beginning, break them down into small action steps? Or instead, do I prefer to just have a sense of direction or purpose in my head and abhor lists and outlines?" Maybe neither of these approaches is your style, so how do you set goals? After reaching some clarity about your way of approaching tasks and setting goals, have your supervisees do the same exercise and compare notes.

Note: For further information about the Myers-Briggs Type Indicator, contact Consulting Psychologists Press, 3803 East Bayshore Road, Palo Alto, CA 94303.

Think of a supervisee with whom you are now having some difficulties as a supervisor and ask, "Do I think we differ from each other on any or all of these four dimensions of the MBTI?" If so, ask, "What things need to be changed to make this relationship go better?"

Other personality differences can

DON'T FORGET

Personality preferences can be highly influential in creating a successful working relationship. Supervisors need to be self-aware and willing to adapt their style rather than labeling and blaming supervisees for problems in the relationship.

CAUTION

If the supervisor and supervisee are on opposite poles in field independence and field dependence, there can be friction in the supervisory relationship. To avoid conflict, supervisors in the early stage of supervision want to discuss motivation needs with supervisees and follow up with a plan to accommodate any crucial differences.

be influential in selecting a supervision style, such as field independence versus field dependence or internal versus external motivation (Middleman & Rhodes, 1985). Field-independent people are said to prefer freedom and autonomy, the ability to create their own structure and goals, and engage in self-evaluation. They value creativity, experimentation, and have a tolerance for ambiguity. Most field-independent people are self-motivated and self-directed and possess an internal motivational system. As supervisees, they function best with supervisors who encourage independence and self-direction. In turn, supervisors who are field independent and internally motivated prefer a supervisee-centered model of supervision and want supervisees to actively participate in all aspects of supervision from setting goals and planning to evaluation.

On the other hand, field-dependent people have been found to prefer working in groups within an organizational structure and contributing to the group effort. They appreciate set guidelines, supervisor direction, and clearly defined tasks. As such, they favor a supervisor who directs and guides, provides structure, delineates tasks, and retains full responsibility for evaluation of their accomplishments (Middleman & Rhodes, 1985).

Leadership Style

There are many leadership styles available, and much has been written in management literature about this topic. Because clinical supervision is a relationship of unequal power, how supervisors envision their leadership role and how they use their power and authority is an important topic to consider. Currently, the situational leadership model (Hersey & Blanchard, 1996), which views selection of a leadership style as an interaction between the leader and requirements of a situation, seems to dovetail well with the developmental perspective recommended for clinical supervision in Chapter 3. Applying the situational-leadership model, supervisors would move from a directive style of leadership to a more democratic, collaborative one as supervisees' development levels increase and they are able to take on new tasks. In other words, opposite to the authoritarian model of leadership, which is based on the leader's needs for control, choice of leadership style becomes inseparable from the needs of the followers (Kormanski, 1999).

Work Values

Another fruitful area to examine is the area of work values. Similarities or differences in work values hold an important place in the supervisory relationship. Clinical supervision is built on the supposition that supervisees want to increase their effectiveness, aspire to do a better job and therefore will be motivated to seek guidance and support, are willing to acknowledge mistakes, and appreciate corrective feedback. However, conflicting needs and values might interfere with this premise. First, differences in culture can be influential in belief about the importance of being on time with paperwork or appointments. Second, differences in the need for autonomy and self-direction versus teamwork and leader direction can contribute to a poor supervisory experience. Third, personal attitudes and beliefs about achievement, success, and failure can influence the supervisory process. For example, perfectionism and fear of failure can contribute to a supervisor's unrealistic expectations, rigidity, difficulty delegating, and unrealistic expectations. This perfectionism coupled with other differences in cultural values could easily spill over onto supervisees with statements such as "They just don't take work seriously enough" or "They are lazy, just doing the minimum."

Using an instrument, such as the Values Scale by Nevill and Super (1985), or posing self-exploration questions of supervisees, such as "What is success to you?" or "What brought you into the field?" might help initiate a dialogue on work values. After better understanding a supervisee's needs and values, supervisors can then set out to alter their supervisory style and choice of methods and techniques.

Learning Style

A supervisee's learning style is another important factor to consider when deciding on a preferred style of supervision and can guide choice of supervision methods and techniques. People have individual differences in their ability to conceptualize, use abstract reasoning, and form hypotheses, all of which are essential to case conceptualization. Some supervisees are auditory learners and learn best talking about their cases. These individuals

> **DON'T FORGET**
>
> There are important multicultural differences in work values. Continually check assumptions for bias. Understand differences in people and build on them.

CAUTION

Avoid the one-size-fits-all type of supervision style. Customize your supervision style to meet supervisees' individual needs. Open a discussion on personal preferences, work values, and learning style. Offer supervisees a variety of activities besides traditional case consultation.

thrive in a case consultation format. Other supervisees may be more visual and learn most effectively with reading and writing assignments. Supervisees with low analytic ability and those who are visual would benefit from written work sheets, structured questions, and case review forms, whereas those who are auditory learners and able to think abstractly will want more time to explore theory as they consult on cases. Active or kinesthetic learners, who learn best through action and movement, will appreciate supervisors who draw on experiential methods and techniques such as role-play and role-reversal. Naturally, many individuals do not have one dominant learning style but may operate with a combination of these learning styles.

Putting It Into Practice

Case Example

Lisa is a doctoral-level supervisee. She sees therapy as an art, not a science, and so works from a broad theoretical framework and rarely knows ahead of time what she is going to do with a client, preferring to rely on intuition and gut instinct. She likes the big picture and doesn't care much for detail, so she struggles with structured types of intervention strategies where they tell her what to say and do, and her paperwork is always in disarray. She doesn't like the medical model and the diagnosis and labeling required by the *DSM* because she feels it gets in the way of understanding the client's world and seeing their strengths and, therefore, interferes with helping them solve their problems.

To her, being with her clients, building a trusting relationship, and working with their strengths to solve problems is what really matters. Lisa thinks things through by talking, so in supervision she wants to process all of her impressions and feelings about her client cases as a means to understand and make changes.

Lisa's supervisor, Ted, is opposite in nature, personality, and preferences. He is older, and has been in the field for 30 years. His specialty is cognitive therapy, and he is very well known for his expertise in this area. He is also known for being very demanding, directive, and structured as a supervisor, having an explicit model of counseling and therapy that he practices and teaches all his supervisees. He places great priority in supervision on paperwork and uses an extensive number of forms as teaching tools. To him, supervisees should come to supervision with their assessment of the client's problem and plan of approach already prepared. He gets very impatient with supervisees who wish to process their thoughts and feelings about clients in supervision and therefore is apt to end discussion with the statement "cut the rambling."

Lisa asked to meet with her program director to discuss her feelings about her supervisor, Ted. She said she experienced Ted as dogmatic, insensitive, and critical, and she felt she was being harmed by the experience. Her program director, while well aware of the poor fit between Lisa and this particular supervisor, told Lisa that finding her another supervisor at this time was impossible, and she should just "suck it up" and "quit complaining." Lisa felt let down and misunderstood and left the meeting questioning whether becoming a therapist was the correct career path for her.

Teaching Point: There are significant difference between Lisa's style and learning needs and that of her supervisor. In such instances, open discussion by the supervisor about differences in learning styles, personality preferences, strengths, and deficits and how they vary in approach to clients would be essential if both are to work effectively together. Differences in style, if not addressed, can leave supervisees feeling unheard and misunderstood and detrimentally impact the supervision relationship. In a few extreme instances, supervisees can be severely harmed by the behavior of their supervisor, so much so that they may leave the field. Her program director's insensitivity to Lisa's need to process her concerns and general disregard for her feelings is another example of how differences in personality preferences identified by the MBTI can create relationship difficulties. The program director jumped to the conclusion that Lisa wanted to be transferred, rather than exploring exactly what her needs were at their meeting. A better question for the program director to ask of Lisa would have been "What do you want to get out of our meeting together?" or "How do you see me being helpful to you?" Transferring Lisa to another supervisor is just one of several options to resolve relationship difficulties.

Another important learning point to take away from this case example is that by not having a discussion of preferences and style be a natural part of supervision and her professional growth, Lisa was unable to articulate her difficulties and needs in a more effective fashion.

🖋 TEST YOURSELF 🖋

1. **The purpose of orientation is to build understanding and the working alliance.** True or False?

2. **Taking time to structure supervision and think through goals, evaluation, and administrative tasks can be helpful in preventing burnout.** True or False?

3. **The most important task of the clinical supervisor at the beginning of supervision is to do a personality assessment of the supervisee and to use that as the primary means to evaluate the supervisee's competence.** True or False?

(continued)

4. **In order to improve motivation, it is best to include supervisees in setting goals for supervision and deciding on topics, methods, and techniques to be used along with ideas for evaluation.** True or False?

5. **The evaluative function is a key component of ethical supervision practice.** True or False?

6. **Fair evaluation means**
   (a) supervisors share evaluation methods, techniques, and criteria for success at the beginning of supervision.
   (b) supervisors overlook mistakes made by beginning supervisees.
   (c) supervisors tell supervisees in the beginning that evaluation is really not very important to them.
   (d) evaluation is only done once at the end of a supervision experience.

7. **Supervisors can help supervisees manage their anxiety about receiving evaluative feedback by**
   (a) telling them that mistake making is natural and they can learn from those mistakes.
   (b) sharing personal thoughts and feelings about evaluation.
   (c) never discussing the subject of evaluation with supervisees because it makes them anxious.
   (d) cutting off any feedback from supervisees about mistakes you have made, as this is not conducive to effective leadership.
   (e) doing a and b.
   (f) doing c and d.

8. **If you are beginning to have problems with a supervisee, it is best to**
   (a) sit down immediately and discuss these concerns with the supervisee.
   (b) just wait awhile; things may get better.
   (c) talk immediately to your administrative supervisor about the need to terminate supervision with this person.
   (d) keep it to yourself but write your personal impressions and feelings down in the supervisee's files.

9. **Minimum standard of documentation for supervisors would include a supervision log. This log would contain**
   (a) a complete record of everything discussed.
   (b) a record of how often you met, how long, and modality (group or individual) for each supervisee.
   (c) the supervisor's subjective opinions about the supervisee and assessment of the supervisee's mental health.
   (d) nothing. Don't bother with a log; it is just more busy work.

10. **Because there are so many changing rules and regulations concerning client documentation and paperwork, it is better that clinical supervisors leave the responsibility for correct paperwork in the hands of supervisees.** True or False?

11. **When experiencing difficulties with a particular supervisee, supervisors would want to**

    (a) document the problem according to the terms of the *DSM*.

    (b) document problems using observable behaviors.

    (c) document problems directly into the client's file who is involved in the difficulty.

    (d) not write anything down at all.

12. **The informed consent agreement for supervision should contain**

    (a) a description of the supervisors approach to supervision.

    (b) the ethical demands for the relationship.

    (c) the parameters of the relationship.

    (d) a line for supervisor and supervisee to sign and date.

    (e) all of the above.

13. **Personal style includes**

    (a) personality.

    (b) leadership.

    (c) work values.

    (d) preferred learning style.

    (e) all of the above.

14. **Flexibility is a hallmark of effective supervisors.** True or False?

15. **If a supervisor has problems with a supervisee,**

    (a) the fault is with the supervisee.

    (b) the supervisor needs to tell the person to do what they are told with no arguments.

    (c) consider the role of style, personal preferences, culture, and work values in seeking a solution to difficulties.

    (d) everyone knows that all supervisees are lazy, so having problems just goes with the territory.

16. **The Myers-Briggs Type Indicator**

    (a) can be helpful tool in clinical supervision.

    (b) is not very reliable or valid and so clinical supervisors should ignore it.

    (c) might provide supervisors with data to use when firing employees.

    (d) could be used to evaluate a supervisee's ability to be in social service work.

    (e) does all of the above.

Answers: 1. True; 2. True; 3. False; 4. True; 5. True; 6. a; 7. e; 8. a; 9. b; 10. False; 11. b; 12. e; 13. e; 14. True; 15. c; 16. a

Seven

THE BEGINNING STAGE OF SUPERVISION

All supervisory relationships have a beginning, and all supervisors and supervisees whether they know each other or not share common concerns from the beginning about the future of that relationship. New supervisors will wonder if they have the skills and expertise to be successful. Supervisees will worry about being treated fairly and with respect. Each is asking, "Will I be heard and understood? Will my competencies be valued? Will I be safe? Is this experience going to be valuable?" Answering these needs in a positive manner is a necessary requirement for the beginning stage of supervision.

Supervisors must be active from the start to build a collaborative working relationship. Because the supervisory relationship is so central to a successful supervision experience, much time and attention must be given to cultivating it. Don't assume everyone, even a very experienced supervisee, knows why he or she is there and what is expected of him or her. Just as therapists have to explain to clients the therapeutic process in order reduce client anxiety and ask clients what their goals are for therapy in order to build a working relationship, supervisors need to do the same thing with supervisees. Supervisors need to work resolutely at the beginning to build understanding and agreement concerning expectations and tasks, reduce anxiety, and create a safe place for supervision to take place.

> **DON'T FORGET**
>
> Beginnings are important. If supervisors do not take time to establish the context for supervision, time and energy will be wasted as supervisees seek information and understanding about the goals and purpose of supervision.

> **DON'T FORGET**
>
> The quality of the supervisory relationship is critical to the success of clinical supervision. It is more important to emphasize relationship issues rather than techniques, especially in the beginning of the supervisory relationship. Spend more time on developing skills and less time on managing.

To accomplish these objectives, the most important task for supervisors becomes setting the stage for supervision through orientation, where all supervisees are informed of the expectations, goals, requirements, tasks, structure, and timing for supervision; the procedures for evaluation and monitoring; and provisions to assure the safety of super-

CAUTION

Before beginning supervision, it is important to review with supervisees the specific supervision requirements, such as licensure requirements, ethical codes and standards that apply, as well as the final evaluation forms.

visees through ethical and fair treatment practices. Significant barriers to building trust, such as dual relationships, multicultural differences, and the evaluation process, should be discussed openly and in some detail during this orientation.

The supervision informed consent agreement and the supervision contract, or a combination of both, are basic tools for the building of the supervisory relationship (see Chapter 6 for a discussion and examples of an informed consent agreement and contracts for supervision). Additionally, during this introductory process, supervisors will need to use all of their rapport-building skills and relationship knowledge in order to establish an open and safe environment. Anderson et al. (2000) found the more open the supervisory environment, the more respect, support, and encouragement are communicated and the more available and involved the supervisor, the better the supervision experience. Rapid Reference 7.1 lists the tasks of the beginning stage of supervision.

One helpful approach to building an effective relationship is to use a developmental perspective. Following the premise that supervisor, supervisee, and the supervisory relationship will grow and change over the course of supervision and that inexperienced supervisees will have different needs than those more advanced, embracing the developmental perspective can be helpful in several ways. First, taking into account the developmental level of supervisees as to skill and experience will assist in goal setting, planning, selecting methods and techniques, evaluation procedures, time management, and monitoring. Inexperienced supervisees take more time and need more structure, direction, and close monitoring than experienced supervisees who will want more autonomy and self-monitoring. Second, understanding the changing relationship needs of supervisees as time passes will also help supervisors be more effective. For example, in the beginning of supervision, attention needs to be paid to establishing safety, whereas later in time, the focus shifts to challenging and giving corrective feedback. Last, the developmental perspective will aid supervisors with evaluation. Ownership and participation in the evaluation process shifts from supervi-

≡ Rapid Reference 7.1

The Beginning Stage of Supervision

Goal: To establish an effective supervisory relationship with supervisees

Tasks for supervisors
- Build the working alliance
- Orient supervisees to supervision—the tasks, goals, and expectations
- Create a supportive environment and build a safe place to learn
- Work actively to reduce anxiety
- Discuss openly the barriers to trust (dual relationships, multicultural differences, and evaluation)
- Validate differences in perspective and approach
- Normalize mistake making and encourage risk-taking
  —Focus on successes, not just failures

Tools
- Relationship- and rapport-building skills
- Informed consent agreement and supervision contract
- Orientation session

sor to supervisee as skill and experience level increases so that in the advanced stage, supervisees are involved in self-supervision and self-evaluation.

Developmental issues also come into play in the beginning of supervision from another direction, the developmental level and experience of the supervisor. If the supervisor is new to supervision or relatively new to the field, it can sometimes be difficult to establish expertise and authority. In fact, Rau (2002) recommended inexperienced supervisors should view themselves more in a collaborative role with supervisees and, in the beginning, seek to find a common ground, rather than attempt to establish their authority. What this tactic means is that new supervisors must acknowledge their newness to the role of supervisor, solicit support and cooperation at the start, and ask supervisees what they would like to get out of supervision rather than tell them what will happen.

BUILDING THE WORKING ALLIANCE

The supervisory relationship, while similar in some ways to counseling and psychotherapy, is by its nature a different relationship with a different purpose. Although good counseling and psychotherapy skills are definitely an asset in building rapport and creating a positive environment, supervision should not be confused with therapy. The term *supervisory working alliance* has been coined to capture the essence of the relationship (Bordin, 1983). The supervisory working alliance is a collaborative relationship of change based on a mutual agreement on the goals and tasks of supervision along with a strong emotional bond of caring, trust, and respect. Research findings suggest that the quality of the working alliance is correlated to greater supervisee satisfaction (Chen & Bernstein, 2000; Ladany et al., 1999). Further, and perhaps more important, a study by Patton and Kivlighan (1997) found that the quality of the supervisory working alliance was predictive of the supervisee's counseling alliance with his or her clients.

In order to move forward in the working alliance, the goals for supervision must be clearly delineated. Supervisees must understand the purpose of these goals and how mastering them will improve their own success and effectiveness as professionals. In other words, they need to understand what is going to happen and how they fit in. They must also develop trust in the supervisor and his or her willingness to provide for their safety while learning. Thus, establishing the working alliance is a critical part of the orientation and contracting phase of supervision. When there is disagreement on the tasks, a misunderstanding about the value of these tasks, a lack of trust, or any combination of these, it is hard to move forward in supervision.

A number of issues may adversely affect the development of the working alliance: distrust in the supervisor, dual relationship issues, role confusion and conflict, anxiety concerning evaluation procedures, and misunderstanding of the value of the goals and tasks required. A lack of investment by supervisors in supervision, a harsh and unfriendly style, and excessive criticalness and dogmatism also impact trust and the working alliance. It takes trust for supervisees to open themselves to supervision, to hear feedback, and to take risks, and it takes the supervisor's relationship skills and ability to convey understanding, caring, and respect to

DON'T FORGET

Supervisors have to create an atmosphere of trust and a commonality of goals and purpose in order to be successful.

DON'T FORGET

There are three elements important to build the working alliance:

- Explanation of tasks and goals for supervision
- An agreement on the meaning of these goals and tasks
- A sense of liking and caring between supervisor and supervisee

Rapid Reference 7.2

Tips for Building the Working Alliance

- Establish mutuality and collaboration to accomplish tasks
- Use self-disclosure to foster openness, honesty, and willingness to admit mistakes
- Talk openly about the hierarchy of power and the means available to resolve problems
- Include supervisees in setting goals, planning, and the evaluation process

develop that trust. Having empathy and compassion for supervisees and a belief in supervisees' abilities and strengths to achieve mastery are all part of the formation of trust. In actual fact, Muse-Burke, Ladany, and Deck (2001) found across the board that facilitative conditions such as empathy, genuineness, warmth, trust, and positive regard are common to virtually all effective supervisors regardless of their theoretical model of practice.

Rapid Reference 7.2 summarizes tips for building the working alliance.

Anxiety and the Working Alliance

Anxiety is a natural response to supervision and may play a significant role in shaping the working alliance and the quality of the supervisory relationship (Bischoff et al., 2002; Campbell, 2000; Fitch & Marshall, 2002). Supervisors need to consider its impact on the supervisory relationship and how to best work with it. Supervisees may feel anxious about their performance and ability to be successful working with clients. Additionally, they may also be concerned about the quality of the relationship with the supervisor. "Will I be liked?" and "Will I be seen as competent by my supervisor?" are typical beginning concerns.

The supervisee's level of anxiety may vary depending on issues of power and choice, personality factors, developmental stage, the purpose of supervision, familiarity with the supervisor, and the importance of the evaluative component. For example, postdegree supervisees seeking licensure may experience supervision differently from those just starting out in the field. Postdegree supervisees who are also employees may be concerned about job safety and job performance along with anxiety about obtaining their license. They may experience low choice in selecting a supervisor and considerable role confusion. All of these considerations, if not addressed, can influence open communication, self-disclosure, and trust.

The hierarchical nature of supervision is another area that can create anxiety and interfere with the working alliance. Anxiety might also be fueled by the supervisee's previous experiences in supervision, confusion about his or her role as a supervisee, and the supervisor's expectations. The existence of multiple relationships, or role conflict, in clinical supervision on both the part of the supervisor and supervisee can also generate considerable anxiety and confusion (Bordin, 1983; Herlihy & Corey, 1997; Kaiser, 1997; Ladany & Friedlander, 1995; Ladany, Waterman, Molinaro, & Wolgast, 1999). For example, the clinical supervisor may also be the administrator or major professor of a graduate program. Supervisees may be former peers, colleagues, and, in some cases, especially in the substance abuse field, former clients.

Another contributing factor to anxiety is the fact that supervisees are encouraged to be open, honest, and truthful about their mistakes and to be willing to discuss their limitations at the same time their supervisor is evaluating their competence and suitability for the profession. Bordin (1983) called this *role ambiguity*. This same confusion may occur for supervisors as they try to avoid providing therapy to supervisees while being ethically bound to explore personal issues if they interfere with quality of care or are potentially harmful to clients. If areas of confusion about role and expectations are not addressed properly, the working alliance can suffer (Ladany & Friedlander, 1995).

Issues about privacy of communication can also contribute to anxiety. Privacy in clinical supervision may be limited. For example, when supervision is delivered in a job setting, supervisors are going to exchange information with administrators and other supervisors. If supervision is required for licensure, a final evaluation must be sent to a licensure board. Thus, supervisors need to think about the extent of privacy and strategize how to protect a supervisee's confidentiality to the best of their ability so as to create a safe environment for self-disclosure. This information should be part of orientation and included in the informed consent agreement for supervision.

ORIENTATION

One of the best ways to minimize anxiety and improve the working alliance is to begin any supervisory relationship with a well-thought-out orientation experience that includes an open discussion of supervision goals, expectations, evaluation procedures, as well as plans to address any relationship problems as they arise. The use of a written informed

> **DON'T FORGET**
>
> Three main responsibilities of supervisees in supervision:
>
> - To protect clients from harm
> - To actively participate in supervision
> - To be open, honest, and truthful about what they don't know and forthcoming about mistakes

≡Rapid Reference 7.3

Supervisee's Responsibilities in Clinical Supervision

This list could also be included as part of a supervision contract or informed consent agreement.

- To provide service to clients in an ethical manner and adhere to ethical standards of one's profession
- To seek to become the best professional possible
- To take supervision seriously: prepare, participate, attend
- To avoid all dual relationships with clients that may be harmful and to agree never to engage in a sexual relationship with clients
- To follow rules of confidentiality and protect clients from harm
- To work always within the limits of competency, skill, and training
- To seek supervision immediately in crisis situations
- To be honest reporting mistakes and identifying areas of bias or where one lacks competence
- To submit documentation of clinical work in timely and accurate form
- To be open to supervision, suggestions, and feedback
- To accept referral to outside help such as counseling, psychotherapy, support groups, or more training if need indicated
- To provide supervisor with honest feedback about supervision and supervisory process
- To seek consultation and guidance on how to proceed in cases of impairment or unethical behavior of supervisor

DON'T FORGET

When orienting supervisees to supervision, be sure to do the following:

- Discuss expectations, goals, needs, evaluation methods, and documentation
- Explain your role and function and that of supervisees
- Use an informed consent agreement and contract as basis of discussion
- Ask supervisees what they need and want from supervision

consent agreement, a supervision contract, or both might be a part of this introduction (see Chapter 6 for a complete discussion of informed consent agreements and contracts for supervision). Rapid Reference 7.3 outlines the main responsibilities for supervisees as they participate in clinical supervision.

Creating a structured orientation plan with an outline of introductory information to be obtained from any and all supervisees, regardless of experience, along with topics to be covered in the first session may be useful to avoid difficulties and overcome anxiety, especially for beginning supervisors.

Assessing Supervisees' Preparedness for Supervision

Because supervisees may come from a variety of backgrounds, the supervisor needs to take time to go over the supervisee's previous training and work experiences before the orientation. Moreover, with graduate interns and postdegree supervisees, it is important not to confuse experience or graduation from a highly regarded program with clinical competency. As a consequence, supervisors need to find ways to quickly establish a supervisee's actual baseline of skill and expertness. This necessity is further bolstered by the ethical and legal requirement that supervisees not be asked to function with clients outside the parameters of their knowledge and skill.

There are a number of sensible methods for assessing the supervisee's basic skills and knowledge base, the most common being a review of a supervisee's graduate school transcript or a resume of work background if the supervisee is more experienced. One other easy and effective method to quickly evaluate the knowledge level of new supervisees is to request a short, structured written summary of their education and experience. This summary could include the following: a brief description of their preferred theoretical model and philosophy of working with clients; a summary of the type of clients they have seen; a description of any specialized training or skills they've developed with particular populations; a summary of their previous supervision experience (good or bad); an assessment of strengths and weaknesses; and a statement of their goals and expectations for supervision. This assignment could easily be adapted for paraprofessionals and become part of the selection process.

Additional material could be collected from supervisees who have experience, such as a sample of client progress notes, a case review sheet, or an audio- or videotape. The snapshot technique described in Chapter 5 is also an excellent suggestion for

DON'T FORGET

Supervisors should be prepared the same as supervisees to share information about their background and experience, preferred model, and areas of expertise.

CAUTION

When supervising a known colleague or former peer, don't ignore the collection of background information or active review of knowledge and skills. It could prove harmful at a later date.

this purpose. The most practical suggestion, however, is to give prospective supervisees a written case vignette and ask them how they would address certain issues with this particular client scenario. If questions remain, these same supervisees could be asked to participate in a short role-play of a client situation, which should also be revealing.

How to Structure Orientation

Because of time constraints and with so much material to cover, any orientation needs to be well planned and include both written materials as well as formal discussion. For example, during the screening stage, much of the background material suggested in the previous section could be collected. Supervisees could be given a packet of materials to review along with a copy of the informed consent agreement or supervision contract.

At the first meeting, supervisors need to go over the expectations, goals, tasks, ground rules, and structure for supervision, including record-keeping requirements, evaluation procedures, and the means available to supervisees for resolving problems. Thereafter, the focus of orientation will vary for each supervision setting based on client needs; organizational setting; role of the supervisee; and the supervisee's level of development, skills, and expertise. On-site supervisors may want to stress organization issues in contrast to those off-site who may need to thoroughly discuss procedures for communication and the handling of crises. Supervision of a colleague or coworker necessitates emphasis on dual relationship issues and evaluation procedures, whereas the focus with a graduate intern might be on program requirements. Depending on the educational level of supervisees, services provided, and the client population, a number of additional sessions may have to be devoted to a systematic review of the code of ethics, laws, and regulations. Rapid Reference 7.4 gives a step-by-step list of topics for the first supervision meeting.

CAUTION

If you are promoted to clinical supervisor in your work setting and now you are supervising former peers, do not skip orientation and jump immediately into a review of cases. Take time to discuss the new state of affairs, and process everyone's thoughts and feelings about the new situation. Be sure to collect ideas from everyone on how to enhance the supervision experience.

CREATING A SAFE PLACE

The basic ethical premise of clinical supervision is that supervisees will be open to supervision; they will seek guidance, be open to corrective feed-

≡ Rapid Reference 7.4

Preparing for the First Supervision Session

1. Discuss by phone or in person the purpose, requirements, needs, administrative details (i.e., logging, record keeping, evaluation), and expectations for clinical supervision.

2. Obtain information from supervisee: Request resume, transcripts, or other documents required by the graduate school, licensing board, or national certification organization, such as supervision contract, evaluation forms, logging forms for hours, license forms, etc.).

3. Read copies of ethical codes, standards, and requirements for particular license or discipline. Have supervisees do the same.

4. Describe your background and experience, including special skills and supervision model. Provide supervisees with a copy of your supervision certificate or credentials.

5. Discuss goals for supervision.

6. Explain time, location, frequency, methods, and fees, if any.

7. Review informed consent agreement or supervision contract or both; sign and date.

8. Obtain a copy of supervisee's malpractice insurance (if desired).

9. Discuss ethical issues as they relate to supervision (vicarious liability, negligence, monitoring, and confidentiality) and crisis management strategies.

10. Bring up areas of potential conflict such as dual relationships, monitoring needs, differences in discipline, model, or to client care and how to resolve them.

11. Provide supervisee with any necessary forms (evaluation forms, logs, sample record keeping, case review sheets, etc.).

---

back, and be honest and truthful in supervision, including admitting what they don't know, owning their mistakes, and be willing to make themselves vulnerable. This premise underlies most traditional supervision activities, specifically the heavy reliance on self-report in case consultation as the primary means for supervision. However, studies indicate that supervisees' willingness to be open and honest depend on a number of variables. For example, Ladany et al. (1996) found 44 percent of trainees surveyed withheld information about clinical mistakes due to

DON'T FORGET

Golden Rule of Supervision

Treat supervisees in the same way you wish to be treated and the same way you wish them to treat clients.

concern about the supervisor's evaluation of their competence, whereas Webb and Wheeler (1998) found greater rapport with supervisors correlated to a willingness on the part of supervisees to self-disclose mistakes.

Other studies point to the supervisors' sensitivity to needs and concerns of supervisees, their openness to consider different points of view or a low level of dogmatism and criticalness, as well as how important evaluation is to the relationship (graded internships) as significant factors that also influence supervisees' openness in supervision (Bischoff et al., 2002; Daniels & Larson, 2001; Fitch & Marshall, 2002; Halgrin, 2002; Magnuson et al., 2000; Steven et al., 1998).

Consequently, another task in building a successful working relationship with supervisees is to create a sense of safety and trust. Supervisees need to feel a sense of worth, belongingness, safety, and security. If they don't feel safe and don't trust the supervisor, then it is hard to build the working alliance. Likewise, if supervisees are afraid to make decisions or be honest, it is hard for them to learn and grow. Because supervision is a relationship of unequal power and supervisees, especially beginners, can be very anxious, supervisors need to focus considerable time and energy on a strategy to build trust and establish an atmosphere where supervisees feel free to take risks and discuss openly their deficits and problems with the work.

One easy place for supervisors to locate ideas on how to build a positive working relationship with supervisees is to review the work of Carl Rogers. Rogers believed that warmth, genuineness, empathy, positive regard, and unconditional acceptance are essential on the part of counselors in order to build trust with clients. "If I can provide a certain type of relationship, the other person will discover within himself or herself the capacity to use that relationship for growth and change, and personal development will occur" (Rogers, 1951, p. 33). His ideas continue to receive validation through research in psychotherapy where these same relationship variables, called *common factors,* have been found to be vital to successful outcome with clients (Norcross, 2002). Supervisors need to use the same rapport-building skills to facilitate a positive outcome in supervision.

For example, encouragers such as "Tell me more; I'm interested" or "Keep going; you're on target" are

DON'T FORGET

Being supportive of supervisees and building trust does not mean supervisors must always be warm, fuzzy human beings who never disagree with supervisees or give them any corrective feedback. Instead, it refers to *how* supervisors relate to supervisees and *how* they give them feedback—that is, by showing a basic respect for the supervisees' needs and abilities.

simple ways to encourage discussion. Paraphrasing and summarizing are used to clarify understanding, while reflecting feelings and empathic responding usually indicate the supervisor is fully present in the relationship. Repeating significant words in a question, such as *no one?* or *the whole time?* helps elicit clarification of meaning. Most counselors and therapists learn early on in their training that open-ended questions are considered better than why questions because they sound less critical. The same is true for supervisors.

Rapid Reference 7.5 gives a list of supportive skills for supervisors.

Even though supervision is a different relationship from psychotherapy, research in supervision clearly supports the relevance of traditional rapport-building skills used in counseling and psychotherapy to supervision. If supervisors are open to supervisees' thoughts, feelings, experiences, and viewpoints; have compassionate and genuine regard; and are willing to offer support and encouragement, a more trusting relationship can be formed (Bischoff et al., 2002; Magnuson et al., 2000). The bottom line is that when supervisees feel heard and understood by their supervisors, they are more likely to be motivated and open to feedback.

Occasionally supervisors in organizational settings rebel at such suggestions. They see no value in pandering to peoples' need for encouragement and support. Instead, they think, "Why should I have to go out of my way to talk about successes or people's strengths or to thank people for their efforts? After all, we are all adults here. These people are not clients. Everyone knows what is expected. We all have a job to do so just do it. I don't have time for such nonsense." However, there is some danger in this attitude. Supervisees who do not feel appreciated or safe avoid supervision, withhold important information, and, in times of need, run the opposite way. Additionally, and perhaps most importantly, studies are beginning to show a positive relationship between the relationship with supervisors and the relationship with clients (Freitas, 2002; Patton & Kivlighan, 1997). Supervisors model by their behaviors with supervisees in

≡ Rapid Reference 7.5

Supportive Skills

Attending	Summarizing	Agreeing
Paraphrasing	Clarifying	Encouraging
Reflecting feelings	Open questions	Empathic responding
Reinforcement	Self-disclosure	Behavioral descriptions

CAUTION

Ignore supervisees' basic needs for safety and support at your own peril. You will not be able to rely on supervisees' willingness to come to you with mistakes or to pitch in and help when things get tough.

supervision how they wish them to behave with clients. For example, the more friendly and supportive supervisors were perceived to be by their supervisees, the less dominant and controlling supervisees were seen to be by their clients.

Supervisors are sometimes confused about what being supportive means in terms of actual supervisory behavior. They interpret the recommendation to mean that all interactions with supervisees should be warm and friendly and should contain only positives and praise, avoiding altogether any corrective feedback or challenge to supervisees' behavior with clients. These supervisors act as cheerleaders who continually repeat, "you are doing a great job" throughout supervision. While everyone likes to hear that they are doing a good job, most supervisees intuitively want more from supervision. They want to explore options and be challenged. Furthermore, a great number of outstanding supervisors are not particularly warm human beings but are still able to convey their appreciation for supervisees' needs.

Similar confusion exists about the term *unconditional positive regard*. Unconditional positive regard is another way of saying supervisors have respect for supervisees, valuing them as persons of worth regardless of whether they agree with them. A supervisor can have positive regard for supervisees without agreeing

Putting It Into Practice

During a review of a client case, Maria's supervisor suggested she try something that did not sound right to her. She felt it would lead the client session in a different direction from where she wanted to go. With some trepidation, Maria inquired of her supervisor "Don't you think that suggestion will take my client away from talking about her grief? I think she needs to do that."

Bad supervision: The following are examples of a supervisor's lack of positive regard: The supervisor responds defensively to this remark and says, "If you had received better training in graduate school, you would know this is not the time to do that." Or "Maria, I think you have problems with authority." Or "Well, you can disagree with me all you want, but I am telling you to do that."

Good supervision: The following are examples of a supervisor's positive regard: "Good point, not sure I agree, but tell me more. I am interested in your viewpoint." Or "Well, that is a good question. Why did I make this particular suggestion at this time with this client? Let me share my reasons with you, and then let me know what you think."

≡ Rapid Reference 7.6

Creating a Safe Environment for Supervision

1. Be genuine, show respect, and be tolerant. For example, "I'm not sure I understand your approach to that client. Can you share with me more about your thoughts and feelings underlying that strategy?"
2. Be available, consistent, and reliable.
3. Focus on supervisees' strengths: Begin case consultation by asking for successes, not just problems. For example, "Tell me what went well for you this week."
4. Use empathic responding and express understanding. For example, "Working with this family is really going to be challenging. However, I think you are up to it."
5. Acknowledge the supervisee's efforts, and when they do something exceptional, point it out. Make a special effort to do so publicly or in writing. For example, "You did an amazing job with that client."
6. Normalize mistake making and support risk-taking. For example, "Even though what you did with that client didn't turn out as planned, I think you will really grow from the experience. Let's talk about it together and see what can be learned."
7. Address at the beginning of supervision the natural causes of anxiety, such as having to hear corrective feedback and being evaluated as to one's competency.
8. Offer hope for success.
9. Use humor.

with everything supervisees do or say or approving of their beliefs and values. Unconditional positive regard does not mean that supervisors cannot disagree with a supervisee or point out something they did wrong. Instead it describes *how* supervisors treat a supervisee and respond to differences of opinion when they occur.

Supervisors at all stages of development and experience need to pause and consider how to use their skills and knowledge to create a safe place for supervisees. Rapid Reference 7.6 presents a list of actions that will promote a safe environment in supervision.

Normalize the Making of Mistakes While Learning

Undoubtedly the best approach is to talk openly at the beginning of supervision about the importance of safety and trust and the need for risk-taking and mistake-making as a part of the learning process. The supervisor's attitude toward

DON'T FORGET

The role of clinical supervisor is to point out what went well, not just mistakes.

the making of mistakes would be reflected in the choice of words, tone of voice, and feedback style. Some supervisors do not even like the term *mistake* as to them, it implies criticism or an attack on a supervisee's self-esteem. Instead, they like to ask supervisees for ideas or options they could use with a particular client or circumstance rather than come out directly and say what they did was wrong.

Three techniques found helpful to reduce supervisees' anxiety about making mistakes include: *self-disclosure, empathic responding,* and *metaphors.* Self-disclosure along with empathic responding is a common method supervisors use to build rapport and create a sense of safety in supervision. By sharing their own mistakes, failures, and problems, supervisors model for supervisees that it is acceptable for them to talk about their own mistakes and misgivings in supervision. Many times this self-disclosure by supervisors mirrors the same thoughts and feelings of supervisees, which creates a sense of commonality that goes far toward building the working alliance (Baker, Exum, & Tyler, 2002; Ladany & Walker, 2003).

The use of metaphors is another way for supervisors to convey understanding and empathy and to make it safe for supervisees to explore issues in a deeper way (Lyddon, Clay, & Sparks, 2001). Metaphors are an easy way for supervisors to capture complex and difficult issues in a positive manner. Popular metaphors involve gardening, sports, and life experiences of real or fictional people. Mary Langan (Langan & Milioti, 2002) begins her practicum supervision using the metaphor of learning to ice-skate to describe the ups and downs of counselor training. She continues to refer to this metaphor throughout supervision by asking, "How is your skating going today?" as a means to check how learning is progressing.

DEVELOPING SELF-AWARENESS

One important aspect of clinical supervision is the development of personal self-awareness on the part of supervisees, with special attention given to how supervisees' personal issues, beliefs, assumptions, and attitudes—particularly gender, culture, and race—affect client care. Griffith and Frieden (2000) used the term *reflective thinking* to describe this as an active, ongoing process of self-examination whereby counselors and therapists explore theories, beliefs, and assumptions so as to better understand and respond to their clients.

Putting It Into Practice

Case Example

Martha had just been hired by an agency. She had almost no experience working in social service and was very worried about seeing her first clients. In fact, she had very little work experience except some babysitting and summer jobs at the mall. She wanted to do a good job and be seen as very competent because she was planning to apply to graduate school sometime in the next few years and needed a good reference from her supervisor. Martha was a top student and always had gotten A's in her classes, so doing well was of particular concern to her. She had majored in sociology and was aware of all the problems in society. She wanted to make a difference, not just sit on the sidelines. That is why she took this job.

She had no idea what supervision really was and what her role would be, so she was highly anxious at the first supervision session. Her supervisor, Mark, who had been at the agency for many years, knew this and wanted to put her at ease. He shared his own experiences starting out, his desire to help all the clients and to have all the clients like him, and how he came into the profession because he wanted to make a difference in the world. He saw himself as the great rescuer of these "poor people who life had treated unfairly." Following this self-disclosure, Martha felt immediately at ease with Mark and openly began to share her thoughts and concerns. As she spoke, Mark responded that these concerns were normal and natural and that was what he was there for—to help her as best he could to be successful in her job and to learn skills and develop competency. However, he also wanted to caution her about her mind-set and possibly distorted beliefs about helping, so he used a metaphor to describe the work at the agency as resembling mowing the grass to mean that there are a number of ways to help clients. Listening to the metaphor, a number of thoughts and questions began to swirl in Martha's head. It dawned on her that this job was going to be a real challenge to her personally, not just professionally, and that Mark was going to be a great resource of support as well as someone to teach her skills. Before the end of the first supervision session, Mark asked her about her goals, what she wanted to learn, what she thought were her strengths as well as weaknesses, and anything she might need from him to make the relationship go better. Because he had already talked about the role of corrective feedback and evaluation earlier in the meeting, she had already mentioned her perfectionist tendencies and how hard it was sometimes for her to hear feedback without getting upset, but, still, she wanted to make sure he understood this as an issue for her. Mark not only heard her, but he also said that was the hardest part of supervision for him in the beginning and that, frankly, it still was. Martha felt relieved and reassured and left her first supervision session eager for more time with Mark.

Teaching Point: Mark understood how important it was to start supervision by orienting supervisees, especially novice ones, to supervision in order to build a working alliance. He understood from his own experiences how natural it would be for Martha to be anxious about supervision, and so he used self-disclosure to create understanding. Mark also included a metaphor as a means to normalize anxiety and bring a number of important topics quickly to the table. He also knew how important it was to have Martha, even when she was so green, participate in goal setting, planning, and have some input into evaluation in order to improve her motivation.

DON'T FORGET

Supervisees should be advised at the beginning of supervision about the importance of self-awareness and ownership of problems such that if entrenched problematic patterns of responding are uncovered during supervision that could be harmful to clients and interfere with the quality of service and these problems are not successfully worked out in supervision, it is the supervisees' ethical duty to seek counseling, psychotherapy, coursework, or other means to resolve the problem.

Personal issues can limit the professional development and success of supervisees within their chosen field. Such things as discomfort with intimacy and closeness or the expression of feelings by clients are a major factor in the building of rapport and creating an atmosphere of understanding and acceptance. Distorted or illogical thinking along with perfectionism on the part of supervisees can also limit effectiveness with clients. Thus, it is the ethical responsibility of all clinical supervisors to assist supervisees to grow in self-awareness and to uncover any problem areas that could have a detrimental impact on supervisees' work with clients. William Glasser, in a panel discussion about excellent therapy practices, said the best advice he ever got from his supervisor was the "need to be in better shape than the client" (Glasser, 2004).

In fact, self-awareness is considered to be one of the cornerstones of ethical practice within all health disciplines, and all practitioners are reminded to know themselves, their limitations, and not let their personal problems or issues negatively impact their care of clients. Furthermore, if any mental health practitioner becomes aware of personal problems that might be detrimental or harmful to clients, they are admonished to take responsibility and seek help to resolve them.

The amount of emphasis placed on developing supervisees' self-awareness varies depending on the type of client services being provided. It probably is a more important supervision subject matter for psychologists, counselors, or psychotherapists, who are involved in intense interpersonal relationships with clients, than for case managers, nurses, and paraprofessionals, who are providing task or education services. However, some effort to include exploration of supervisees' mind-sets and basic attitudes and beliefs about people should be a part of everyone's clinical supervision plan.

Another issue is when to begin the process of exploring self-awareness. Stoltenberg and Delworth (1987), in their developmental model of supervision, suggest raising self-awareness should take place later in supervision after supervisees have been acclimated to the work and have seen a number of clients. However, others such as Kagan & Kagan (1997) with IPR believe this process should begin immediately after the first client session. It is this author's recommendation that inserting thought-provoking questions that ask supervisees to put themselves in relationship to their clients should begin immediately. A straightforward inquiry about where the supervisee is in relationship to his or her client, or how connected he or she feels to the client, will start

> **DON'T FORGET**
>
> It would be unethical *not* to challenge supervisees about issues that may be harmful or interfere in some manner with providing ethical client care.

the process. As supervisees become more experienced and more comfortable, self-exploration questions can become more complex. Studies by Protinsky and Coward (2001) and Bischoff et al. (2002) of experienced clinicians indicated that it was this process in supervision of connecting oneself and one's thoughts and feelings to the client relationship that was most powerful in helping them develop competency.

Differences between Supervision and Psychotherapy

One of the inherent struggles supervisors face in facilitating a supervisee's personal development is understanding and respecting the difference between supervision and personal counseling or psychotherapy. The key difference is when discussing personal issues with supervisees—the processing must remain anchored solely to the relationship between the supervisee and the client rather than probing deeply into the background facts or causes of a supervisee's specific issue or working with them to resolve background issues in supervision. Supervisors must understand that to go beyond this context may be unethical as it constitutes a dual relationship.

It is always a dilemma for supervisors as to how to raise supervisees' level of self-awareness without falling into the role of therapist. Having had a supervisor who was able to process personal issues in a helpful and ethical manner would certainly be advantageous. Moreover, it is undoubtedly easier to maintain good boundaries and encourage self-exploration on the part of supervisees when working with a group in

> **CAUTION**
>
> For those working with a psychodynamic orientation, examination of transference and countertransference is an integral part of that model, and more permission is given supervisors to explore personal background issues with supervisees. However, even in these situations, supervisors will need to use caution to keep appropriate boundaries in supervision and to be clear that the purpose of any exploration of transference is the impact on client care.

≡ Rapid Reference 7.7

A Three-Step Process for Ethical Self-Exploration with Supervisees

1. Promote self-exploration. Use a variety of methods and techniques to promote self-awareness on the part of supervisees in their relationship with clients, such as thought-provoking questions, a family genogram, experiential exercises, or audio- and videotaping.

2. Connect supervisees' self-awareness to their relationship with clients by asking supervisees to ponder how their family background and thoughts, feelings, beliefs, and attitudes about people might impact their relationship with clients in general or with one in particular. This could be both positive and negative. For example, the supervisor can inquire, "Is there anything about this client that makes you reluctant about confronting her? Anything in your background that might make you hesitate?"

3. Follow up any self-exploration experience by prompting supervisees to explore options for change as a result of their self-awareness. Ask "What will you need to do as a result of this awareness?" or "Let's explore together some ideas for what to do differently with this client as a result of this awareness."

supervision than in an individual session, especially if adopting a psychoeducational training perspective. However, self-exploration can be done successfully in any supervision format by practicing the following guideline: Keep the supervisee's self-exploration focused on the impact of their thoughts, feelings, and background on client care, and avoid an extraneous discussion of the roots and causes of such awarenesses in supervision to the fullest extent possible. Rapid Reference 7.7 summarizes the steps for ethical practice in regard to exploration of the self in supervision.

How to Increase Self-Awareness in Supervision

There are numerous ways to bring the topic of self-awareness into supervision. Traditional techniques include journaling, process recording, genograms, experiential training exercises, and the employment of thought-provoking questions during case consultation. Other means to promote supervisees' self-exploration might be a discussion of parallel process or transference and countertransference within the context of case consultation, review of audio- and videotapes, psychodrama, role-play and role reversal, and the Gestalt empty chair, to name a few (Campbell, 2000; Griffith & Frieden, 2000; Rambo, Heath, & Chenail, 1993).

Putting It Into Practice

Case Example: How to Work with Supervisees' Self-Awareness

Patty had recently graduated with her master's degree in counseling and just began working at an agency that sees cancer patients and their families. Her supervisor is very concerned that Patty (as all counselors at the agency) explore her personal history of grief and loss because of the strong impact this history could have on how she responds to her clients.

Supervisor: One issue that is important for you to explore in supervision before too much time passes is your own history of grief and loss, what types of losses you have had in your lifetime, and what happened as a result of those losses. I have found over the years that a person's history of loss will powerfully influence what happens with clients during counseling.

Patty: I know right now one experience I have had that may be really significant in my work; my mother died of cancer five years ago. It is part of my desire to work here, to help family members deal with cancer and loss.

Supervisor: I am glad you shared that with me. Sounds as if it will be important to explore this issue more deeply. Can you share with me more about the loss of your mother? Let us start with what you took away from the experience.

Patty: Well, one thing I learned from my mother's death is that talking about your feelings is important. It is important to let them all out, to cry, to get angry, and if you don't do that, then grief will fester and may lead to depression or worse.

Supervisor: Take a look at what you just said from the aspect of how these thoughts may impact your work with clients here at the agency. Can you think of anything that you just said that might interfere with your hearing a client?

Patty: Absolutely. As I spoke my thoughts, I realize how strongly I believe in the importance of expressing feelings out loud. However, I may have a client who doesn't express their feelings openly. As a result of my belief, I may see something wrong with that and start to demand that he or she do grief my way. Wow. I wouldn't want to do that. I will really have to be vigilant and will need your help to make sure this doesn't happen with any my clients.

Supervisor: Sounds like a really good awareness to have at this point. I have some ideas about things you can do to keep your personal material out of your counseling sessions. Why don't we talk about one of your cases where you think this issue of your experiences with loss might be present? Anyone you are struggling with?

Mary: It just occurred to me how frustrated I feel with Mr. Jones. He comes to counseling, but I have so much trouble getting him to talk about his feelings. He told me he hasn't shed one tear yet over his wife's death; he didn't even cry at his wife's funeral! I have thought he obviously didn't care about his wife. Now, I am wondering about my assessment of the situation and how I am approaching him. Any ideas on something different I might try?

DON'T FORGET

A supportive environment is a necessary prerequisite for open and effective self-exploration by supervisees.

DON'T FORGET

A series of thought-provoking processing questions should be included with any self-awareness exercise to boost the learning curve.

For example, to highlight the impact of personal issues on therapeutic effectiveness, the supervisor might require supervisees to tape one of their client sessions and then review the tape together in supervision applying IPR.

To accomplish this difficult task of maintaining boundaries and to keep the focus on training, it is best if supervisors see themselves in a consultant role to the supervisees' self-exploration. Rapid Reference 7.8 furnishes a number of examples of consultant-style process questions appropriate for supervision.

One of the oldest and best-known means to encourage self-exploration on the part of supervisees is the requirement of a personal journal. Journals are customarily made use of in graduate programs as a private venue for supervisees to explore emotions without fear of censorship as well as a means to track events, make sense of experiences, and organize thoughts and integrate learning. Particular questions or exercises, such as a genogram, are often assigned to help structure the journal and increase learning. Supervisors do not as a matter of course ask supervisees to share the actual journal with them, thereby circumventing any problems with dual relationships. Rather, most supervisors usually request supervisees share only insights or concerns that could potentially affect their work with clients. Asking supervisees to keep such a journal has numerous benefits. However, in certain circumstances, such an idea

Rapid Reference 7.8

Processing Questions for Supervisors

- "Where are you with this client? Any buttons being pushed?"
- "How does it feel to be with this client?"
- "What is the client doing or saying that causes you to feel this way?"
- "Why do you think you feel this way? Does this client remind you of another person or situation?"
- "Is there anything happening in your life right now that may be contributing to your response to this client?"
- "As a result of this discussion, what might you want to do differently with this client?"

Putting It Into Practice

Case Example

After several months working with the probation department as a case manager, David told his supervisor that he disliked one of his clients, Mr. Donothing. The supervisor asked David, "What does Mr. Donothing do that makes you dislike him?" To that question, David launched into a description of his client's behavior during their first meeting. In response to this, his supervisor then inquired if Mr. Donothing reminded David of anyone. To this question, David looked blank and then suddenly said, "He reminds me of my no-good younger brother. He never took responsibility for anything he did. Any mistake was always someone else's fault. No wonder I don't like Mr. Donothing." At this admission, his supervisor thanked him for his openness, telling him that making these kinds of connections is very important to ethical practice. Then the supervisor asked, "So, now that you have made this connection, what do you think you will have to do with to work with Mr. Donothing?" Whereupon David began to talk through his ideas with the supervisor.

Teaching Point: The supervisor in this instance maintained good boundaries with his supervisee and avoided any dual relationship by keeping the focus on David's relationship with his client, rather than spending time in supervision on David's relationship with his brother.

may not be feasible because of legal and regulatory parameters.

Whatever method or technique is chosen, supervisors need to be fully trained and competent in its usage before application to supervision. Learning new methods and tech-

DON'T FORGET

The end point of any self-exploration on the part of supervisees is to help them make any changes necessary to protect their clients from harm.

niques for supervision can be rewarding and invigorating. It is also suggested that supervisors first practice on themselves or with a colleague before using any self-awareness exercises with supervisees.

Application of the Family Genogram for Developing Self-Awareness in Supervision

The use of genograms in psychotherapy is based on the premise that past relationship patterns affect current personal and family functioning. Thus, generational issues and patterns of conflict, distancing, boundary setting, and triangulation can be explored using a genogram (McGoldrick & Gerson, 1985). In supervision, a genogram can provide an excellent source of family background information that can be used to explore the effect of those experiences on supervisees' current work with clients, such as transference reactions, parallel process, anxiety, and other relationship difficulties (Kuehll, 1995). The cultural genogram (Hardy & Laszloffy, 1995) and the spiritual genogram (Frame, 2000) supply additional means to help supervisees explore their cultural and religious heritage and the impact of these variables on present behavior. Topics such as grief and loss, substance abuse, sexuality, intimacy, gender roles, divorce, stepfamilies, social support, and family resources can all be explored via the genogram (Magnuson & Shaw, 2003). A study of seasoned therapists found that exploration of their own family of origin was a significant part of their professional development and an excellent bridge between the personal and professional self (Protinsky & Coward, 2001).

To use a genogram in supervision, the supervisor may first request supervisees to make a genogram of their family and then answer a series of written questions designed to get them to identify family patterns of coping with such topics as anxiety, anger, loss, or conflict. After responding to the questions, supervisees then would be asked to think through how any of these recognized family patterns might present themselves in their current relationships with clients. Afterward, the material could be processed further in supervision by application to particular client cases. Supervisors can add the use any number of action techniques, such as role-playing, role reversal, psychodrama, and Gestalt empty chair, to facilitate the processing and integration of material by supervisees. Adler's lifestyle inventory could also be easily included with the genogram exercise (Campbell, 2000). See Rapid References 7.9 and 7.10 for an example of how to use genograms in supervision.

One specific area where using a genogram is especially helpful in supervision is the role of the supervisees' family history in how they respond to clients' expressions of feelings. For instance, those supervisees who saw their role in the family as peacemaker will often struggle to confront clients. Teyber (1997) termed a person's dominant mode of responding to life situations as the *affective constellation,* a sequence of interrelated feelings such as anger, sadness, and guilt that repeatedly recur throughout one's lifetime. The affective constellation develops through experiences in one's family of origin and is seen to mask deeper feelings of pain, hurt, or shame. Helping supervisees uncover their affective constellations and dominant mode of responding to life events can increase understanding of their responses (transference) to certain clients and client problems.

≡ Rapid Reference 7.9

Making a Genogram

A genogram is a pictorial representation of family relationships across several generations.

Male ☐   Female ◯   Miscarriage or abortion △

Sex unknown △   Adopted ◈ or ⬖   Death ⊠ or ⊗

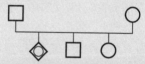

Twins

| Marriage |
| Separation or divorce |
| Death |
| Living together, but not married |

Children are denoted by vertical lines. Place oldest on the left and youngest on the right.

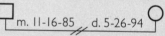

Ages are written inside the squares or circles.   32   ㉜

Names can be written inside or outside the squares or circles.   ㊶Jill

If desired, include marriage, separation, and divorce dates on the horizontal line.

 m. 11-16-85   d. 5-26-94 ◯

Additional information may include vocations, temperament, hobbies, or other pertinent attributes about each person.

㊲Julie Doctor   ㉙Sam Alcoholic

Genograms may also include "feeling faces" such as happy, sad, angry, numb, and scared.

Rapid Reference 7.10

Employing the Family Genogram in Supervision

1. Make a genogram of your family going back three generations. See Rapid Reference 7.9 for instructions on how to make a genogram.
2. Look at the genogram, noticing relationship patterns in your family of origin:
   • Do you see significant patterns of loss or connection?
   • Next consider multicultural issues such as interracial marriage, gay or lesbian members, adoption, or changes in the socioeconomic status in your family of origin.
3. Explore the genogram more deeply with a series of thought-provoking questions:
   • How was anger handled in your family? What were typical patterns of responding to conflict? Was there any difference in how it was handled between generations? Certain people?
   • What does the genogram tell you about the role of loss in your family? What type of losses occurred, and what happened to family members as a result of these losses?
   • What did you learn in your family of origin about people of a different race (ethnicity, gender, socioeconomic status)? (Hardy & Laszloffy, 1995)
   • What was it like to grow up in your family? Did you feel acceptance and caring? Did your parents give feedback in a way that was reassuring, or was it painful?
4. How might your family of origin impact your work with clients?
   • For example, do you see a relationship with your model or approach to clients? Your choice of population or problems with which to work?
   • How might family patterns of coping with events and feelings influence your response now to a client's expression of intense feelings or your assessment of a client's problems or personality?
5. Answer the same in terms of supervision.
   • Any thoughts on how your family history may come into play in your relationship with supervisors (i.e., transference)? For example, experiences with critical parents may spill over into supervision.

Challenging Distorted and Illogical Thinking

Another fruitful subject for supervision is distorted and illogical thinking such as a tendency toward perfectionist thinking on the part of supervisees, especially in the early stage of development. Thoughts such as "I can never do enough" or "I can never do it right" usually lead to feelings of guilt and self-doubt or a sense of failure and incompetence. Before endeavoring to help others, supervisees must be able to accept their own mistakes and imperfections and to believe that even though they are not perfect, they are also not failures. Demands for perfection can also play a significant role in how supervisees respond to corrective feedback in

Putting It Into Practice

Case Example

Sarah was a new supervisor in an agency that specialized in victims of violence and sexual trauma. After reviewing cases with George, a therapist who had been at the agency for a number of years, Sarah began to suspect the presence of some personal history that was affecting how George interacted with his clients. Recognizing the touchiness of the situation given that she was new, she wanted to go slowly. Remembering how effective making a family genogram had been for her when an intern, she decided to ask all of her supervisees to do the same exercise. She couched this suggestion by talking about her own experiences and the usefulness of such an exercise. As expected, George balked, saying he did not see any need for any such thing. "I have been working here for eight years, and no one has ever demanded we get so personal. It sounds more like therapy to me, and I know my rights. No one is going to snoop into my past." In response, Sarah reiterated her reasons for the exercise and reassured everyone that she would not ask to see anyone's genogram. All she was interested in as a clinical supervisor was any connections they made between themselves and their past to their current practice with clients and then for them to look for as many ideas as possible to correct any problems that might affect clients. After all, one of the main ethical guidelines for all mental health practitioners is to know themselves and their limitations and not work out their own personal issues with clients. Sarah said to George, "I know you care deeply about your clients and what happens to them, so I am rather surprised at your response. Because you are the senior therapist, and using genograms with our clients is standard, I just assumed you would be open to this suggestion as I know you believe how important self-awareness is in ethical practice with clients. Maybe I wasn't very clear about how I envision using a genogram in supervision. It is different than the way we use them with clients. However, if you are so uncomfortable with my suggestion to make a personal genogram, it's okay by me to back off." George was a silent for a long period of time and then said hesitantly, "I guess it might be a good idea. We can try it and see how it goes. Maybe something good will come out of making a genogram and examining the past. I just want to be sure this doesn't turn into therapy." Sarah responded reassuringly, "I will make my best effort not to cross over the line. However, I am going to count on you to keep me straight if for some reason what I ask seems inappropriate. How does that sound?"

Teaching Point: Sarah felt the need for all her supervisees, regardless of years of experience, to continue to grow in self-awareness. She was clear the purpose of the genogram in supervision was different than in therapy, thus avoiding a dual relationship with her supervisees. When George objected, rather than becoming defensive she showed positive regard for his thoughts and feelings and so opened the door for him to reconsider his objections.

≡Rapid Reference 7.11

Challenging Distorted Thinking on the Part of Supervisees

1. Make a list of distorted and illogical thoughts or beliefs prevalent to novice supervisees. For example, the need to be liked, the need to be needed, the need to have all clients change in order to feel successful, and the need to be 100 percent available in order to be helpful. Be sure to include generalizations such as *always, never, everyone,* or *no one* that indicate irrational thinking.

2. Review the list with supervisees and have them identify which of the listed beliefs or illogical thoughts they commonly have, noting any that they believe are especially significant in their work with clients.

3. Take these hot thoughts and work with supervisees to create a list of statements to dispute each one.

4. Have supervisees write them down and practice saying these new thoughts out loud.

5. To reinforce the learning on this topic, take a typical client case scenario (or just make a list of client requests that typically trigger illogical thoughts) and then do a role-play with supervisees. As the client, act or do things that normally will trigger illogical thinking on the part of supervisees—such as unreasonable requests for attention, changes in the way things are done, desire for outside contact, and so on. Have supervisees respond to the client requests and then correct themselves if any illogical thoughts appear in the role-play. This would be an excellent activity for group supervision.

6. Ask supervisees to pay attention to the existence of distorted or illogical thinking as they talk about client cases in supervision. Do they use words such as *always, never,* or *everyone?* Do they hear themselves use a number of *shoulds* or exhibit perfectionist thinking?

7. Make note of supervisees' favorite illogical thoughts, and watch for their appearance during case consultation. When noted, ask supervisees on the spot to dispute their illogical thoughts. "What are you saying to yourself right now that leads you to this evaluation of your work with this client?"

Putting It Into Practice

Case Example

Joy was reviewing a case involving a mother who had just been referred to hospice. As she talked, tears formed in her eyes, and then she began to sob. Her supervisor sat quietly, letting Joy cry. But after several minutes, when Joy did not seem to be able to stop crying and the sobs were more intense, the supervisor reached out and took Joy's hand, murmuring comforting words. Slowly, Joy returned to the present, and her crying stopped. After blowing her nose, Joy said in a quiet voice, "I thought I was over my grief, that I had worked it all out, but something with this client just got to me. I keep seeing my mother. I don't know what to do now." Her supervisor responded, "This often happens to counselors here. Many times old grief will well up unexpectedly. I still sometimes have the same response to my client's pain. Out of nowhere the tears come. My first concern now is to check to be sure you are okay, and then we can talk about your client. Is there anything you need from me right now?" Joy thanked her supervisor for her concern and her sharing how normal crying was at the agency. However, Joy also stated that she realized that if she was to continue working with cancer patients, she was going to have to go back and do some more therapy around her mother's death. "Somehow what you said makes me feel stronger. I think your being real with me gives me courage to do what I need to do."

Teaching Point: In this example the supervisor stayed with the supervisee in the here and now and responded to her with caring. Through self-disclosure, she normalized the expression of intense affect in that setting and thereby gave Joy permission to be open about her feelings in supervision. However, the supervisor did not attempt to become Joy's therapist nor did she tell Joy what to do but instead allowed Joy to come up with her own solution to the problem.

supervision. They may have trouble hearing positive feedback or may be deflated if supervisors suggest any changes to their work with clients. Perfectionism can be an underlying factor as well in patterns of overfunctioning with clients. For example, if supervisees believe that they can never do enough, it will lead them to difficulties in setting realistic boundaries with clients. Rapid Reference 7.11 describes a strategy for exploring distorted thinking in supervision.

COMMON PROBLEMS TO ADDRESS IN THE BEGINNING STAGE OF SUPERVISION

Dress and Appearance

Dress and general appearance are one area of difficulty that is quite common with beginning supervisees, especially younger ones. In today's world of casual

CAUTION

Many times there are established rules in an organizational setting, such as mode of dress, that are not open to change in an organizational setting, regardless of the supervisee's personal feelings. However, clinical supervisors should still want to help supervisees see a relationship between their behavior and client outcome. By holding a focused discussion that validates supervisees' thoughts and feelings but encourages them to connect their behavior, such as their dress, to their goals for clients, accommodation and compliance *are more likely* to be the outcome rather than continuing conflict and bickering about rules and regulations.

dress and hip style, supervisors may find themselves having to bring up this issue with increasing frequency. Some organizational settings, such as hospitals, may require uniforms and hence avoid some problems in this arena. However, the concept of professional dress can be very broad in its interpretation depending on the client population and setting. What is considered acceptable in one setting might be problematic in another.

The easiest strategy is to ask supervisees at the beginning of supervision how they see dress (hairstyle, exposed tattoos, body piercing, jewelry, etc.) coming into play in building their relationship with clients, looking at both the positive and negative aspects. If a dress code were in place, it still would be beneficial to process the role of dress in professional demeanor. This type of discussion, however, requires supervisors to be open and tolerant of a variety of thoughts and feelings on the topic and willing to hear what supervisees have to say. Supervisors who are playful by nature could lend some humor to the conversation by putting on several different outlandish outfits for a counselor, nurse, case manager, or therapist and then have supervisees role-play being clients in such circumstances. For example, the supervisor could state "Your hair length, styles of dress, and jewelry all come into play in building relationships with clients. They make an important statement. How does your dress [hairstyle, jewelry] help you accomplish your goals with clients? How does it get in the way? If it is having a negative effect, what can you do about it?" Rapid Reference 7.12 provides suggestions for initiating a sensitive discussion, such as personal appearance, with supervisees.

Sexual Attraction to Clients

Ethical codes for all of the mental health disciplines are very clear that sexual relationships with clients are harmful and should be avoided at all cost. Yet statistics across the board for all disciplines indicate that sexual relationships with clients is still a top ethical complaint and one of the leading causes of malpractice suits.

A number of studies have indicated that feelings of sexual attraction to clients is perhaps more common than realized (Cardona, Brock, & Sandberg, 2002; Ladany et al., 1997). In fact, sexual attraction is a normal and natural phenomenon experienced by human beings, so it is only to be expected that sexual attraction will emerge in therapeutic relationships that are emotionally intense. However, few participants in these studies reported discussing the subject of attraction to clients with their supervisor. In fact, a study by Harris (2001) found that most graduate students were reluctant to discuss the issue of attraction to clients for fear of being seen as maladjusted or perverted by their supervisor.

Furthermore, only a small number of clinical supervisors report they received any training in this topic while they were in supervision (Campbell, 2001–2005, informal

≡ *Rapid Reference 7.12*

How to Talk to a Supervisee about Problems with Dress

Own your own feelings: "It makes me uncomfortable to talk to you about this issue."

Remind supervisee of goals for supervision: "I know you shared with me at the beginning of supervision your deep desire to help our clients, how you wanted to learn to be the best counselor possible. That is why I am going to say this to you."

Use empathic responding: "You may hear this feedback as critical or maybe think I am too conservative and out of date."

State the problem clearly from your perspective. Stay away from character or motive: "I am concerned that the way you dress is interfering with your effectiveness as a counselor. I am not sure it is having a positive effect on your groups, and, in fact, from my observation, it is actually distracting the men from the purpose of the group."

Give specific behavioral examples: "When you wear really short skirts that hitch up above your knee when you sit down, attention is drawn to your legs rather than what you are saying. I don't think you want that. And when you wear low cut blouses that accent your breasts, the same thing happens."

Ask supervisee to own the problem: "I wonder what your thoughts on this are? Have you thought about how you present yourself and how it may be helping or hindering your counseling relationships?"

---

feedback, supervision workshops; Cardona et al., 2002; Nickell, Hecker, Ray, & Bercik, 1995). The exception to this statement comes from practitioners with a psychodynamic orientation where examination of transference and countertransference reactions is an integral part of training. Coming from the perspective of transference and countertransference, it is an easy step for supervisors to introduce the topic of personal attraction to clients into supervision. When reviewing cases, the subject of personal feelings toward clients would be considered a normal topic for discussion.

At this point, even as professional ethical codes and standards warn about inappropriate personal relationships with clients, when attraction occurs, it is usually left up to the practitioner to manage the situation in a way that is not harmful to the client.

CAUTION

Not all feelings of attraction to clients are sexual. Similarity in life experiences, upbringing, interests, as well as analogous problems can lead unwary practitioners into less easily identified inappropriate dual relationships with clients. Supervisors need to explore the whole issue of attraction and friendship as a general topic of intimacy, closeness, and how a sense of similarity with clients can lead supervisees to boundary violations with clients.

Obviously, there is a need for a different approach, and that task falls squarely on the shoulders of clinical supervisors. Not just sexual attraction to clients, but feelings of attraction in general are important but frequently overlooked training issues that need to be given more attention by every clinical supervisor, no matter the circumstance. It is critical that supervisees are able to recognize situations where issues of attraction might be present and be prepared to handle them appropriately. Supervisors need to educate and normalize attraction as a therapeutic issue and promote ethical responses to such situations. Rather than treating the topic as taboo, this is an issue that needs to be on the forefront of clinical supervision, regardless of degree, education, or experience. Housman and Strake (1999) found overwhelmingly that those therapists who did discuss attraction to clients with their supervisors felt more comfortable and better able to cope with such a situation. What is at stake here is how supervisors handle the topic so as to encourage openness and promote ethical practice. Rapid Reference 7.13

≡ Rapid Reference 7.13

Responding to the Topic of Personal Attraction to Clients

Supervisor: How comfortable do you feel with this client?

Supervisee: I don't feel very comfortable working with him. I find myself having problems concentrating during the session.

Supervisor: Can you identify anything the client is doing that makes you feel uncomfortable?

Supervisee: Well, it's hard to talk about. I feel embarrassed. You probably will think it's my fault and that something is wrong with me, but actually I find myself attracted to him. He reminds me of my first high school boyfriend. I know this is wrong, and, of course, I wouldn't do anything, be assured of that, but, still, it makes me uncomfortable to work with him.

Supportive Supervisor

"Thanks for letting me know how you feel. I appreciate your honesty. This type of situation crops up occasionally in our work with clients, and it is good to talk about it without feeling ashamed. We are just people, not robots, and most everyone, myself included, have had this happen at one time or another. Let's explore this situation in more depth and see what actions need to be taken. I want to be sure you receive whatever support you need from me to act ethically here."

Punishing Supervisor

"Well, this is a very serious problem, and you can bet your bottom dollar, you won't do anything with this client. I am going to refer him to another therapist immediately. I thought you had better training than this. I am really disappointed in you. From now on, I will have to think about whether I will allow you to work with any other young male client."

supplies an example of both a supportive as well as a punishing approach by supervisors to the subject of supervisees' personal attraction to clients.

Documentation of Client Care

A great deal of documentation is now required in the mental health field, and teaching proper paperwork has become one of the main clinical supervisory tasks. Good documentation is considered fundamental to ethical practice as well as necessary to meet numerous regulatory guidelines. All mental health professionals are expected to document what services were rendered to clients and the effectiveness of those services. In spite of the importance of good documentation of client services, Prieto and Scheel (2002) noted the absence of much literature or information about structured methods for case notes to use to teach counselors and therapists, except for the SOAP model. While the SOAP model for client record keeping is probably the most well-known structured method to help beginners learn the correct way to keep client progress notes (see Rapid Reference 7.14), it is derived from the medical field, and some question its application to counseling or case work in organizational settings. Further, there are many details and dos and don'ts attached to the SOAP model so that supervisors would need to be very well versed in the method themselves in order to meet all ethical and legal guidelines and requirements (Cameron & turtle-song, 2002).

In some instances, for teaching or training purposes, it might be easier for supervisors to collect outstanding examples of required paper work from their setting, such as client intakes, progress notes, charting, and documentation of crisis situations, and make those available to supervisees as models. Of course, in such instances all clients' identifying data would be removed.

Structured forms are another excellent training vehicle to increase success of supervisees with documentation and paperwork. Possibilities include a sample case review form (see example in Chapter 5), a sample intake form, or forms for treatment plans, charting, progress notes, or any other sample of the documentation required of supervisees in that setting. In actuality, many forms as well as the responses to questions on the forms are now so standard-

≡ Rapid Reference 7.14

The SOAP Model for Client Record Keeping

Subjective:	Quotes from client
Objective:	Data collected by therapist
Assessment:	Include suicide lethality check here
Plan of action:	Recommendations and follow-up

DON'T FORGET

Remind supervisees of the following:

- Client progress notes and charts are public record and can be subpoenaed.
- Don't write anything down that you don't want to be read in court.
- At the same time, good progress notes are an important part of ethical practice. They assure quality of care so that in an emergency another person would be able to continue the treatment. They are also necessary to show what services were rendered to the client and the quality of those services.
- Don't leave important information out or change the diagnosis to help clients or to collect insurance (this is fraud).
- Use behavioral descriptors, and avoid emotions or subjective impressions that cannot be substantiated.
- Remind supervisees' to write clearly, accurately, and succinctly in black ink, not pencil; avoid abbreviations and codes that cannot be understood.
- Be brief and concise. Avoid excessive quotes and lengthy detailed description of a session.
- Don't write disparaging statements about clients, their lifestyle, parentage, cultural or racial origin, or diagnosis.
- Try to make notes immediately after each client session.
- Always keep client files in a locked place. If kept on a computer, follow security procedures to protect confidentiality. Control access to files by unauthorized personnel.
- When using computers and other forms of electronic communication, use caution to protect client privacy.
- Be up to date on record keeping requirements and procedures, laws, and regulations.
- Follow HIPAA rules and regulations when applicable.
- Periodically make a random check of supervisee's progress notes, intakes, charting, or other client documentation.

ized and repetitive that supervisors may well save time and energy by constructing fill-in-the-blank samples to acclimatize supervisees to requirements of the setting.

Providing structured forms may also assist those supervisees who struggle with the written word. Another helpful proposal is for supervisors to break larger, more complex questions found on forms down into simpler questions that lead up to the more complex answer or create a basic outline to guide supervisees' thinking.

Taking time to think through typical problems that novice supervisees may face with regard to paperwork and being ready with a few solutions is worth the effort. Rapid Reference 7.15 lists popular strategies for helping supervisees with paperwork problems (Campbell, 2001–2005).

Ideas to Help Supervisees Solve Paperwork Problems

Problem: Supervisee has a hard time completing progress notes.

Solution: Suggest supervisee spend three minutes between each appointment jotting down a few sentences about each client visit.

Problem: Supervisee has difficulty finding time for paper work.

Solution: Have supervisee set time in the morning to do paperwork before meeting first client. Whenever a cancellation occurs, use the available time for paperwork.

Problem: Supervisee is not sure what to say in the progress notes.

Solution: Provide supervisees with a list of important questions to answer and several examples of correct progress notes.

Problem: Supervisee has trouble getting paperwork done because of phone interruptions.

Solution: Suggest supervisee put phone on voice mail. Ask receptionist to hold calls for short periods. Move self to a place away from phone, such as a conference room.

Problem: Supervisor has difficulty finding time to do paperwork because of interruptions.

Solution: Close door and explain to everyone when door is shut, you need quiet to do paperwork. Put sign on door saying how long you will be unavailable. Find a place to go hide and do paperwork if asking people not to interrupt you doesn't work.

Problem: Everyone is overwhelmed by too much paperwork.

Solution: Get together as a team for an hour on Friday afternoon and do paperwork together as a group. Include treats.

Problem: Supervisee dislikes doing paperwork.

Solution: Suggest supervisee reward self when paperwork is complete.

Problem: Supervisor is desperate to get supervisee's completed paperwork because of important deadlines.

Solution: Use negative reinforcement. When it is not done, make supervisees stay until it is done.

Problem: Supervisee has poor writing skills and must fill out the same paperwork repeatedly.

Solution: Give supervisee a fill-in-the-blank form to use with this type of documentation.

Problem: Supervisee is trying hard to get caught up but not making much progress and supervisor has run out of ideas and patience.

Solution: Assign a mentor who can offer support and suggestions.

Problem: Supervisee admits not liking to do paperwork.

Solution: Ask the supervisee "How do you get yourself to do something you don't like to do?"

TEST YOURSELF

1. The term *working alliance* is used by Bordin (1983) to describe the supervisory relationship. True or False?

2. The quality of the supervisory relationship is critical to successful supervision, and so supervisors must take responsibility for the quality of the relationship. True or False?

3. Supervisors can build a working alliance with their supervisees by
   (a) telling supervisees clearly what is expected of them, and then hope for the best.
   (b) discussing goals and tasks openly in orientation and working to create trust by offering support and being empathic.
   (c) giving supervisees a list of their jobs and telling them to come find you if they have any questions.
   (d) not making any demands on them during the first month or so of supervision.

4. It is better for the working alliance if the clinical supervisor is also the administrator. True or False?

5. Identify one thing a supervisor has to do to build the working alliance.
   (a) Tell them everything they say in supervision is confidential.
   (b) Stress that you will be evaluating them, and so they better watch out.
   (c) Use self-disclosure about some of your mistakes and assure them making mistakes is a good part of learning.
   (d) Ignore this topic completely as it makes everyone uncomfortable.

6. The working alliance between the supervisor and supervisee can be affected by
   (a) anxiety.
   (b) role conflict and role ambiguity.
   (c) the organizational system.
   (d) disagreement or misunderstandings about goals.
   (e) all of the above.
   (f) none of the above.

7. In order to facilitate trust, supervisors need to
   (a) be self-aware.
   (b) be able to create a climate of care and respect.
   (c) be able to tolerate differences.
   (d) be supportive and encouraging.
   (e) treat supervisees in the same way they wish them to treat the clients.
   (f) do all of the above.

8. **With advanced supervisees there is no need to hold an orientation session. Everyone knows what to do.** True or False?

9. **Taking time to think through orientation—what information to give supervisees and what information is needed from supervisees—will help prevent problems and increase effectiveness of supervision.** True or False?

10. **Using an informed consent agreement or contract are excellent ways to help build the working alliance with supervisees.** True or False?

11. **Personal development is an important area of supervision because personal issues, when not identified, can have a negative impact on the quality of client care.** True or False?

12. **The supervisor's role in personal development of the supervisee is to**

    (a) help supervisees to identify areas of personal difficulty that may impact clients.

    (b) tell them all to go get therapy.

    (c) act as their therapist in supervision.

    (d) assume they already know what they need to do because it is in all of the ethical codes.

13. **Self-awareness exercises are excellent tools to facilitate a supervisee's exploration of personal issues in supervision.** True or False?

14. **Name two topics that may be important to explore with supervisees in the area of self-awareness.**

15. **One of the hardest tasks many supervisors face is how to increase a supervisee's self-awareness and ownership of personal problems and at the same time avoid becoming a therapist. To do this, supervisors should**

    (a) be sure to include at the beginning of supervision a discussion about the role of personal self-awareness and its importance in ethical practice with clients.

    (b) avoid exploring roots and causes of these personal issues as they come up.

    (c) help supervisees connect their awarenesses to their work with clients.

    (d) ask supervisees to come up with suggestions for what they need to change in order to work ethically with clients.

    (e) do all of the above.

16. **If you suspect a supervisee is attracted to one of his or her clients, it is better to**

    (a) ignore the problem altogether because it makes you uncomfortable.

    (b) talk to the supervisee about the observation as soon as possible.

    (c) suggest immediately terminating that supervisee because feeling attraction to a client is not natural.

    (d) call the supervisee's licensing board or university program and report them for unethical behavior.

(continued)

17. If a supervisee comes to work improperly dressed, it is not the job of the clinical supervisor to tell them to follow the rules. True or False?

Answers: 1. True; 2. True; 3. b; 4. False; 5. c; 6. e; 7. f; 8. False; 9. True; 10. True; 11. True; 12. a; 13. True; 14. Attraction, especially sexual attraction; beliefs and attitudes toward people who are different, such as a client's race, ethnicity, and sexual orientation; experiences with loss; comfort with conflict and confrontation; need to be liked; perfectionism; distorted or illogical thoughts; transference and countertransference; theoretical model and openness to new ideas. 15. e; 16. b; 17. False

Eight

THE INTERMEDIATE STAGE OF SUPERVISION

After the beginning stage of orientation and settling in, the real work of supervision begins. For many, this is the stage that demands the most skill and effort. The main goal at this point is to simultaneously support and challenge supervisees to mature into effective, ethical, independent practitioners. Shulman (1993) refers to this skill as the *demand for work:* the need to empathize and understand the supervisee's anxiety yet still challenge and push him or her to get the work done. To be successful in the intermediate stage, supervisors must be active and involved in supervision, use a variety of methods and techniques to stimulate learning and improve monitoring, provide ongoing constructive feedback, confront problems as they develop, and help promote self-awareness and ownership of goals by supervisees.

The timeline for this stage varies depending on the situation and the capabilities of the supervisees. With interns on rotations of 6 months or less, supervisors have to quickly get supervisees focused on the required tasks. On the other hand, with postdegree supervisees, several years might be spent in this stage.

Hopefully, supervisors have begun early building the working alliance as a platform for the intermediate stage through orientation and the use of a written informed consent agreement or contract. However, it is easy for busy supervisors to leap immediately into review of cases with supervisees and forget to take time to establish the supervisory relationship. If supervisors forget to take care of relationship issues, precious time can be wasted as supervisees seek to calm their calm anxiety or settle disagreements and get ready to work. As

> **DON'T FORGET**
>
> The main tasks of the intermediate stage are to challenge supervisees to solve problems, overcome obstacles, and get the work done; give and receive feedback in a climate of caring and concern; promote development of self-awareness and ownership of goals; move supervisees toward independent functioning and decision making; and confront problems and difficulties in the working alliance.

CAUTION

Supervisors must always keep in mind the potential for harm in *not* challenging supervisees when their behavior might be harmful to the welfare of the client.

mentioned previously, research in group dynamics and psychotherapy outcome has shown that until an individual's needs for safety and inclusion are addressed and he or she feels understood and accepted, little progress on tasks occurs.

Most beginning supervisors are much more comfortable with the supportive role and may shy away from challenging or confronting their supervisees because they believe this to be negative to the working relationship. However, to be effective, supervisors must also be able to question supervisees and give them corrective feedback in order to help them grow. It is important for supervisors at this point to begin to challenge supervisees, especially novice ones, in order to help them develop self-efficacy and an accurate view of themselves and their competency (Steward, Breland, & Neil, 2001). Additionally, supervisors need to encourage supervisees to speak up and challenge them if they are to advance toward independence. The key factor to all of this challenging is how willing and comfortable the supervisor is in giving corrective feedback and confronting problems head-on, such as saying things to supervisees that they may not want to hear, and how skilled they are to do this effectively.

This chapter presents ways and means for supervisors to accomplish all of the tasks and challenges presented during the intermediate stage of supervision including how to give corrective feedback, promote self-awareness and ownership of goals, challenge supervisees to grow, and confront problems in the supervisory relationship, as well as teach practical skills, such as proper documentation of client sessions.

PROVIDING CORRECTIVE FEEDBACK

Providing corrective feedback need not always be an unpleasant experience. When perceived as an integral part of the learning process and the development of competency, it can be regarded in a positive light. When done correctly, it may be the keystone of any successful supervision experience and the development of self-efficacy in supervisees.

Increasing interest is being paid by supervision researchers to the concept of *self-efficacy* as it pertains to supervision. Self-efficacy refers to a person's level of confidence in his or her own ability to handle prospective situations (Bandura, 1997). Belief about one's ability to carry out specific tasks influences learning and performance of tasks. In supervision, how the supervisor gives corrective feedback and what the supervisor emphasizes in supervision has been found to enhance the supervisee's confidence and satisfaction with supervision (Bischoff et al., 2002; Ladany, Constantine, Miller, Erickson, & Muse-Burke, 2000).

Nonetheless, individuals vary in their comfort with providing and receiving corrective feedback. Some supervisees are more sensitive and uncomfortable with challenges, whereas others relish them. Rapid Reference 8.1 lists several questions for supervisors to use to explore their own comfort, as well as their supervisees' comfort, with corrective feedback.

Although some challenging and confrontation may be necessary to stimulate the supervisee's growth, constant correction can be detrimental to building the working alliance. Supervisors should strive to limit the amount of corrective feedback given at any one time as it can overwhelm supervisees and create non-productive anxiety. Taping a supervision session and counting the number of interruptions and corrections will help beginning supervisors to monitor this problem. A second option is to ask supervisees directly how they are experiencing corrective feedback or use the questions in the corrective feedback test in Rapid Reference 8.2.

One difficulty facing most mental health practitioners is focusing corrective feedback on behavior and away from personality. The best feedback, whether positive or negative, is specific, behavioral, and directly related to the learning goals of supervision rather than to global generalizations about

≡ Rapid Reference 8.1

Stimulus Questions for Supervisors and Supervisees to Encourage Personal Self-Exploration around the Topic of Corrective Feedback

1. If someone says to you, "I want to give you some feedback," what thoughts or feelings does this question trigger?" Do you think, "Oh, oh, here we go," or do you assume the feedback will be by and large positive?

2. When giving feedback to another person, do you assume (1) it will hurt the other person and lead to problems in your relationship or (2) do you see this feedback as more often than not improving your relationship?

3. What are some things that will make you more comfortable receiving feedback? For example, do you prefer to receive feedback in writing versus orally? Do you prefer to hear positives first, then corrections, or are you partial to the opposite?

Source: Adapted from Hulse-Killacky and Page (1994).

≡Rapid Reference 8.2

How Do I Give Corrective Feedback to My Supervisees?

Ask yourself:

Do I talk about strengths and successes as well as making corrections when giving feedback to my supervisees?   Usually ___ Sometimes ___ Never ___

Do I listen without interrupting when my supervisee is making a point?   Usually ___ Sometimes ___ Never ___

Do I notice extra effort or risk taking on the part of my supervisees?   Usually ___ Sometimes ___ Never ___

Do I give regular, ongoing corrective feedback concerning changes desired?   Usually ___ Sometimes ___ Never ___

Do I keep my feedback focused on behaviors such as frequency and amount, not my supervisee's personality?   Usually ___ Sometimes ___ Never ___

Do I work to limit the amount of corrective feedback given to my supervisees at any one time?   Usually ___ Sometimes ___ Never ___

When I give supervisees feedback, do I try to focus on exploring options for improvement, not just mistakes?   Usually ___ Sometimes ___ Never ___

Note: Inspired by the work of Irwin Rubin, PhD.

the person. For example, it is more productive to say, "You seem to be having trouble getting your process notes done on time," rather than saying "I think you are lazy," or "You just don't care." Supervisees will respond better to specific feedback about behaviors they need to change than to global assessment of their personality. Rapid Reference 8.3 summarizes the characteristics of good and bad corrective feedback.

DON'T FORGET

To make corrective feedback effective, supervisors must be good observers as well as describers of behavior and guard against mixing their own thoughts and feelings, or interpretations, about the behavior into the feedback.

Therefore, supervisors need to hone their observational skills and learn to separate behavioral observations from their thoughts and feelings *about* the behavior. While this statement sounds simple, many supervisors in the mental health field have difficulty turning off the interpretive voice so essential today in diagnosis and assessment of patients.

≡ Rapid Reference 8.3

Providing Corrective Feedback

Good Feedback
- Highlights areas for improvement and gives specific suggestions for change
- Focuses on improvements
- Creates cooperation
- Instills trust
- Improves confidence
- Clarifies action

Example of good feedback: The focus is on a specific situation and behavior. "It seems to me that you are really struggling with what to say to this client about his anger."

Bad Feedback
- Uses generalizations and replays what went wrong
- Creates defensiveness
- Focuses on blame
- Makes the person feel judged
- Undermines improvement

Example of bad feedback: The focus is on personality and is global in nature. "I think you have problems with anger. It is obviously getting in the way of your work with clients."

Another common problem faced by supervisors is that in an effort not to sound critical or accusatory, they tend to be too tentative and use too many disclaimers, so the real message is lost. Studies have shown that feedback that is clear and specific without numerous qualifiers is more effective (Hulse-Killacky & Page, 1994).

Feedback will be heard and more readily accepted in a climate of caring and concern. Self-disclosure and empathetic responding will help supervisors defuse anxiety and facilitate openness. For example, statements such as "I know I struggled with this same problem when I first started out," or "Sometimes it must feel pretty overwhelming," might break the ice and make the supervisor seem more understanding and approachable.

Also, starting feedback with "I" statements rather than with "you" statements will decrease the accusatory feeling of the feedback and reduce defensiveness. For example saying "This is my assessment," or "It seems from my perspective," sounds a lot different than "You did or didn't do that," or "You are this or that." Absolutely avoid beginning corrective feedback with statements such as "Other people think that you . . ." or "Everyone else does . . ." because these global anonymous generalities tend to rile supervisees and have no benefit in terms of actual behavioral change.

Pointing out discrepancies, that is, noticing differences between verbal and nonverbal communication or stated goals and action, is another accepted feedback skill. "As you talk about how well things are going with this family, your voice dropped and you appear sad." Or "You tell me that you really want to get your paperwork done on time but after two weeks, I still don't have your paperwork."

One of the best suggestions for corrective feedback is *sandwiching* (Powell, 1993). Here unfavorable feedback is sandwiched in between positive comments. The main point is to keep feedback specific, behavioral, concise, and timely. Also, starting first with one or two specific comments that are positive before moving to any correction is usually appreciated. For example, "I like how you did . . ." However "I see you still struggle with . . ." so "and maybe you could try . . . next time. You seem to be moving in the right direction" (Powell, p. 189). Try to avoid the word *but* when delivering praise as it tends to negate all that comes before it. Also, it is recommended to place any general statement of praise at the end rather than the beginning of the feedback sandwich. Statements such as "You are doing a great job" when said first go unheard as people prepare to hear the proverbial "but" and all the exceptions. Instead, place specific statements of praise at the beginning.

A variation on sandwiching from the solution-focused model is to ask supervisees to name one or two things they liked and one or two things they didn't like about what they did in a client session. Or ask a scaling question such as "on a scale of one to ten, rate how you think you are doing so far with this client [or with your clients in general]."

Another suggestion to try is Haim Ginott's *xyz* formula in which parents give feedback to their children to correct behavior without criticizing the person (Goleman, 1995). The *xyz* formula is "When you do *x*, I think or feel *y*, and I want you to do *z*." Supervisors can combine this technique with empathetic responding: "I know you are struggling with my feedback; however, when you say or do *x* . . . I think or feel *y* . . . and I wish you would do *z*."

Metaphors, along with storytelling, are also effective tools for providing corrective feedback. They can be particularly helpful when trying to tackle complex thoughts and emotions as it is frequently easier to hear and understand corrective feedback when given in this way. For example, the supervisor could say, "It's as if you are on a sinking ship and searching for a life preserver." Or, employing the

≡Rapid Reference 8.4

Examples of Corrective Feedback Skills

Empathic responding: "This is a problem most supervisees at your stage of development have," or "I realize that clients like this can be very stressful the first time you have to work with them."

Self-disclosure: "I struggled with the same thing when I was just starting out," or "It is still sometimes difficult for me to know what to do with this type of client."

"I" statements: "I have observed a pattern here that when a client begins to talk about his or her anger, you interrupt or change the topic. This is what I see going on. I wonder what you observe?"

Pointing out discrepancies: "I noticed even though you told the client it was okay to cry in the session, when she began to do so, you asked a question, and that cut her off. What do you think this is about? Have you seen yourself doing this at other times?" or "When we started supervision, you told me that it was really important for you to expand your knowledge about intervention strategies, yet when I make suggestions, you usually tell me they won't work. I guess I am confused right now about what it is that you do want."

Sandwiching: "I like the way you asked the client.... I would like to see you do more of ... Overall, I see you are making great progress. You seem to be much more comfortable in your sessions" (taken from Powell, 1993).

xyz: "When you do x with your clients, this is what happens ... y ... and so I suggest you try ... 'z.'" or "When you come late to supervision, it really disrupts my schedule with my clients, so I would really appreciate your coming to supervision on time."

Metaphors: "You appear right now to be a ship without a rudder, spinning around in a circle. Let's see if you can get hold of the wheel. In what direction would you like to go with this client?"

storytelling technique, "I had another supervisee who struggled with a similar situation with a client." Rapid Reference 8.4 offers examples of each of these feedback skills.

USING COACHING IN SUPERVISION

The coaching model has a number of applications for clinical supervisors. A coach helps clients by offer-

DON'T FORGET

Provide challenging or corrective feedback in a climate of acceptance and understanding, include specific examples of positive and negative behaviors when providing praise or correction, and use corrective feedback focused on behaviors, not on the person.

> **DON'T FORGET**
>
> When working as a coach-supervisor, your job is to help supervisees forward action, move from ideas and dreams to actuality, and overcome blocks and resistances.

ing support, challenging them, and continually focusing attention on forwarding an individual's action toward stated goals. Change is not seen as automatic; it requires energy, thought, and courage. Because coaching is felt to both challenge and support people to achieve either personal or professional goals, it is logical that the field of coaching has much to offer supervisors.

An important facet to any successful coaching relationship is that the coachee owns the goals for change, and the relationship is a clearly defined contractual one. Therefore, one area in which coaching principles may assist clinical supervisors is in promoting the supervisee's ownership of goals for supervision during the contracting phase of supervision.

Coaches work best with clear objectives and goals. Coaching won't work if the energy and commitment for change belongs mostly to the supervisor or if the supervisor's definition of success is noticeably different than that of the supervisee. Therefore, supervisor-coaches need a number of thought-provoking questions to challenge supervisees during the contracting phase. For example, ask each supervisee "What is it that you would like to get out of supervision? What will you need to know and be able to do to be a competent professional?"

Coaching requires trust, reciprocity, and a commitment to change. If there are issues between supervisor and supervisee that prevent trust and reciprocity, it will be almost impossible to establish a coaching relationship. Supervisors who wish to use the coaching model must work through such relationship problems first or bring someone else in as a consultant to do the coaching.

> **DON'T FORGET**
>
> For supervisors to be successful as a coach, there needs to be agreement on the tasks and goals as well as a commitment to change on the part of supervisees. Coaching requires the following:
>
> - Trust
> - Commitment and reciprocity
> - A climate of honest and open communication
> - An ability to seek and hear feedback

Rapid Reference Box 8.5 lists a number of coaching techniques that are transferable to clinical supervision.

The instant payoff technique (Landsberg, 1997) is an example of a coaching technique that is useful in situations where supervisors become prone to nagging and haranguing

≡ Rapid Reference 8.5

Coaching Skills for Supervisors

Encouraging: "I know you can do that!"

Acknowledge success: Cheerleading: "Wow, that was great. I'm impressed. I can see you really worked hard on that."

Holding the focus: When supervisees are rambling or talking about extraneous things in order to avoid supervision, interrupt and say, "Let's get back to supervision and your clients."

Bottom line: When supervisees are easily bogged down in details and have difficulty formulating a problem focus, interject, "Bottom line. What do you need from me right now?"

Powerful questions: "What do you think you will have to do to solve this problem? How long do you think it will be before you do that?"

Challenging: When supervisees are contemplating solutions to a problem suggest, "I think you know the answer. You don't need me to tell you what to do now." or, "I challenge you to do ... x ... by next week."

Asking permission to tell the hard truth: "When you come in here week after week and tell me that you want to do a better job on your paper work, and get it in more timely. Yet nothing is happening. We need to go back to the beginning and take another look at your goals."

Contracting: At the beginning of supervision, ask "What would you like to work on in supervision? What are the areas of interest to you?"

Creating an action plan: After supervisees have selected a goal or solution to a problem, add, "Now that you have decided to do ... x ... Let's get out our calendars and make a plan. Give me a date and a time for ..."

Asking for success and reporting accomplishments: After a plan is created by supervisees for change, say "How do you want to tell me about your successes? Send me an e-mail or call? This Friday afternoon?"

Mission statements: At the beginning of supervision, suggest that supervisees create a mission statement that captures the meaning of their work with clients. Ask "What do you really want to accomplish with your clients? What is your vision of helping people?"

Goal sheets: At the beginning of supervision, to build the working alliance, suggest supervisees fill out a supervision goal sheet. "I'd like you to identify five goals for supervision this year. For each one, develop two to three examples of some activities that will be necessary for you to accomplish each of one of these goals. For example, read two to three articles on the topic, make a short presentation in our team meeting, attend a training, bring in a case that involves your goal and work on it in supervision, and maybe make a tape of one of your clients. I am sure you have some great ideas for topics for supervision. Bring your sheet in to supervision next week, and we will go over it and put together a rough plan for the next six months."

Source: J. Campbell (2001).

> ## CAUTION
> ....
> If there is to be any hope for successful change by supervisees, an action plan with exact dates and times for each step of the selected solution has to be completed before the problem-solving session is brought to a close. Please reserve sufficient time for this step.

supervisees to try to convince them to solve a chronic problem. The purpose of the instant payoff technique is to move ownership of problems and solutions from supervisor to supervisee. The key point of the instant payoff technique is to have supervisees, not supervisors, define the problem and come up with their own personal ideas for a solution. Instead of supervisors attempting to persuade supervisees to see problems from their perspective and trying to motivate them to adopt the supervisor's solutions, the supervisor as coach begins the problem-solving session by asking supervisees to describe the problem from their perspective. After that, supervisees are invited to identify as many obstacles to solving this problem as they can produce and then generate a list of likely solutions to each obstacle. Out of that list, supervisees may select the most promising idea for solving the problem, and it is this idea that becomes the basis for the last problem-solving step, creating an action plan that includes the exact dates and times for each step toward the solution.

At each step along the way with the instant payoff technique, the supervisor as coach serves more in the capacity of a consultant to the supervisee's problems, rather than the actual solver of those problems. Hence, the energy for change belongs where it should—with supervisees, not supervisors.

IMPLEMENTING PROBLEM-SOLVING STRATEGIES

A problem is present when there is a gap between what is happening and what is preferred or desired. People's comfort and ability to respond to problems vary, but most practitioners, especially counselors and psychotherapists, already have a vast repertory of problem-solving skills to draw on. For example, most trained clinicians already have the ability to listen to a client's extensive list of difficulties and then are able to quickly capture the chief problem. *Gaining a problem focus, compartmentalizing, partializing,* or *Swiss cheesing* are other names for this problem-solving skill, that is, the ability to identify the main problem and subsequently break it down into smaller parts as a means to encourage the taking of reasonable steps toward change.

Another well-known problem-solving method with broad application in supervision is *brainstorming.* Brainstorming requires the suspension of critical judgment in order to generate as many creative solutions to a problem as possible. Brainstorming can be employed at any time or in any situation given that most people are already familiar with the process, and it doesn't require much time. Supervisors can insert brainstorming into case consultation, group supervision, or couple it with coaching techniques.

CAUTION

Suspend critical judgment while brainstorming. Avoid statements such as "It won't work; we have tried that before," or "We don't have enough time or money for that." Postpone the tendency to analyze suggestions as they are being made as it kills creative energy.

Putting It Into Practice

Brainstorming

Frank had been a clinical supervisor for several years in a busy hospital setting that utilized both masters- and doctoral-level interns from a nearby university. Previously there was a training director at the hospital, but due to budget cuts, the position was axed. Frank, as the most senior supervisor, was asked to pick up the slack and "think of something to do that wouldn't cost any money." Frank decided this would be a good topic for brainstorming with the whole staff. Getting everyone together, he asked the group to tackle the issue of limited resources for training. The staff responded enthusiastically as everyone felt the training program had real value. Using brainstorming, the following ideas were generated:

- Create a training seminar to be offered at a brown bag lunch on the last Friday of each month. Rotate leadership among the staff. Include everyone. Collect ideas for topics. Explore receiving CEU credits for the seminar, and open it up to other professionals.

- Check with the local university that is sending the interns to see if the would cosponsor a series of CEU training seminars at the hospital in return for an internship site. Make these open to professionals outside the hospital, and charge a nominal fee.

- Create teams of two or three experienced staff members. Each team will create a case vignette that represents a typical situation supervisees will be faced with at the hospital. Include in the case scenarios the most common ethical issues that come up regularly.

- Have experienced staff members prepare short demonstrations of approximately 5 minutes each where they will model for supervisees through role-play a variety of basic skills and intervention strategies. Videotape each demonstration, and make tapes available to all supervisees.

- Build a videotape or CD library of training materials. Ask the university for assistance with this project.

(continued)

- On another day of the month, have a 1-hour brown bag lunch for case presentations. Put a sign up list on the board with meeting dates for the year, and ask all the staff to volunteer to lead at least one meeting.

After the brainstorming session, Frank asked the group to select one of the ideas from the list that most intrigued them. Surprisingly, everyone was excited and immediately began to volunteer to head small committees to implement each idea. Understandably some ideas, such as working with the university to hold CEU training seminars, might take several months whereas starting a brown bag training series could be done immediately. Being a savvy supervisor, before adjourning, Frank wrote down the names of leaders and members for each committee and had each committee chair agree to report his or her findings at the next staff meeting. He also had the group select a date to begin the brown bag series and found a volunteer to lead that session. Following this meeting, it took some time and energy for Frank to follow up with each committee and get the various ideas off the ground. However, the benefit was improved team spirit and reduced turnover of staff at the hospital.

Teaching Point: Rather than giving up because of an organizational change, the supervisor used his problem-solving skills to come up with a solution. By employing brainstorming, and keeping the the meeting focused on the problem, he was able to tap into the positive energy and resources of his staff.

Situational problem solving (Komanski, 1999) is another particularly helpful method to free up energy for solutions to nagging problems. It could be used with one supervisee or a group of them. Situational variables can be divided into three groups: (1) blocks in the situation (e.g., inadequate resources, shifts in agency or organizational focus, state and federal laws, organizational guidelines, professional standards, loss of grant monies); (2) blocks that exist in others (e.g., stressed out staff, clients, and anxious or stressed administrators); and (3) blocks that exist in the supervisee (e.g., lack of skill/knowledge, low motivation, personal attitudes and beliefs). To apply situational problem solving, supervisors and supervisees examine a problem from the three perspectives and together develop a broad list of things that get in the way of attaining particular skills or completing tasks. As pieces of the puzzle unfold, new solutions or plans are then generated. The strength of this approach is that it normalizes and depersonalizes many problems and challenges supervisors to look beyond the supervisee's personality as the root of all difficulties.

For example, many inexperienced supervisees struggle mightily with the proverbial problem of paperwork. Causes can run the gamut from being overwhelmed by the demands of client services and possessing an inability to organize time efficiently to no training in how to complete paperwork satisfactorily, continuous changes to the paperwork requirements, computer problems, negative attitude about paperwork on the part of other staff members, ingrained fears of writing, and perfectionism that precludes starting or prevents finishing anything written. Supervisors, along with supervisees, can generate a wide list of possible obstacles to completing paperwork, and, after that, supervisees may select the one obstacle from the list that best describes their personal problem with paperwork. (Note: They may wish to select more than one.) After choosing the obstacle, apply brainstorming to stimulate creativity. Next, have supervisees select the solution out of the brainstorming that sounds most workable and create an action plan based on it. After that, don't forget to ask how they will reward themselves for effort expended.

One general caution for new supervisors is to be sure to leave sufficient time at any problem-solving session to create a plan for implementing suggested solutions. Many times much energy is spent on identifying problems and creating solutions, but little attention is given to implementation of solutions, resulting in motivation taking a nosedive. Watch the clock, and before the meeting adjourns, request that anyone involved in the problem-solving session take out their calendars and set actual dates and times for follow-up. Rapid Reference 8.6 summarizes the steps involved in good problem solving.

≡ Rapid Reference 8.6

Problem Solving Steps for Supervisors

1. **Define the problem:** "How is this a problem for you? Can you give some examples? What does the problem look like? Feel like? Any metaphor that comes to you that fits this problem?"

2. **Identify contributing factors:** "What factors might be contributing to this problem? For example, what are the system's variables that may be contributing to the problem? Multicultural differences? Dual relationships? Anxiety? Lack of information or skill? How does this problem affect you? Others [your department or organization]?"

3. **Reassess the definition of the problem before moving on to solutions:** Be careful not to jump to solutions until certain of the actual problem.

4. **Visualize the ideal outcome:** "What would success look like?" Or "If you had a magic wand to wave over the situation, tell me what would be different."

5. **Identify obstacles:** "Tell me the all the obstacles that exist between where you are now and where you said you'd like to be." (Supervisors please note if these obstacles are internal or situational.)

6. **Brainstorm ways around these obstacles:** "When brainstorming, suspend critical judgement and just let your imagination and creativity soar. Anything is possible!" Avoid "I've already tried that." Or "There isn't enough time or money for that."

(continued)

7. Select out of the brainstorm list the answer that most interests you: "Which of the ideas that we have generated so far intrigues you the most?"

8. Examine the positives and negatives for that solution: "Draw a line down the center of a page and put on one side all of the positives for that solution and on the other side all of the negatives."

9. Tackle the negatives. Be innovative: "Take the list of negatives, and ask your what could be done about each of the negatives."

10. Create an action plan to implement your solution: "Okay, let's get down to the details of creating an action plan around this solution. Get out your calendar, and let's pin down who will do what and when. Get some dates and times."

11. Choose dates and means for reporting back on progress. Celebrate all successes, no matter how small: "How do you want to report back to me about your success?"

UNDERSTANDING RELATIONSHIP DIFFICULTIES

Though the overall goal in postdegree supervision is to form a collaborative working alliance, there are times when both supervisor and supervisee may experience tension and discomfort. Each may want to avoid discord, but conflict is normal and natural in any close relationship, especially given the complexity of roles and relationships in supervision (Nelson & Friedlander, 2001). Although it likely will be unnerving when it occurs, supervisors need to understand that it is their responsibility to address problems in the supervisory relationship in a fair and respectful manner, not avoid them. The standard in supervision should not be the absence of conflict but one in which resolution comes without blame, with equal participation, and where all are treated with dignity, fairness, and respect.

There are many causes for friction. Supervision is a multifaceted relationship with many intrinsic problems, such as dual relationships, role conflict, and role ambiguity. Tension in the relationship can indicate any number of troubles, such as concern for safety on the part of supervisees or the need for more or less structure, direction, or support from supervisors. Sometimes the issue is fit between supervisor and supervisee on style, approach, model, or methods. Other times it is an indication of the lack of skill on the part of the supervisor. Problems can go both ways.

The main point is for supervisors to understand that because super-

DON'T FORGET

The first job of the supervisor is to create an atmosphere of support and positive good will with supervisees—a win-win environment.

vision is a relationship of unequal power, supervisors have to act responsibly when trouble occurs and not let problems fester. Changing relationship dynamics takes openness on the part of supervisor (and supervisee), as well as creativity, honesty, and respect. Just as with clients, resolving difficulties also requires skill and the expenditure of considerable time and effort, along with a little inventiveness, but the return can be enormous. Rapid Reference 8.7 gives a number of suggestions for solving problems with supervisees.

Solving difficulties also requires assertiveness and a willingness to

≡ Rapid Reference 8.7

Strategies for Resolving Relationship Problems

- Change methods, techniques, and style
- Depersonalize problems
- Try relating to the supervisee differently
- Use a variety of relationship skills and techniques, such as active listening, coaching tools, paradoxical intervention techniques, storytelling, and metaphors
- Talk directly to the supervisee about relationship problems

confront problems, no matter how tough. When experiencing problems in the supervisory relationship, the only truly effective way to resolve matters is to address them openly with supervisees. Nonetheless, supervisors are just like most people when faced with uncomfortable situations; they generally want to avoid strife. One common supervisory response to friction is to focus more on tasks and procedures and to talk more about what needs to get done in order to avoid any discussion of personal thoughts or feelings.

Supervisees may follow similar avoidance patterns by appearing in supervision with a list of clients they wish to cover and then racing through the list, not stopping for any feedback or discussion. Other avoidance strategies are rambling, jumping from topic to topic, ignoring the supervisor's suggestions or being so busy they do not have time for supervision. For example, instead of expressing doubts, raising personal thoughts or feelings, or contradicting supervisors, supervisees use busyness to mask underlying problems. A wall of words can mean many things: a lack of trust, a response to the supervisor's perceived criticalness or dogmatism, a lack of respect for the supervisor's expertness, or a disagreement concerning the supervisor's style, direction, or focus. Shulman (1993) coined the term *illusion of work* to describe this phenomenon.

When such behavior occurs, the obvious tactic is for the supervisor to stop and think, "What is this person telling me or not telling me by this behavior?" Supervisors might also ask themselves, "What issues or problems are we not talking

CAUTION

Use the facilitative confrontation model. Confront supervisees in order to make improvements and solve problems, not to blame or punish. Avoid merely labeling the person as the problem. Look at the relationship.

about right now? What does this wall of words represent?" As a result of such self-questioning, it follows that supervisors need to stop and challenge the supervisee's behavior in supervision: "I hear all of the things you are doing that are going well, but I don't hear about any difficulties? I wonder what that means? Is there something I am doing, or not doing, that causes you not to share? Do I seem too critical or dogmatic? Is there anything I can change that will make supervision go better for you?"

It is hard to generalize about what types of relationship issues will create the most difficulty for supervisors. However, there are several categories of supervisee responses to supervision that can be described as generally problematic: highly dependent, helpless, or too agreeable supervisees; closed, resistant, or defensive supervisees; externalizing and oppositional supervisees; and apathetic or uninvolved supervisees.

Models for Understanding Relationship Difficulties

Applying Karen Horney's (1950) model concerning how people cope with the unknown can be exceedingly helpful to supervisors as they seek to understand difficulties in supervision. She used the terms *moving away, moving towards,* and *moving against* to describe strategies that people use to cope with anxiety. Beginning supervisees who lack practical experience with clients may respond with these characteristic patterns of behavior as they attempt to manage their anxiety about what lies ahead. However, it is easy for beginning supervisors, who are also anxious and unsure of themselves, to misunderstand how these behaviors can be indicators of a supervisee's anxiety and an expression of a genuine need for safety and support from the supervisor. Instead, they might

CAUTION

It is important to avoid jumping the conclusion that all relationship difficulties are an indication of a supervisee's impairment. Instead of labeling the person as the problem, work to depersonalize them. Ask yourself "What am I doing, or not doing, that is the problem here? What factors may be contributing to our relationship tension? How might the supervisee's behavior be an expression of anxiety? What do I need to do differently as a result of these awarenesses?"

mislabel the supervisee as Passive Aggressive or Dependent Personality Disorder. Once given the label, the supervisor may then give up on any attempt to explore how these behaviors might be a result of factors present in the situation rather than an indication of psychological problems.

Parallel process is another model that can be helpful to supervisors as they try to understand and resolve relationship difficulties. The parallel process model suggests that problems between a supervisor and supervisee mirror problems the supervisee is having with clients. For example, a client in a crisis situation may feel overwhelmed by a number of contributing factors. Supervisees in response to the client's state of helplessness may feel similarly stuck and so present themselves in supervision as overwhelmed and unable to assist the client. Applying parallel process, supervisors would note the similarity between the supervisee's and client's response to problems and so guide the supervisee to change actions as well as the session focus.

Parallel process thinking is also helpful in self-examination. Because supervisors continually model ethical practice for supervisees, they must be careful to monitor their own assumptions and behavior. For example, if they want supervisees to be sensitive to multicultural differences in clients, they need to pay close attention to their own negative remarks and stereotyping of supervisees. If they want supervisees to be compassionate and caring with clients, supervisors in turn need to watch how they treat their own clients as well as how they treat

Putting It Into Practice

Applying the Parallel Process Model in Supervision to Resolve Difficulties

Tom, a supervisor, finds himself struggling with one of his supervisees, Joan. She appears to get overwhelmed by client problems, and even though he gives her numerous suggestions for things to try, he never feels Joan follows through with them. During a supervision session, Joan said she felt helpless and overwhelmed to aid a particular client family. She kept asking Tom "What should I do to help this family? They are so overwhelmed with problems. Everything is falling apart. I keep making suggestions but they never seem to follow through." Noting parallel process, Tom said "Joan, I am noticing a parallel between what you are saying right now in supervision with me and what you describe as feeling with your clients. I wonder if you are aware of this, too? If so, what does it tell you? Can you think of anything different you need to try with your clients?"

Teaching Point: Pay attention to the process, not just the content, in supervision. Address relationship issues directly. Share insights, and be open to supervisee's feedback.

their supervisees. Novice supervisees watch their supervisors and imitate the supervisor's behavior with their clients.

Applying a systems perspective to supervisory relationship problems is also advantageous. Just as there are parallels in relationships between individuals, there are parallels or isomorphic relationships between systems. For example, just as clients may feel their needs are not being met in an organizational system because of limited resources or regulations, supervisees may feel exactly the same with supervisors. Similarly, just as clients become angry and defensive in such circumstances, supervisees can act the same in supervision. Here, however, the supervisee's defensiveness is questioned not in terms of individual dynamics but as a result of system variables. Seeing this behavior as a systems problem, and not that of an individual, assists supervisors in altering their responses.

By taking a system's perspective, such things as overfunctioning and underfunctioning become easily recognized patterns in supervision (Getz & Protinsky, 1994; Lerner, 1989). Many new clinical supervisors are classic overfunctioners. They were made a supervisor because they work hard, have good skills, are responsible, and follow through on tasks. They may carry anxiety about having everything exactly right, which can also contribute to overfunctioning. As overfunctioners, these supervisors may have trouble delegating work. Instead, they take over the work of the supervisees and work harder than they do to get things done right. In response, many supervisees assume the role of underfunctioner, acting helpless and stuck to solve problems and unable to assume responsibility, which feeds the supervisor's anxiety and keeps the dynamic going. Recognizing this cycle as a systems interaction assists supervisors to make necessary changes and improve the supervisory experience.

The Transtheoretical Model has considerable application in supervision, as it provides supervisors with a means to rethink relationship difficulties and work more effectively with supervisees (Watkins, 1997). This six-stage model describes the cycle of change that will occur when anyone is faced with solving problems: precontemplation, contemplation, preparation, action, maintenance, and termination (Prochaska, Norcross, & DiClemente, 1994). Rapid Reference 8.8 describes these six stages in more detail.

Applying the transtheoretical approach to supervision should be an easy stretch for most skilled clinicians. As with clients, the movement through the change cycle is not linear, and it may take as many as three attempts, stops, and starts before supervisees successfully complete the cycle (Prochaska et al., 1994). Supervisors who look at difficulties with supervisees from a transtheoretical perspective know automatically to utilize different methods and techniques to work with supervisees, depending on where they are in the cycle. They also

≡Rapid Reference 8.8

The Transtheoretical Model

1. **Precontemplation:** The precontemplation stage represents the period when a person may deny they have a problem or insist it is someone else's problem. Supervisees, especially highly experienced ones, who are required by state rules or organizational regulations to be in clinical supervision, can be excellent examples of people in the precontemplation stage because they may believe that they do not need supervision, they are fully competent to do their job and, as a result, resist any attempts by supervisors to engage them in supervision. Paradoxical techniques; indirect techniques such as story telling and solution-focused questions; along with confrontational methods are the best strategies for supervisors with this stage.

2. **Contemplation:** At this stage, the person may begin to be aware they do have a problem but still have no solid commitment to take any action to change. The time frame for the contemplation stage can be lengthy, with some people spending years or even a lifetime wishing, hoping, and waiting for change without actually doing anything to bring it about. In supervision the contemplation stage will regularly be seen in supervisees who talk extensively about things they need to do differently, but very little actual change occurs. Noting discrepancies between what a supervisee says and does, keeping a focus in supervision on the problem, and challenging supervisees to do better are all good suggestions for this stage of change.

3. **Preparation:** According to Yalom (1989), the assumption of responsibility for one's problems only brings the person into the "*vestibule of change; it is not synonymous with change*" (p. 9). Therefore, the preparation stage serves as a bridge between thinking about change and action. Sometimes this bridge seems poorly built and dangerous, while in other instances, the bridge is solid and easy to cross. Supervisors cognizant of how natural it is for novice supervisees to be anxious as they approach the tasks and goals in supervision will want to tailor their interventions around this phenomenon. For example, discuss openly how normal it is for supervisees when they begin supervision to have worries about making mistakes and having the supervisor criticize them. Supervisors can also raise the issue of anxiety about change and how people frequently sabotage success by introducing the transtheoretical model. It then becomes an easy step to ask supervisees to identify what stage of change they are in when tackling some of the problems they are experiencing in supervision.

4. **Action:** This stage is perhaps the trickiest as it is easy to confuse action with actual change. Supervisees at this stage can say they really want to make changes and look very busy with a flurry of activity, but, in fact, nothing is really changing. Most of the investment in accomplishing goals is still with the supervisor, who is more worried than the supervisee about the problem

(continued)

and so works diligently to help supervisees by continually making numerous helpful suggestions. Checklists, regular reporting, rewards, and celebration of successes are all typical methods used with the action stage to help ensure true change is made.

5. **Maintenance:** For some this is the most difficult part of any change process. According to research by Prochaska et al. (1994), new behaviors must be repeated for a minimum of 6 months before the maintenance stage is achieved. This means that supervisees, in order to consolidate change, will have to work hard over a long period of time. Supervisors can assist them in this process by offering support and checking frequently to see if supervisees need a boost to maintain any new behaviors.

6. **Termination:** Termination represents the point at which a person really feels finished with a problem because there is no need to invest any effort to maintain the new behavior. The changes are integrated, and there is no danger of any return to old behaviors. In supervision, this stage may be represented several ways. First, the previous problem disappears completely and after 6 months or longer does not reappear. Second, supervisees are actively self-correcting any reappearance of a previous problem during supervision.

understand that the more specific the behavior change is and the more reasons the supervisee has to make the change, the more likely they are to be successful. Consequently, changing one's role from the *expert on* problems to the consultant *to problems* becomes the preeminent strategy.

Applying the transtheoretical model of change has other benefits in supervision. It can be very useful to engage supervisees in a discussion of the model in terms of their clients, asking them to identify what stage of changes they think a specific client is in. This can subsequently free supervisees to consider other ways to approach clients and client problems. Supervisors may at that point be able to recognize how to offer suggestions and ideas in a way that can be heard.

Contributing Factors to Relationship Difficulties

It is always challenging to identify all of the factors that may contribute to difficulties in the supervisory relationship and detract from the working alliance. Rapid Reference 8.9 lists a number of issues that can cause relationship difficulties.

Anxiety

Anxiety is one of the most often cited factors leading to problems in supervision. As the supervisory relationship is one of unequal power, issues of control, responses to authority (transference and countertransference), and anxiety concerning safety will be present in the relationship to some extent, regardless of circumstances. Situational factors, administrative attitudes, policies, and budgets all contribute to anxiety and difficulties in building the working alliance. Dual relationships, use of power and authority, and ambiguity concerning role are also major factors in generating anxiety. In situations where the clinical supervisor is also the administrative supervisor and the supervisee's job as well as professional development is involved, issues of trust and safety can be a major source of difficulties.

=== Rapid Reference 8.9

Contributing Factors to Relationship Problems

- Anxiety
- Transference and countertransference
- Differences in personality, style, or viewpoint
- Dual relationships
- Multicultural differences
- Environmental factors and organizational culture
- Stress, burnout, and compassion fatigue

Externalization of Control or Blame

Externalization of control or blame is a common issue with many clients at the beginning of counseling or therapy as they attempt to manage anxiety and the need to be safe. Be-

CAUTION

The more their jobs are on the line, the more supervisees will defend themselves and deny weaknesses.

ginning supervisees do the same. When challenged by a supervisor about what he or she is doing with a particular client, it may be easier for a supervisee to say, "The client wouldn't let me do that," or "There wasn't enough time," rather than say "I don't know what to do." In such situations, supervisors need to gently assist supervisees, just as they would clients, to move from externalized thinking about problems to a more internalized ownership of the issues.

Transference and Countertransference

Psychodynamic theory of transference and countertransference is also helpful in understanding and exploring relationship difficulties with supervisees. Even if one does not subscribe to the theory or feel comfortable with the terms, the idea that both supervisors and supervisees might respond to each other in the context of other relationship experiences with authority is generally understood. Such things as prior experiences in supervision, past problems with parents or teachers, and attitudes and beliefs about authority may all contribute to problems in supervision. Overly emotional responses to the supervisee's actions, serious dislike of a supervisee, and personality labeling can indicate the existence of countertransference in the supervisory relationship. Similarly, supervisees may experience a transference reaction to their supervisor's behavior or style. However, most supervisors outside of psychodynamic training models receive little training in how to address countertransference reactions to their supervisees (Campbell, 2001–2005; Ladany et al., 2000, anecdotal reports by workshop participants). Most indicate they handle such a situation by consulting with colleagues.

It is very important in order to prevent harm from such reactions that both supervisors and supervisees are educated as to normalcy of transference and countertransference reactions in supervision and prepared with ways to respond. The first suggestion is for supervisors as well as supervisees to continually engage in a process of self-exploration concerning their response to each other in supervision. Periodic consultation with other supervisors, videotaping supervision sessions, or even trading supervisees and supervisors helps to check perceptions and objectivity. Furthermore, both supervisors and supervisees are advised to consider engaging in personal psychotherapy to uncover any relationship triggers or hot spots in order to prevent injurious reactions in supervision and with clients.

Differences in Viewpoint

Differences in viewpoint can also contribute to relationship problems. Theoretical models form a lens through which to view the world. For example, many psychologists, psychiatrists, nurses, and clinical social workers use a medical model, whereas marriage and family therapists take a systems approach, and alcohol and drug abuse counselors subscribe to a support model. Differences may also exist in terms of a preferred model of counseling and psychotherapy, such as psychodynamic, cognitive-behavioral, or Gestalt.

Certainly, the supervisor's theoretical framework will influence how he or she responds to difficulties. For example, those who practice rational emotive therapy (RET) or cognitive therapy might want to pursue the subject of distorted or illogical thinking on the part of supervisees. Psychoanalytic therapists might rather look at transference, whereas family systems practitioners might concentrate on system factors. Thus, tension can exist between various practitioners over viewpoint, theoretical model, and suggested intervention strategies.

Differences in Needs and Goals

Differences in needs and goals can also contribute to difficulties. Resistance itself could be seen as a response to any number of factors. For example, clinical supervisors may believe that correct documentation, progress notes, and other paper work is absolutely essential and focus the lion's share of attention on that domain. Supervisees, especially beginners, although they may understand the importance of this area, may be more concerned about what to do in a crisis situation or how to handle an angry client. They also may be struggling with how to manage all of the demands and expectations of the work. Therefore, what is seen as resistance in supervision may merely be an expression of differences in needs and goals.

Differences in Personality

Personality and personal style also can contribute to misunderstandings and conflict. For example, placing supervisees who like autonomy and independence with supervisors who emphasize structure and engage in close monitoring will surely lead to struggles. Placing supervisees who express their feelings and wish to process them as part of supervision with supervisors who think such discussion is not relevant to supervision can also be problematic. A supervisor's saying, "I don't care what your feelings are; just go do it," communicates to supervisees a lack of support or caring. Please see Chapter 6 for an extended discussion of personal style in supervision.

Multicultural Differences

Another important area of concern is multicultural differences. Such differences are sometimes overlooked as a source of relationship problems in supervision. However, a growing body of literature indicates this is an important cause for misunderstandings. Some multicultural differences are easily identified (race, ethnicity, gender), whereas others are less obvious (age, education, model of practice). However, what is problematic for many new supervisors is how to approach the area of cultural differences in a safe and ethical manner. The easiest means to address differences is to begin to discuss them in the context of client cases. Supervisors might begin by asking supervisees what differences they can identify between themselves and clients. The discussion should easily evolve to how these recognized differences might affect their assumptions and viewpoint about clients, client problems, and intervention strategies. Questions such as "How might this client's being African American [older, physically challenged,

> # DON'T FORGET
>
> Supervision is a multicultural relationship. Multicultural differences both energize the relationship as well as contribute to misunderstandings.

and so forth] affect your intervention strategy, diagnosis, or treatment planning? If the person were … , how would that change things for you?" can stimulate a broadening of perspective on this important issue. As the supervision relationship develops, conversation could be initiated about differences between supervisors and supervisees and how these differences might have both a positive and negative effect on the supervisory relationship, especially in the development of trust.

Environmental Factors and Organizational Climate

Environmental factors can also play a sizeable role in supervision. In today's world of shrinking resources, issues of staffing, budget considerations, paperwork, and regulations are seemingly always factors in clinical supervision. Supervisees are being asked to see more clients with complex cases and potential danger before becoming fully trained, while at the same time, clinical supervisors do not have adequate time to monitor or train them. Another issue that is creating problems for some supervisors and supervisees are burgeoning numbers of state laws and regulations governing supervision. In much of the country, groups outside of an organization are mandating the structure and requirements for clinical supervision, and this situation is triggering frustration and even anger on everyone's part.

Organizational climate is another powerful factor that either supports or blocks the success of clinical supervision and strongly influences motivation and level of stress. Organizational climate, sometimes called organizational culture, refers to the explicit and implicit values, assumptions, and beliefs of an organization (Hawkins & Shohet, 2003; Towler, 1999). The role of organizational climate in supervision can best be seen in how much time, resources, and support are actually given to clinical supervisors. A large amount of time is spent in the health professions talking about ethical practice and how important it is to maintain high standards for client services. Yet resources and support for clinical supervision is often lacking. Supervision is commonly deemed as something only necessary for new and inexperienced practitioners. When budgets shrink and demand for services swell, the first budget item cut is training and supervision.

Another dynamic that can contribute to a negative climate in organizations is a strict focus on productivity and bottom-line numbers rather than on people and relationships. Rubin (2000) termed these *toxic environments,* where the culture

≡ *Rapid Reference 8.10*

How to Supervise in a Toxic Environment

- Have a firm grounding in ethical codes and standards for your discipline.
- Be clear with supervisees on ethical action with clients (even if not occurring in one's organization).
- Distribute the ethical codes and standards for supervisors from each discipline.
- Attend workshops on ethical practice and collect information to bolster ethical position.
- Join a consultation group for supervisors outside of your setting.
- Take risks. Speak up. Become an advocate for ethical practice.
- Try denial.
- Polish up your resume and find another situation.

is one of blame, punishment, and scapegoating. Clinical supervision in such a world takes on a crisis function that is designed to put out fires, not a teaching, training, and mentoring one. If things are not going well, there is a person at fault. No wonder experienced practitioners in this atmosphere see supervision as punishment, not an opportunity to grow, and new supervisees learn quickly to distrust supervisors and keep problems to themselves. As a result, environmental factors and organizational climate can contribute to high levels of stress and burnout and lead to relationship difficulties, discouragement and poor motivation. Rapid Reference 8.10 recommends a series of activities for supervisors in toxic environments.

Stress, Burnout, and Compassion Fatigue

Stress, burnout, and compassion fatigue can also be significant factors in how supervision progresses. As supervisees, especially those who are inexperienced, attempt to manage the workload and productivity requirements along with the needs of their clients, they can experience high stress, and if supervisors do not spend sufficient time assisting them with learning how to cope with the demands of the job, a number of relationship difficulties can occur. For example, when overstressed, supervisees may act irritably toward clients and other staff members, or they can be apathetic or very short in response to requests from supervisors. Others may become ill or act out their feelings by absenteeism and lateness with paperwork. Understanding the presence of stress, burnout, and compassion fatigue with various problems in the supervisory relationship can go a long way in helping clinical supervisors respond effectively. A full section on this topic can be found in Chapter 9.

Strategies for Working Through Relationship Difficulties

After engaging in self-exploration and reviewing possible areas of misunderstanding and conflict, the next step is to decide on a strategy to resolve difficulties. In most instances, as any trained mental health professional knows, the best suggestion for resolving difficulties is to engage in an open dialogue with the supervisee about any difficulties. While this recommendation sounds like common sense, sometimes supervisors forget their training and simply react to situations, which usually is a poor tactic. Stress can certainly contribute to this type of ineffective problem solving.

A better strategy is for supervisors to think about what the goal is for the discussion and how they want to approach that particular supervisee before sitting down with him or her. Simply asking, "What is my goal with this person? How would I like the relationship to be with this supervisee?" can get the ball rolling. Another technique is to put oneself in the supervisee's shoes through role reversal, which can be extremely illuminating. Other techniques to try are the use of miracle questions or imagining a successful solution to the problem.

Rapid Reference 8.11 suggests steps to take when approaching problems in the relationship with supervisees.

Self-disclosure and *empathic responding,* along with other rapport-building skills such as *open-ended questions* and *summarizing,* are all great tools to help resolve relationship difficulties. Starting the supervision session with an empathic statement demonstrates caring and understanding of the supervisees' world and opens the door so supervisees hear what the supervisor has to say. Process comments, or what Teyber (1997) termed *self-involving statements,* express the supervisor's here-and-now reactions to what a supervisee has just said or done in a session. This type of remark also provides a means to bring relationship issues to the foreground in supervision. A list of a few of these relationship skills with examples follows in Rapid Reference 8.12. Those new to supervision will quickly realize that many of these skills are identical to those used with clients.

A number of techniques may be employed with specific types of relationship difficulties. For example, *solution-focused questions* offer supervisors a good resource to work with both highly dependent and seemingly

DON'T FORGET

Always begin any problem-solving session with supervisees from an empathic position of caring and understanding, rather than one of anger or blame.

≡≡*Rapid Reference 8.11*

How to Resolve Relationship Problems in Supervision

Please note that it is strongly suggested to consult with a colleague to check out your viewpoint on the problem with a supervisee and practice through role-play what you want to do or say before the meeting, particularly if the situation is difficult.

1. Take responsibility for solving problems.
2. Rate your relationship with your supervisee on a scale of 1 to 10 (1 is the pits, and 10 is glorious).
3. Check into your thoughts and feelings in response to the situation.
   • "How is this person a problem for me? What are they doing or saying that pushes my buttons?" Get some specific examples of behavior. Pay attention to how much is behavioral observation and how much is your explanation or interpretation of the behavior.
   • Check to see if these specific examples represent potential harm to clients, or is this a person who is just difficult for you to work with?
4. Determine contributing factors to relationship problems.
   • "How might this behavior be a cry for help or a message for you to change your style?"
   • "What about anxiety and safety? Do I have multiple relationships with my supervisee that need to be addressed?"
   • "What about evaluation? How important is my evaluation to this supervisee?"
   • "Is supervision required, and is there no choice as to supervisor?"
   • "Do I come across as mostly critical? Are most of our sessions focused on what this supervisee does wrong and not much attention to what is going well?"
   • "How about conflicting theoretical models or viewpoint on working with clients? Are we from different disciplines?"
   • "What about multicultural differences? Can that be a factor?"
   • "Could we have differences in our goals for supervision and in our work with clients?"
   • "How might the work environment be affecting our relationship? Are there factors outside that could be contributing to tension?"
   • "Is this problem I am having with my supervisee a symptom of burnout or compassion fatigue?"
5. List all of the things you have tried so far to solve the relationship difficulty. Did anything work partially or for a brief time?
6. Then ask yourself, "What is my goal with this person? How would I like the relationship to be?"
7. Ask the miracle question: "If I went to bed tonight and a miracle occurred, when I wake up tomorrow, what will be different in this relationship?"

(continued)

8. Now do a role reversal and see if you can become the person in mind. How might they see the problems with you? What might be their miracle?

9. Imagine you could sit down with this person and say anything, what would you want to say?

10. Review your answers to these questions and ask yourself what you would like to have happen as a result of talking with your supervisee and what you will need to say and do to get that result.

11. Arrange a time to meet and talk with your supervisee. Meet in a neutral setting or pull your chair away from the desk and talk to the person without barriers. Stop all interruptions for the duration of the meeting. Give the supervisee your full attention.

12. Make the relationship the agent of change. Focus on creating a climate of caring and concern.

13. Talk directly to the person about the relationship problems.

14. Be emphatic and share desire to have a better relationship. Take a position as a consultant to the supervisee, rather than one of authority.

15. Keep feedback and discussion focused on behaviors, not personality.

16. Talk about strengths and positives, not just problems.

17. Be respectful. Ask for the supervisee's point of view on difficulties, and be open to hearing the response. Use open-ended questions to solicit feedback.

18. Remind supervisees that the bottom line in resolving any relationship difficulty with you is the welfare of clients as there is a tendency for problems in supervision to spill over onto client care.

19. If talking doesn't help, try out different techniques such as role-play, role reversal, or videotape to increase understanding and improve the relationship.

20. Document the session.

21. If emotions run high and nothing positive seems to be occurring, end the session and set up another time to try again. Recommend someone else be involved in the next meeting in a consultant role. Set some ground rules.

22. When problems continue with the supervisee and your problem solving strategies do not seem to be successful, seek help from others. Consult with other supervisors and your administrator about the problem. If possible, consider referring this supervisee to another supervisor who may be able to build a better relationship.

resistant supervisees. The solution-focused brief therapy model is built on the premise that clients already have the answers to their problems. This also applies to supervisees. Whether the supervisee is dependent on the supervisor or, conversely, is resistant to the supervisor's suggestions, the solution-focused model suggests supervisors change tactics. Instead of supervisors jumping in with their own ideas about how to solve the supervisee's problem, supervisors may ask instead, "What have you thought about doing?" or "What have you tried so far?"

≡Rapid Reference 8.12

Skills for Addressing Relationship Difficulties

Creating an internal, or "I," focus (Teyber, 1997): Process comments are used to help the supervisee move from complaining about others and wanting others to change, to looking at him- or herself. For example:

"What are you feeling right now as you are saying that?"

"When the client said that, what did you really want to do or say?"

"What is it like for you when clients act that way?"

Exploring meaning (Ivey & Ivey, 1999): These questions are designed to explore the inner thoughts, beliefs, values, and motivations behind the supervisee's behavior.

"What does it mean to you to be ...?"

"As you look at this situation, what thoughts or beliefs underlie your actions?"

"When the client said ..., how did you interpret that?"

"What personal values do you think are important to the client?"

"Why ask that particular question of your client?"

Moving from the general to the specific: If supervisees use generalizations when discussing clients, supervisors need to challenge them to be more specific.

Supervisee's statement: "You can't really help these people."

Supervisor's response: "You mean you are having trouble helping this specific client?"

Getting to the point: When supervisees flounder in details and have trouble getting around to what they actually need, supervisors may ask:

"What do you need from me right now?"

Summarizing: Periodically interrupting supervision to summarize one's understanding communicates interest and improves the flow of conversation. For example, "Let me see if I understand you?" or "What you mean is ...?" or "Before you go on, let me see if I am following you."

Open-ended questions: Asking supervisees *who, what, where, when,* and *how* questions rather than *why* questions will facilitate better discussion and understanding between supervisor and supervisee. For example, "Please share with me what happened ..." or "Where were you trying to go with the client?" or "How was it that you asked or did that?" or "When did you try to ...?"

Warm questioning: Asking supervisees why they did something often appears accusatory. Instead of saying, "Why did you do that?" or "I think you

(continued)

really screwed up here," use a more kindly approach. For example, "Help me out; I am not sure I understand your thinking." or "I am wondering . . ." or "I'm intrigued; what did the client say or do that led you to that conclusion?" or "I'm not sure I am following you. Can you tell me exactly what you said and did?"

Self-involving statements (Teyber, 1997): Self-involving statements, which are sometimes called *process comments*, represent supervisors sharing here-and-now responses to whatever is happening in the moment in a supervision session. The purpose is to improve relationships. For example, "I fell really stuck now in how to help you." or "I don't seem to be able to give you corrective feedback or suggestions without wounding you." or "How can I share my comments or suggestions without taking away your feeling of competency? Can you give me some specific suggestions?"

Paradoxical interventions also offer supervisors a means to change relationship dynamics. Paradoxical interventions were originally created to help therapists interrupt clients' entrenched patterns of responding to situations, particularly with defensive or oppositional behavior (Fisch, Weakland, & Segal, 1982; Haley, 1976). These techniques, although they appear too complex or manipulative to some clinicians, carry an important message for supervisors about changing relationships; pay attention to the relationship process, and if something isn't working, try out the opposite behavior.

Sometimes applying paradoxical interventions can also change the quality of a supervisory relationship in unexpected but profound ways. For example, a suggested paradoxical intervention technique to use with defensive supervisees is to start supervision by saying "I know you have the best interests of the client in mind. I know you care deeply what happens to them. So, my suggestion is that you try . . ." While this statement is considered paradoxical as it sets up the supervisee to agree with the supervisor's suggestions or else be seen as uncaring, this same statement is extremely affirming of the supervisee's motivation. Often in this situation, the supervisee hears the compliment and responds to that rather than the paradoxical statement. "I'm astonished. I didn't think you had any positive thoughts about my work and me. Most of our interactions are so critical. I do care deeply and want to do the best job I can and am glad you finally recognized that fact. Thanks." The vital message here is that by trying out new behaviors, supervisors can change relationship dynamics with supervisees.

Working with Anxious or Perfectionist Supervisees

A large number of supervisees, especially those at the doctoral level, bring into supervision weighty personal demands to be successful and do things right.

Certainly these qualities and attributes have much to recommend them. After all, to get into graduate school and finish a degree requires high achievement and serious effort. However, occasionally, the demand to achieve translates into perfectionism and feeds a supervisee's anxiety so much so that it interferes with learning. This can be particularly true in the early stage of development. Hence, supervisors have to be accepting of the normalcy of perfectionism in relatively inexperienced supervisees and have a number of possible strategies ready to reduce its impact in supervision.

Exaggeration is one suggestion to try with perfectionists as it points out the absurdity of trying to be perfect. For example, rephrasing supervisee statements using percentages or grades captures the essence of the anxiety. "You want an A with this client." Or "You want to be one hundred percent successful." If done with some lightness and humor, supervisees are given permission to talk about their worries in a nonjudgmental way.

Reframing is another technique to assist supervisees, especially those who are self-critical, to view situations from a different perspective. "I hear you focusing on what didn't go well with this client, but I am curious about what did go well?" or "Even though you have only talked about what you did wrong, I see a lot of success with this client such as . . ."

Another idea to use with supervisees who get overwhelmed by internal demands to be perfect is to ask them to take small steps for change. Thus, when supervisees sound stuck and overwhelmed, ask, "What is one thing you could do differently with this client?"

Approaching the problem of perfectionism and accompanying high anxiety from the angle of paradoxical interventions brings several techniques to mind: (1) suggesting the supervisee do more of the thing that is causing problems ("I don't think you are really trying hard enough to help that client; you need to do more of . . ."); (2) agreeing with the supervisee that the problem is to big to be solved ("I agree, the situation is impossible. I'm not sure how you are going to solve it"; or (3) encourage risk-taking by indicating that the supervisee is probably not ready to attempt new things ("You are probably not ready to try this . . .").

Working with Defensive and Resistant Supervisees

In instances where supervisees respond defensively, rejecting directions or suggestions, supervisors should ponder possible sources of such behavior. Rather than seeing resistance as a personality trait, the relationship model suggests resistance and defensiveness can indicate a problem in the way supervisors are

DON'T FORGET

Most experts say that the best way to defuse conflicts and reduce defensiveness or resistance is to agree.

relating to their supervisees. Many times supervisors sound critical and judgmental, or they focus supervision on what supervisees are doing wrong, rather than what they are doing right, which implies supervisees are incompetent or stupid. Time and again, supervisors can solve relationship difficulties by simply changing their approach so that supervisees will hear them better.

To resolve problems with resistance or defensiveness on the part of supervisees, supervisors need to begin by looking at their own behavior in supervision, which is obviously not an easy task. Supervisors have to ask themselves some hard questions, "Do I come across as dogmatic, closed, intolerant, or critical? As a result, is the supervisee's response to my behavior exceedingly realistic? Or is my supervisee's resistance an expression of a difference between us in needs or goals? Do I focus most of supervision on issues and topics that are important to me but not of primary concern to my supervisees, and, therefore, they respond as they do?" Certainly any time supervisors are struggling with supervisees, seeking out a trusted colleague for some honest feedback is always a good idea.

After some period of self-exploration, the next task for supervisors is to explore others ways of relating to supervisees. Perhaps the easiest means to change relationship dynamics when faced with supervisees who seem to be closed and defensive is the paradoxical technique of *going with* or *honoring the resistance* (Haley, 1976; Minuchin, 1987; Teyber, 1997). Going with the resistance means that supervisors stop trying to push and exhort supervisees to do certain things and instead pull back and agree with the supervisee's position. "I agree; you are right; my idea probably won't work. I see I can't help you with this client." Another suggestion is to use more *tentative language*. "I don't know if this will help or not." Or "Here is an idea to try. It might be helpful, maybe not, so you can use it if you want." *Acting confused,* or the *Colombo technique,* can also be disarming. "I'm somewhat confused here, are you telling me . . ." or "Help me out; I am a little bit confused. Is there something I am missing here?"

David Burns (1989) suggests that if someone attacks or criticizes, it is best to agree with them. For example, when a supervisee disagrees with a suggestion, a supervisor might respond, "Glad you let me know you don't agree. Tell me more about your thoughts." In other situations, saying, "I am glad you pointed that out. I hadn't looked at it that way" can change relationship dynamics. Another suggestion that may be helpful with chronic complainers or criticizers is to inquire, "I hear a lot about what is wrong with the way I do things, so I wonder, what do you think is going right? Anything?"

Storytelling also is another approach to take as it tends to depersonalize feedback. Stories can be drawn from the supervisor's own experiences but retold as if they are about someone else. Sometimes parables, Sufi tales, or myths could also be used to talk about differences in a relatively safe way. Storytelling can be particularly effective with supervisees who have a rigid model for their work with clients and, as a result, are resistant to any of the supervisor's suggestions that entail a different approach. Applying parallel process thinking, supervisors can hypothesize this same supervisee has the same difficulty hearing clients' thoughts and feelings. In this situation, the supervisor could say to the supervisee, "I hear you are having a problem getting Mr. Smith to follow your recommendations. This is a problem many case managers face. I heard about a case similar to that in a workshop I went to recently. Let me tell you what happened with that client and see what you think about it."

Another idea along similar lines is to remove oneself from the discussion by calling in a consultant or a *phantom supervisor* (Campbell, 2001–2005). "I don't know if this will help, but when I had a similar situation with a client, my supervisor suggested I try...." Or "One thing my supervisor did with me that I found useful was . . . I am not sure if it will help you, but I thought I would share it; see what you think." Just be careful to keep self-disclosure to a minimum; use short examples in order to avoid turning the supervision session into an autobiographical lecture about the supervisor's own supervision experience.

Another powerful proposal that may be borrowed from family systems to use with supervisees who have a standard negative response to anything the supervisor says is to *preempt the objection.* Applying this technique, the supervisor would begin feedback or suggestions with an opening statement that employs the supervisee's characteristic negative responses to whatever the supervisor says, thus preempting it. For example, "I know you are going to disagree with this suggestion, so tell me why it won't work." Or "If you've been unhappy about my feedback before, just wait, you *really* are not going to like what I am going to say now."

Finally, consider using *humor* to defuse uncomfortable situations. Laughing at oneself and one's situation can be disarming and change the affective climate. "I can't believe we are spending all our time bickering. We sound like an old married couple. Maybe we should just take time out and laugh at ourselves and then figure out a better way to get along." Others may use quips and off-the-cuff remarks such as "Since I am never wrong, I just can't imagine what your problem

> ### CAUTION
> ....
> Check with the supervisee to see if they hear the response as humorous and not critical.

is with taking my suggestions." Metaphors and stories can also add a humorous touch.

Defusing Anger

In certain instances, such as when new regulations or supervision requirements are being instituted, supervisees can feel frustrated, helpless, and out of control, which then leads to angry outbursts in supervision. While not pleasant for supervisors, many times expressing anger can lead to improved relationships (Lerner, 1997). Searching for a way to defuse anger and calm the waters without shutting off conversation on a touchy topic is always the optimum choice. In such a situation, the best strategy is for supervisors to show empathy and understanding of the supervisee's feelings. By doing so, supervisors are not necessarily agreeing with what the person is saying but showing they hear the supervisee's feelings and have some understanding of his or her perspective. "I see you are very frustrated by this new regulation, and I can certainly understand why this is so upsetting to you. It seems as if someone is saying we are not adult enough to do this on our own. That's how I am experiencing this, too. As if we don't have enough to do already."

Working with Ambivalence

Many times what supervisors call resistance in a supervisee is actually the expression of ambivalence: Part of the supervisee wants to change, and part of the supervisee has various worries and concerns about that change. Ambivalence about change is normal in everyone (Prochaska, Norcross, & DiClemente, 1994). Many times it is easier to talk about goals than to actually strive for them because of worries about failure or, conversely, success. For example, one common concern for supervisees is whether they have the capabilities to actually accomplish the identified supervision goals. Supervisees may be asking themselves, "What will happen if I strive toward these goals and fail? What if my best effort is not good enough for my supervisor? What does that say about me as a person?"

Therefore, understanding how a supervisee's behavior may be an expression of his or her ambivalence about change can lead supervisors to more effective interventions. One obvious strategy is for supervisors to remove themselves from the supervisees' struggles to successfully complete identified goals. Such a strategy requires a shift in the supervisor from trying to push and persuade supervisees to change to becoming a consultant or coach to their efforts to change, to learn, and to grow. In other words, "You can lead a horse to water, but you can't make it drink" is the best advice experienced supervisors can give to those new to the role.

A first-rate metaphor to help supervisors understand the notion of ambivalence is that of a baton that on one end has all of the positive reasons to make a change and on the other end all of the negative reasons (Coleman, 2001). If the supervisor grabs hold of the positive end of the baton, the only place left for the supervisee to grab hold of is the negative end. Supervisors grab the positive end of the baton by listing all the reasons supervisees need to change or by trying to help the supervisee with suggestions ("Why don't you try this?") or inquiries such as "What can we change in your environment to make it easier to for you to do your paperwork?" However, if the supervisor goes toward the negative end of the baton instead and begins to question the supervisee's motivation or suggests reasons not to change, the supervisee metaphorically has to grab the positive end of the baton.

Putting It Into Practice

Working with Ambivalence

Sam, a clinical supervisor was working with Grace, a doctoral-level intern. Grace was having trouble meeting all of the demands of the work setting. She was coming late to appointments, and her progress notes for her clients were weeks behind. Sam met with Grace to discuss the troubles. Grace insisted in the meeting that she understood how important it was for her to be on time for her appointments with clients and get the paperwork finished. She agreed to change her behavior and work harder at the internship. However, after several weeks went by, Sam noticed that although Grace did better at first, she was back to her old behavior. In fact, she was, if anything, more behind, coming later and later to the center, and had none of her files complete.

Sam again met with Grace and said "Grace, we talked about some serious changes you needed to make in your behavior here at the center, to see clients on time and get all of the progress notes up to date for each one of them. You agreed to make changes in these two areas as it was important to you. In spite of this commitment, nothing is really different now. I saw some effort in the first week to be timely, but at this point, we are back to where we started and, if anything, further behind. So have you ever really considered the fact that you don't really want to be here now?"

To this statement Grace responded strongly that she did want the internship. It did matter to her. Sam, being an expert on ambivalence, followed this declaration by observing, "Part of you may think it is important to be here, but there is another part of you that doesn't." Grace looked tearful and then said to Sam, "I guess you are right. In order to graduate next May I need to do my intern-

(continued)

ship this semester. At the same time, I also have to get my dissertation proposal completed this semester so I can begin my research. I am having a lot of trouble with my proposal. It just isn't coming along very well. I am so worried; it takes me forever to go to sleep, and that leads me to oversleep in the morning. That's why I am always late getting here and late with my progress notes. Every time I sit down to do my notes, I start thinking about my dissertation. I guess I am running in circles now and not doing anything right."

In response to this honesty, Sam expressed his concern for her. "Well, I appreciate your sharing your situation with me. I have a better understanding of the problem. I struggled in the same way when I was in graduate school, trying to do everything at once and not only to do everything, but also to do everything well. So I resonate with your problem of feeling like you are running around in circles. Any idea about how you might get out of the circle and get on a straight line toward your expressed goals?"

Teaching Point: Sam as clinical supervisor realized the need to change his approach to helping his supervisee, Grace. Rather than interpreting Grace's behavior as resistance to supervision or lack of motivation, he used his skills to uncover the root of her lateness with appointments and paperwork. Sam's knowledge of the central role that ambivalence about change can play in any problem solution was central to his intervention strategy.

Working with Apathetic and Uninvolved Supervisees

Another group of problematic responses to supervision that sometimes gets overlooked are from those supervisees who appear disinterested or uninvolved. Apathy and lack of interest in supervision can represent a host of problems, such as discouragement, anger, burnout, anxiety, and even confusion. For example, sometimes what is seen as indifference on the part of supervisees is in fact their inability to grasp or understand what the supervisor is asking. Consequently, along with exploring the roots and causes for apathy, supervisors will need a full toolbox of ideas to try out in such circumstances. Rapid Reference 8.13 furnishes a number of helpful suggestions.

Nevertheless, the best approach to use with supervisees who seem disinterested in supervision is to be direct. This type of strategy will be more successful if made from a position of genuine caring and concern. "I have noticed that you appear disinterested in supervision. When we meet to talk about cases, you tell me everything is fine; you have nothing to talk about. I am not sure if I understand all that is going on here, but I am concerned. We need to talk about what is happening between us because whether you like it, we have to develop some sort of supervisory relationship. It is required. Is there something I need to know? Something that needs to change?"

Rapid Reference 8.13

Working with Apathetic, Uninvolved, or Burned Out Supervisees

Refocusing: "Even though you are telling me that everything is fine with all of your clients and there are no problems, is there any client you wish you did have a better relationship with?"

Changing the question: "Perhaps my question is too general. Let me say it this way; I am curious why you say everything is okay with all your clients. Can you get more specific? Can you give me an example of one thing one of your clients did or said that led you to the conclusion that everything is fine?"

Acting confused: "Not sure I understand what you mean by everything is okay. You mean everyone of your clients is one hundred percent happy and satisfied?"

Honoring the resistance: "Perhaps there is nothing we can do to improve things here between us in supervision; the situation is hopeless."

Changing the session focus: "I am so delighted everything is going so well with all of your clients, and you don't need any supervision. I wish I could say the same for myself. Perhaps you would be willing to share how you do that?" Or "Could you share with me one or two things you are doing with your clients that are so successful? I would love to learn from you."

Suggesting a new role: "Since everything seems to be sailing along okay, and you don't need supervision anymore, I would love for you to share some of your wisdom with our new counselors. I know that Susie, particularly, could use some real mentoring. Also, would you be willing to come to our next supervision group and talk about boundary setting with clients? That is a topic they all are struggling with at the moment, and I know you have good ideas on that subject."

Using Videotape to Improve Supervisory Relationships

Overall, the optimum method to assist supervisors who wish to improve their relationships with supervisees is to videotape a supervision session. A myriad of possibilities exist for its use. (See Chapter 5 for a detailed explanation of how to use taping in supervision.) First, supervisors could review the tape of the supervision session and make observations about their style, nonverbal behavior, number of critical remarks, interruptions, and demonstration of caring and concern. Second, with the supervisee's permission, another supervisor could be asked to view the tape and give suggestions. However, the third and best suggestion is to sit down with that supervisee and use IPR to

CAUTION

Use videotape early in the supervisory relationship before problems get out of hand.

review the tape. Watching the tape together and then stopping and processing what occurred presents numerous opportunities for supervisors and supervisees to examine and change their behavior. (See Chapter 4 for more in IPR.)

Referral of Supervisees to Outside Help

With planning, skill, and time, most supervision problems can be resolved. The supervisory relationship might not be going smoothly at all times, but clients are receiving adequate care and supervisees are making adequate progress on supervision goals. However, in some instances, problems with supervisees can extend beyond the parameters of supervision, and the solution requires outside intervention. It could be that the supervisee's way of coping in the world or the existence of personal history may interfere with clinical supervision and be of real concern because of potential harm to clients. A lack of skill or competence could also be an issue; no matter what is tried, no improvement is made, and it puts clients at risk. If the supervisor's attempts to be helpful in solving these problems are met with continuing resistance to help, or there is an inability to make the changes necessary to improve service, the situation requires a more radical solution.

One common tactic for helping supervisees who lack basic skills and knowledge is to have them add some kind of coursework. However, when the problem with a supervisee has more to do with the impact on clients of the supervisee's personal history, attitudes, beliefs, or way of coping with stress and anxiety, then the standard suggestion is for him or her to participate in some type of outside

---

CAUTION

Supervisors need to be able to distinguish between a supervisee's poor service quality (need to develop skills and performance) and real harm to clients. Real harm includes the following:
- Refusing to help and withholding service and support from clients
- Belittling, harassing, attacking, and manipulating clients for one's own benefit
- Abandoning clients
- Breaking confidentiality
- Engaging in fraud
- Promoting boundary crossings (sexual relationships, going into business, etc.)
- Using inappropriate diagnosis or intervention strategy
- Failing to recognize a need for referral
- Withholding information from the supervisor, particularly in crisis situations

activity, such as counseling, therapy, participation in a support group, or referral to an EAP (Employee Assistance Program). If the supervisee's impairment is severe due to issues such as substance abuse, severe illness, or some type of family crisis that will take considerable time away from work, the supervisor may need to insist that the supervisee take a leave from his or her professional duties until the situation is rectified.

When made, the suggestion to seek outside help should not come as a surprise to the supervisee. From the beginning of supervision, starting with the informed consent agreement and orientation to clinical supervision, the topic of personal

> **CAUTION**
>
> The need to seek therapy or counseling to clear up family-of-origin issues that affect the supervisee's judgment and objectivity is even more essential for those who are delivering counseling or psychotherapy services because of the particular seriousness of harm to their clients.

> **CAUTION**
>
> Be sure to establish guidelines for resolving difficulties at the beginning of supervision. Spell out expectations in the informed consent agreement or contract. Don't wait until problems develop to decide on a plan.

self-awareness and the need for competence as essential components of ethical practice, along with the supervisees responsibility to ensure no harm comes to clients at their expense, should have been extensively covered. Additionally, supervisees should have been receiving ongoing feedback from the supervisor as to their progress or lack thereof.

How the suggestion is made for a supervisee to seek outside help for problems can make a difference in the response. Being empathic and demonstrating caring and concern usually works better than personal attack. The supervisor's tone of voice and posture are a significant part of what will be communicated. Therefore, supervisors need to arrange a private meeting time and be sure they, themselves, are in a good place to calmly discuss with the supervisee what to do next. It is also advised that supervisors think through what they really want to say before starting this type of feedback session. Arranging consultation with a colleague to work out the details and to practice using role-play is also a smart idea. Another proposal is to place the suggestion for counseling or therapy or more course work into the context of long-term professional development.

Furthermore, in order to avoid problems with various laws and regulations, how the suggestion to seek outside help is made will be significant. It is best if the solution to any problem comes from the supervisee, not the supervisor. In other words, asking supervisees for their ideas on a solution to a problem or offering

Putting It Into Practice

Broaching the Subject of Psychotherapy with Supervisees

Supervisor: "I understand that what I am going to say could be misconstrued by you, but I hope you take it in the positive way it is meant. I see you have both the aptitude and the motivation that will make you a wonderful therapist. At this point in your career, you have invested an enormous amount of time and money to get where you are. However, we have been talking for several months now about your difficulties in handling corrective feedback from me and from others on our team. Even though I see some change in your openness, I still have lingering concerns mostly because, bottom line, my assessment is that this same difficulty affects your therapeutic alliance with clients. If they do not agree with your suggestions, you pull back, and by your voice and facial expression, you look so hurt that the client then begins to take care of you."

"I know we have talked about this problem and have tried various things, but at this point, I don't think we have made much progress. As we have discussed before, and as our ethical codes reiterate, you have to do something about this because it is negatively impacting your clients. My personal answer, if I were in your place, would be to seek out some good therapy. In fact, when I was just starting out, I did just that because I, too, had some family history to clear up. I still go sometimes, even at this point in my career, if I feel I need a booster. I want to share that I found going to counseling had a secondary benefit for me. I learned quickly by being a client what to do and what not to do as a therapist. Anyway, that would be my solution to your problem, but I am not you. What are your thoughts on this? What do you think you need to do at this point?"

a series of suggestions from which they can select is better than the supervisor blurting out, "You need therapy!" For example, if a supervisee becomes ill with cancer and has to miss extensive amounts of work due to treatment, it is ethically mandated that the supervisor discuss openly with this supervisee the plans for what to do with his or her clients. Asking the supervisee to suggest ideas and solutions to this problem rather than jumping in immediately with proper procedures will go far to insure the supervisee feels supported at a difficult time and will take responsibility to do the right thing.

TERMINATION OF SUPERVISEES FROM SUPERVISION

Hopefully, as difficulties with a supervisee develop, the supervisor has made sure the supervisee understands exactly what the problems are, and he or she has been given ample time and support to make whatever changes are necessary. As part of this process, the supervisor should have tried different strategies to help the supervisee change behavior, such as reviewing a tape of a client session or seeking consultation from other clinical supervisors to garner new ideas. Even changing supervisors could bring resolution and so should be considered. However, other times, no matter what is attempted, the clinical supervisor is not successful. Maybe the supervisee refuses to follow through on suggestions, or the various interventions don't bring the hoped for benefit. Sometimes nothing works; the behavior is entrenched. At this point, even if supervisees are upset and threaten to sue, supervisors need to take on their gatekeeping role as protector of the health and welfare of the clients, their profession, and their community.

The most important part of this discussion is that the supervisor begins to seek consultation and guidance on how to proceed early on in the situation and is actively engaged in trying to help the supervisee change. If this particular supervisee is a graduate intern, the internship director should be informed and consulted on appropriate action. If the supervisee is seeking licensure, the ethical codes and standards are utilized for guidance. With an employee, the supervisor should be in contact with his or her administrator early on in the situation and be following correct procedures. Assuredly, whether the supervisee is an employee, graduate student, or someone seeking licensure, there will be legal issues for supervisors to consider as well. See Chapter 2 for a discussion of the ethical and legal issues involved in terminating a supervisee from supervision.

It is also very important how the problems with the supervisee are defined. It is much easier to terminate supervision or counsel a supervisee out of the field when clear ethical or legal mistakes have occurred than in instances where supervisors are concerned about the person's character or fitness for the profession.

The problem many supervisors face in this type of situation is the lack of any formalized gatekeeping procedures and established standards that adequately describe what personal and professional competence is so they can objectively evaluate their supervisees' ability to practice effectively and feel comfortable with their decision to terminate a supervisee if it is necessary (Kerl, Garcia, McCullough, & Maxwell, 2002). Lack of any such standards and procedures in an organization leaves many supervisors feeling vulnerable to lawsuits and, therefore, unwilling to take the necessary steps. What is required in all circumstances is (1) a clear definition

> ## CAUTION
>
> Before terminating supervision, it is important that supervisors have made their best attempts to resolve relationship problems with the supervisee, discussed with the supervisees specific behaviors that need to be changed, tried a number of different strategies to help the supervisee solve problems, given the supervisee opportunity to make changes, sought consultation, involved others, and documented what was done.

of the acceptable personal and professional behaviors necessary to meet ethical guidelines for each profession and (2) supervisees be fully informed of these standards prior to beginning supervision. Rapid Reference 8.14 goes through the recommended steps for clinical supervisors to follow when faced with a negative evaluation of a supervisee.

Another problem for supervisors in situations that involve problematic supervisees is determining what is a realistic amount of time and effort to expend. When has the supervisor done everything possible? What does that look like? What are the standards? These are tricky question as there are really no set answers. Exactly how much time and effort is enough is still very subjective, and it may vary from situation to situation. One popular standard is to try for 6 months to bring changes, the same as with many probationary terms for employment, before referring on the supervisee.

As a result of the lack of clear standards on what represents an intractable problem, many clinical supervisors have difficulty recognizing the point at which they

≡ Rapid Reference 8.14

Steps for Handling a Negative Evaluation of a Supervisee

In situations with graduate interns or those seeking licensure when a negative final evaluation of a supervisee is probable, it is imperative that supervisors do the following:

1. From the beginning, make sure the criteria for success has been clearly defined for the supervisee and given to him or her in writing.
2. Give frequent evaluative feedback to the supervisee about problems and concerns, using behavioral examples that match stated goals and criteria for success. Include a number of suggestions for improvement.
3. Apply a variety of different methods and techniques to help the supervisee succeed and to serve as a basis for evaluation. Never rely solely on subjective opinion that is formed exclusively from case consultation and the supervisee's verbal self-report.
4. Seek consultation to explore other strategies that could be tried, and apply them to supervision with this supervisee.
5. Apprise the graduate intern program or licensure board of the situation.
6. Talk to the supervisee about the probable negative outcome early on in supervision. (Don't wait until the end of supervision to notify supervisees of your decision.)
7. Document what steps were taken to correct the situation.
8. Be prepared for unhappiness on the part of the supervisee.

have really done all they can to try to resolve problems and how to let go of a supervisee without feeling like a failure. It is usually difficult and painful for clinical supervisors, who take their role seriously and want to do the best job possible, to give up on a supervisee and terminate supervision. After all, they think maybe something else could have been done to salvage the situation. This is especially true for those in the helping professions. And, of course, the fear of lawsuits and letters to the licensing board can also prevent supervisors from acting.

There are some recommended strategies to help clinical supervisors keep perspective and avoid a loss of confidence when faced with terminating a supervisee. First and foremost is for supervisors to seek consultation and support from others before, during, and after the development of difficulties. All clinical supervisors need a support network and a safe place to discuss their problems with supervisees. No matter how busy a supervisor is, regular consultation with other supervisors should be a part of any supervision plan. However, it is absolutely vital for supervisors, when faced with such a stressful circumstance as the likely termination of a supervisee from supervision, to take time for this activity. Support could be sought from another clinical supervisor, an administrator, a peer supervision group, or all three. If guilt or nagging thoughts of failure continue, clinical supervisors should follow the same advice they give supervisees and seek personal counseling or therapy. Not only is this good practice, it is also good modeling.

Putting It Into Practice

Case Example

Mary was a psychologist who had been successfully supervising postdegree doctoral interns for state licensure in her private practice. Mary had sought training in clinical supervision and felt after many years in the role that she was very competent to supervise. In previous years, this had been an excellent arrangement not only because her practice was growing and she needed help but also because she really enjoyed mentoring a new professional in her community. Most of her postdegree interns came highly recommended from the local university, so she felt comfortable with their training and references. However, this year's intern was a different story. From the beginning, Mary began to have questions about the intern's behavior with clients. She noticed he was having difficulty keeping clients, and he tended to give all of his clients the same diagnosis and treatment plan. When she questioned his assessment and diagnosis of a client's problems or tried to give feedback to him about what he was doing with his clients, he became defensive and argumentative, frequently telling her that his internship supervisor at his previous site told him to do it this way, so she

(continued)

was wrong and he was right. Using all of her skills, Mary attempted to build a better working relationship to no avail. Worrying about the situation, she called the university internship program director for advice. This professor indicated surprise at Mary's problems with this particular supervisee, stating that he had done exceedingly well in school, and everyone thought he was an outstanding candidate for licensure. His previous internship supervisors gave him high recommendations. This conversation left Mary feeling confused about her judgment of the situation.

However, she still did not feel comfortable supervising this person and was worried about her clients' welfare. She insisted on the supervisee taping several of his client sessions to review in supervision, but, again, she was unable to make any progress even when reviewing the tape together. She tried suggesting he seek some counseling to explore his difficulty hearing feedback from her in supervision, even sharing how this strategy had been helpful to her when she started out. This suggestion infuriated the supervisee, and he stomped out of supervision. Desperate, she sought out another colleague in the building and asked if he would be willing to meet with her supervisee for several sessions and see what he thought could be done, a strategy the supervisee willingly agreed to. After several meetings, however, this colleague told her he had identical concerns to hers and suggested she should probably terminate supervision to protect her clients. He reminded her that under her licensure ethical codes and standards, the supervisor always has to put the welfare of the clients first.

As imagined, when she met with the supervisee and stated her position and why, she was met with a wall of anger, threats, and accusations. Even in the face of this, she stood firm on her position to terminate supervision and referred the supervisee back to the contract he signed at the beginning of their postdegree supervision relationship, which stated clearly that if either party was unhappy with the supervision arrangement, the agreement could be terminated.

Shaken by the experience, Mary began questioning her judgment and her competence as a supervisor, so she decided to meet with another psychologist who was known in the community for his supervision expertise. He began their consultation session by asking her, "How can I be helpful to you with this situation?" Mary responded that she needed to decide if she had done enough with this supervisee and whether she was right to terminate him. Her consultant then asked, "How was this supervisee a problem for you?" She reiterated what the problems were, giving them in specific behavioral terms. He asked her to give him one or two specific examples so he could understand her better.

At that point in the meeting, her consultant agreed with her that these problems appeared very worrisome. He then asked Mary, "What did you do to try to solve these problems?" Mary outlined an extensive list of activities; getting a tape of several of the supervisee's client sessions and reviewing the sessions with the supervisee, reviewing his client progress notes and diagnostic assessments, frequent demonstrations and role-plays, and consulting with several of her colleagues for ideas. All of this was to no avail.

Her consultant paused and waited for Mary to comment on what she just said. Gently, he asked her "As you think about this supervisee and the situation, what do you find yourself saying?" Immediately Mary said "Maybe someone else could have been successful with him. Maybe I am not such a great supervisor." Her consultant then said, "Okay let me play devil's advocate here; how successful do you think another supervisor would have been with this supervisee?" Mary responded that she actually did that. She had asked another psychologist in her building who had attended the same university as this supervisee to meet with him and see what he thought because maybe the problems were gender related and he would do better with a male supervisor. In fact, the other supervisor had exactly the same concerns that she had about this supervisee and didn't feel any more successful with him than she did.

Her consultant commented that she seemed to have put considerable energy and thought into trying to help this supervisee make needed changes, so he was now wondering what enough would look like to her. Mary's response was to say she guessed she had done a lot but had no idea what enough supervision looked like. Maybe the problem actually was what she was saying to herself about this experience, how guilt ridden she felt that she was not able to be successful. "I set awfully high standards for myself, not only at work but in the rest of my life. My dad taught me never to accept failure, to keep striving for excellence. I see now through our processing this situation together that my old critical, never-can-do-enough perfectionist voice is definitely part of my problem. I guess it's time to go back to my therapist and work some more on it."

The consultant agreed with this strategy. At the same time, he shared his own experience with having to terminate a supervisee and how difficult it was to do that without doubting one's competence. He found he needed to process the situation a number of times with several different people before being able to put it to rest and move on. He encouraged her to do the same.

Teaching Point: Mary followed the ethical guidelines for supervisors in this scenario. She tried a number of different strategies to help the supervisee change behavior that she felt was detrimental to clients' welfare. She used a written contract at the beginning of supervision to outline expectations and create understanding and agreement. She sought consultation with others to help guide her actions. Even though she was uncomfortable terminating this supervisee, she held steadfast because of ethical concerns. Last, still experiencing some distress over the incident, she took steps to take care of herself. By seeking consultation with another expert supervisor who responded to her with caring, she was able to recognize how normal and natural it is in circumstances such as this to doubt one's competency and receive support to continue processing the experience in order to put it behind her and move on.

✍ TEST YOURSELF ✍

1. **What are the five main tasks of the intermediate stage? List them.**

2. **To be effective, the clinical supervisor must understand the factors that contribute to problems in the working alliance and be willing and able to respond to the needs of each individual supervisee.** True or False?

3. **Good feedback focuses on improvement and gives specific suggestions for change.** True or False?

4. **Sandwiching is described as**
   (a) placing corrective feedback between two positive statements.
   (b) giving corrective feedback during lunchtime.
   (c) placing the supervisee in the middle of a supervision group and squeezing him or her.
   (d) telling the supervisee what a great job he or she is doing before you tell him or her what was done wrong.

5. **When faced with difficulties with a supervisee, the supervisor should**
   (a) wait awhile to see if things get better.
   (b) review the *DSM* for a proper diagnosis of the supervisee's problem.
   (c) meet the supervisee as soon as possible and talk about the problem.
   (d) focus more in supervision on the task and procedures because obviously the supervisee doesn't understand what to do.

6. ***Illusion of work* is a term Shulman (1993) used to describe how busyness could be a mask for underlying problems.** True or False?

7. **Supervisors must understand it is their responsibility to address problems in a fair and respectful manner, not avoid them.** True or False?

8. **When approaching problems, the supervisor would want to**
   (a) approach the situation from the perspective that any problems in supervision are an indication of deep-seated psychological problems in the supervisee.
   (b) remind supervisees that the bottom line is that the supervisor is in charge, and they better remember that.
   (c) take responsibility, check in to their own thoughts and feelings, review contributing factors, and talk directly to the supervisee about the situation.

9. **Many problems in supervision can be attributed to anxiety.** True or False?

10. **In situations of serious dislike or continual negative labeling of a supervisee, the ethical response on the part of the clinical supervisor would be to**

   (a) seek consultation.

   (b) refer the supervisee to another supervisor.

   (c) engage in personal psychotherapy to avoid possible countertransference.

   (d) do all of the above.

   (e) do only a and b.

11. **No matter what, supervisors must include the issue of multicultural differences in their supervision plan.** True or False?

12. **When applying the coaching model in supervision, it is most important that**

   (a) the supervisee owns the goals for supervision.

   (b) the supervisor just sits back and lets things happen.

   (c) the supervisor tells the supervisee what do to and how to do it.

   (d) the supervisor gets the supervisee to exercise more.

13. **What is the most effective strategy to use when faced with terminating clinical supervision?**

   (a) Get tough. Don't think. Just act.

   (b) Seek consultation before the problem gets out of hand.

   (c) Trust your instincts, and if supervision is not going well, terminate it right then.

   (d) Include discussion of procedures to resolve difficulties and terminate supervision in the supervision informed consent or contract at the beginning of supervision.

   (e) None of the above.

   (f) Only b and d.

14. **When a supervisee seems disinterested in supervision, it is best to excuse them.** True or False?

15. **Name two possible techniques to use when supervisees appear defensive, resistant, or closed in supervision.**

Answers: 1. Challenge supervisees; give and receive feedback; promote development of self-awareness and ownership of goals; move supervisees toward independent functioning; confront problems; 2. True; 3. True; 4. a; 5. c; 6. True; 7. True; 8. c; 9. True; 10. d; 11. True; 12. a; 13. f; 14. False; 15. Supervisors need to check to see if they are part of the problem: How they are coming across? Too dogmatic and critical? Goals or topics in supervision not of interest to supervisees or not fit their needs? Use paradoxical interventions, going with the resistance, storytelling, acting confused, phantom supervisor, preempt the objection, or humor.

Nine

THE ADVANCED STAGE OF SUPERVISION

Near the termination of training in postdegree supervision, it is expected that supervisees at this level of development would be able to practice independently, so the relationship in supervision should almost automatically become more peerlike and collegial. This is definitely true when providing clinical supervision to already licensed or highly experienced professionals. Therefore, the main task for supervisors at this stage is to build a collaborative relationship with supervisees so they are working together with supervisees more as partners or colleagues.

In other words, at this point, a supervisor would want to stop doing things *for* their supervisees and begin to work *with* them. What does this mean? It means that the relationship moves from supervisor-directed to supervisee-directed, where supervisees are in reality supervising themselves. In fact, self-supervision (self-monitoring, self-awareness, and self-evaluation) should be the "universal supervisory goal" for all clinical supervisors from the beginning of supervision (Todd & Storm, 1997, p. 17). What this entails is supervisors having to shift from the expert-teacher role to the consultant one. Supervisors who are committed to the consultant role would ask supervisees at the beginning of supervision how they would like supervision to go rather than telling them what will happen. For example, supervisors could inquire "How do you see the goals and priorities for supervision at this point in your development?" Or "What is the most useful part that I can play in your development now?"

Rapid Reference 9.1 lists the tasks of the advanced stage of supervision.

DEVELOPING A COLLABORATIVE RELATIONSHIP

Collaboration, as a concept, refers to a mutual coordinated effort of two or more people to solve problems and be more effective in service to clients (Staton & Gilligan, 2003). The object of collaboration is to pool ideas and information and come up with solutions that are better than those arrived at by individuals

≡ *Rapid Reference 9.1*

Tasks of the Advanced Stage of Supervision

- Promote independence and self-supervision
- Work collaboratively
- Endorse teamwork
- Encourage the use of consultation and peer support
- Model and teach self-care
- Continue self-exploration and understanding of limitations
- Champion lifelong learning and professional development
- Advocate for mental health services in the community

by themselves. The heart of the collaborative process is that influence, resources, and power are shared equally among collaborators. As a result, truly building a collaborative relationship with supervisees requires a shift in approach on the part of supervisors and a willingness to let go of their power and authority, which is not always an easy task.

Perhaps the best illustration of what is meant by a collaborative working relationship is to draw a comparison between consultation in the expert mode and consultation in a shared-power mode. For example, the supervisor working in the expert mode might state "After reviewing the case, it seems to me.... This is what I recommend you do...." However, when working more col-

CAUTION

When supervising highly experienced supervisees at the advanced level, supervisors are advised to forgo a didactic teaching manner and avoid covering subjects well known by those at this level of development. Instead, the focus in supervision should be on innovations, research, new theories and intervention strategies, and the continuous integration of this new material into current practice (Campbell, 2001–2005).

DON'T FORGET

Supervisors in the advanced stage need to get out of the way and turn over the goals, process, structure, and evaluative piece to supervisees.

laboratively, the supervisor might instead ask the supervisee "What have you thought about doing with this client?" or "What have you already tried?" Even adding "What do you think about this suggestion?" at the end of any suggestion given to supervisees changes the dynamic to be more peerlike.

≡ Rapid Reference 9.2

Collaborative Skills

Brainstorming
Open-ended questions
Probes
Empathic responding
Solution-focused questions
Miracle questions

Process comments
Examination of parallel process
Self-disclosure
Self-involving statements
Scaling questions
Imagining successful solutions

A number of interpersonal skills are necessary for instituting a collaborative relationship with supervisees, most of which have already been discussed in other chapters. These include brainstorming, process comments, open-ended questions, probing, solution-focused questions, empathetic responding, and self-disclosure. Rapid Reference 9.2 contains a summary of collaborative skills.

One skill that is truly essential for the advanced stage of supervision is the use of process comments or process questions. Process comments are any *how, what, where,* and *when* statements that focus attention on the here-and-now relationship between supervisor and supervisee. The purpose of process comments is to improve relationships so they have a natural place in supervision. When used correctly, they come across like remarks that would be made by colleagues. For example, when a supervisor says to a supervisee "I am feeling stuck right now with you. How are you feeling now with me?" he or she is inviting supervisees to speak as an equal. If a supervisor says to a supervisee, "I notice we seem to be spending a great deal of time talking about. . . . Is that what you want?" this process comment establishes the peerlike quality of the relationship.

Rapid Reference 9.3 lists some other consultation-style questions for supervisors.

Another task of the advanced stage is to encourage self-evaluation and self-monitoring by supervisees. The simplest suggestion to encourage self-evaluation by supervisees is to insert a scaling question during the review of a client case. For example, ask supervisees to rate on a scale of 1 to 10 how they feel they are doing with a particular client (or goal or solving a problem). Then ask them to identify one thing they need to do differently to move just 1 point up the scale.

Another means to encourage self-evaluation is for supervisors to comment on changes they have observed in a supervisee. "I notice a change in the type of questions you are asking now in supervision. Six months ago, you would be ask-

☰Rapid Reference 9.3

Consultation-Style Questions for Supervisors

- "What do you want from supervision?" or "What do you want from me?"
- "As you are talking about this client, what are you most aware of?"
- "What was your goal for this session with the client?"
- "Help me to understand. When the client did that, what happened to you?"
- "What do you think is going on between you and this client?"
- "How might the client's gender or race be affecting the problem? Your relationship with the client?"
- "Where were you going with that line of questions?"
- "Let me play devil's advocate here. What do you think might have happened if you had tried...."
- "As you are talking about this client, what comes to you that you might have done differently?"

ing me to tell you what my take is on this client and what I would do with him or her. Now you come into supervision telling me what you perceive the issues are and how you plan to proceed. To me, this indicates major growth on your part. How do you see it?"

PROMOTING TEAMWORK

There is a large body of research and writing spanning decades that reinforces the importance of teamwork in organizations as a means to increase productivity, job satisfaction, and morale. In the area of mental health, promoting teamwork has many advantages for overworked and underpaid clinical supervisors in agencies, hospitals, community centers, and schools. Fostering teamwork, while sometimes not easy, will be well worth the effort.

To be a considered a team, team members must actively participate in decisions concerning the setting of shared team goals, planning, and problem solving. There needs to be a commitment by all members to the team goals and an interdependence and accountability among these members as they work toward these goals. In other words, people in a team may have separate assignments but depend on each other to get the work done successfully.

Lots of lip service is given to teamwork in organizations. Expressions such as "We are all a team here," and "We all need to pull together," and "Everyone is equal" have become standard management clichés. Hiring outside consultants to come in for team-building workshops and sending supervisors to team-building trainings has almost become mandatory. But how many organizations actually support and reward *real* teamwork is questionable, and younger employees soon become jaded as they learn quickly the difference between the teamwork talk and the teamwork walk.

Organizational climate and environmental factors are crucial to the success of any team-building efforts on the part of clinical supervisors. For example, in toxic environments, where staff members don't feel safe because they are constantly fending off criticism and blame, building collaboration and a teamwork model is almost impossible (Rubin, 2000). However, there are a large number of situations in which team building could be a success and add immeasurably to the effectiveness of clinical supervision.

There are a number of suggested strategies that can be employed by clinical supervisors to build an authentic work team. First, in order to create a sense of interdependence among team members and a shared commitment to mutual goals, supervisors have to be facilitators and encouragers—not directors—of group process, and use whatever authority they have to promote a win-win situation for all team members. Second, individuals have to understand the interconnectedness of their work to others on the team and see the rewards for working collaboratively. If the team is to be made up of supervisees from a number of different organizations, identifying a common goal for the team is absolutely essential to success but might require considerable effort to keep everyone on target.

For example, in a school setting, depending on the size of the district, the team might be made up of a psychologist, one or two counselors, the school nurse, a social worker if available, and other ancillary staff such as diagnosticians or special education support staff. The identified common goal for the team might be helping students, and each team member's job could be viewed as a part of that greater goal. Through sharing of information and open dialogue, new ideas could be generated that could benefit everyone.

To get everyone onto the same page, supervisors should start their team-building efforts with an open discussion on a number of topics, such as identifying team goals and what benefits each person will receive from a collaborative teamwork model. To facilitate understanding and personal accountability, supervisors might wish to emphasize the shared aspect of each team member's work, what factors are in team members' control and which are not, and how each person's effort fits into the larger picture. Supervisors should also inquire of each team member what gives meaning to his or her work, how he or she likes to make decisions, and what motivates him or her to do a better job. Through the process of collecting such material, group consensus could be reached on how

≡ *Rapid Reference 9.4*

Six Steps to Build Successful Teamwork

1. Share your vision.
   - Get people excited about goals
   - Sell your passion
2. Communicate expectations.
   - Ground them in expectations
   - Prepare them for hardships
3. Demonstrate respect for differences.
   - Promote feedback
   - Provide safe ways to give feedback
   - Thank people who speak up and give ideas, even if they sound critical
   - Manage conflict
4. Ask for discipline and pride.
   - Explain the supervisee's role in accomplishing goals
   - Reward competence and hard work
   - Ask supervisees how they would like to be rewarded
5. Use teamwork to resolve problems.
   - Bring problems back to the team
   - Serve in a facilitator role
   - Spread authority around
   - Use the brainstorming model

to use this information to build the team structure. Rapid Reference 9.4 lists six steps to build teamwork.

Leadership style is another consideration. Logically, an authoritarian style of leadership would not be conducive to creating the kind of atmosphere of equality and collaboration required for teamwork. At the same time, supervisors, as team leaders, have ultimate responsibility for the team's actions. This places supervisors in a delicate balancing act between managing whatever the current situation is with the team members' current level of skills and at the same time attempting to inspire members to take risks, try out new things, and grow.

At the center of this leadership question is how decisions will be made in the team group. Supervisors who wish to work in the team-building model have to pay close attention to this detail. Traditionally with teams, decision making is regarded as a team task; therefore, supervisors should promote the use of consensus building and compromise along with brainstorming as primary problem-solving strategies. However, these methods all take time, and there may be many circumstances, such as a crisis, when a supervisor's quick action

Putting It Into Practice

Examples of How Supervisors Can Challenge Consensus

- "Let me play devil's advocate. You all nodded in agreement when I suggested we change the way crisis calls are handled. But what I want to know is what are some of the potential problems you see if we implement this strategy?"
- "I notice as a pattern in our team meetings that you readily agree with all my suggestions, just like you did now, and this makes me uncomfortable. I am wondering about this fact. Are all my ideas that great, or is something going on that I need to hear about? Is there something I am doing that makes you feel unsafe to disagree?"

CAUTION

If supervisors continually make quick decisions about problems and ignore input from team members, this strategy can have long-term repercussions. It will create resentment and disillusionment with the teamwork model. For example, "Oh, yes; he says all the time we are a team but when problems occur, he is going to tell us what to do and how to do it. We don't really have any say."

is required, and there is no time for group input. In order to avoid any detrimental effects from this state of affairs on overall team morale, supervisors need to clearly delineate ahead of time to team members what these circumstances might be and then later ask for feedback from team members around any actions that were taken.

Additionally, consensus building and compromise only work when power between people on the team is equal (Kormanski, 1999). Otherwise, the team members may indicate agreement with the person in power but underneath harbor unexpressed concerns about the problem solution, which if not uncovered, can lead to subsequent difficulties.

As noted earlier, from the beginning of supervision, supervisors are responsible for creating a safe, respectful work environment. This means that supervisors apply all of their rapport-building skills, such as paraphrasing, empathic responding, self-disclosure, reflection of feelings, and open-ended questions, to build a safe environment for open discussion of problems and differences in the team.

Another equally important part of team building is motivation. Rewarding team members for efforts made on the team's behalf is one of the best-known means to spur teamwork. For those in the helping professions where monetary rewards are seldom available, just publicly thanking team members for their hard work is an excellent incentive. In addition, many of today's workforce would prefer time off or more autonomy on the job as rewards rather than the traditional one of money. As a consequence, supervisors might consider rewarding extra hard effort by team members with the gift of time—a day or a half day off, permission to come to work an hour late or go home early. Naturally, asking team members what type of team-member behavior should receive extra notice and what would be a suitable reward in their eyes for this effort will lay the groundwork for increasing motivation.

In the advanced stage, when working with supervision groups, the supervisor would definitely want to function more as a facilitator of the group process rather than group leader. In order to facilitate teamwork, supervisors will need to have genuine positive regard for everyone on the team. Supervisors need to be congruent and have consistency between what they say and what they do, both verbally and nonverbally. They model for the team through their behavior how to treat people with dignity and respect, no matter the circumstances. For example, if there is one person dominating the meeting, try redirecting the conversation to include others. "I wonder what the others of you think about what Sam is saying?" Or compliment the person for their input, and then move conversation back to whatever is the group task.

Also important to building safety in the team is how conflict and confrontation are to be managed. Again, just as with counseling and therapy groups, clinical supervisors model how conflict and problem member

DON'T FORGET

Rewarding excellence and hard work is also a key component of motivation and team building. Be sure to publicly praise and thank a team member who did an exceptional job in some situation, team members who demonstrated the team spirit by working together to solve a problem, a team member's particular idea that contributed to the success of the team, and any situation where sacrifice by an individual team member led to the greater good of the team.

CAUTION

In today's world of hype and spin, actions speak louder than words. Behaviors such as interrupting, ignoring, sarcasm, and belittling all will defeat any teamwork model. Thus, give supervisees your full attention when they speak, and be sure to thank them for asking questions and letting you know their concerns. When a supervisee makes a suggestion or points out a problem, say, "I am glad you brought that point up," or "Thanks for the suggestion. What do the rest of you think?" rather than "We have tried that before," or "You must be kidding!"

DON'T FORGET

The two main tasks of a group facilitator are to develop group cohesion and manage harmful conflict. From inception, teams will need to set clear guidelines for group-member interactions and work jointly with the leader to prevent any kind of harmful exchanges.

behaviors should be handled. Therefore, if any members of the team are in open conflict or if someone is irritable and aggressive, puts others down, or says nasty things, supervisors must quickly intervene. If they don't, supervisees will not feel safe, and any team feelings will dissolve.

Putting It Into Practice

Case Example

Erik was a new school psychologist in a moderate-sized school district. Once a month all of the allied health service staff got together at his office for a team meeting. The team was made up of Erik (the only school psychologist and male team member), three counselors, a school social worker, a school nurse, and a special education counselor. None of the members of the team had supervisory responsibilities over anyone else on the team. These team meetings were mandatory under current administrative guidelines.

Erik was confused about the purpose for the team and after several meetings, he was dissatisfied with the experience. He also became cognizant of the fact that everyone in the team looked to him for leadership, and whenever members brought up problems for group discussion, they received very little feedback. If there were any differences in opinion, the group quickly squashed the discussion by changing the topic of conversation. Erik became determined to address these issues at the next meeting. When he did so, other team members chimed in with their dissatisfaction, the fact they also were unclear about the purpose of the group, and uncomfortable with the lack of a designated leader and set guidelines.

From this discussion, the team moved to an agreed-upon structure for the team meetings, with a rotating leadership position and basic guidelines for decision making and handling disagreements. Within short order, the team came up with a solution to a shared problem of shrinking resources in the district. Team members realized that most of their time was being spent on a relatively small group of students who appeared repeatedly with various needs. By calling and e-mailing each other to share information, members were able to avoid much of the duplication of service and leave time and energy for other needs.

Teaching Point: As a result of Erik's willingness to speak up, the team became more effective. By identifying the source of his dissatisfaction and taking a risk to share this with the group, improvements were made and the value of the time spent by the team more meaningful. Not only were new solutions to old problems created but also members began to feel much needed support for their efforts, which resulted in an increase in job satisfaction.

IMPORTANCE OF PERSONAL AND PROFESSIONAL DEVELOPMENT

One area that is sometimes overlooked in clinical supervision is an active program of personal and professional development. Supervisors serve as models for the importance of self-care and continuous growth and development by sharing their own professional growth experiences, such as workshops or conferences attended, what they are reading at the moment that excites them, current research, and new ideas for practice. They also should invite supervisees to go with them to various professional activities, such as lunch programs, grand rounds, CEU seminars, or conferences. Additionally, many supervisees would benefit from encouragement from their supervisors to give a presentation at a state or national conference. This activity could be done in tandem with the supervisor or with other supervisees.

Another important area of professional growth that sometimes is not discussed at all in supervision (and may be controversial in some settings) is the role personal psychotherapy plays in professional development. Some graduate programs require students to engage in therapy as part of their program requirements, but many times, supervisors avoid the topic altogether or look upon psychotherapy as something only needed for situations of severe impairment. However, because ethical codes and standards strongly advise all practitioners to be continuously involved in self-monitoring and seek out therapy as a means to maintain clearness and objectivity, the topic should be integrated into supervision from a growth perspective, not just if deficits are uncovered. Certainly, in many ways, in order to minimize the risk of countertransference or their own personal problems negatively impacting clients, engaging in personal counseling or psychotherapy is an ethical strategy. Supervisors who believe in this standard and are involved in their own personal psychotherapy should share its benefits with their supervisees. (Note that it is not necessary to share the exact issues discussed with the therapist or insights gained, just the value of the activity in professional practice.)

Exchange of information about career development is another area to cover in supervision. How one puts together a successful career in the area of mental or behavioral health in today's world may not be discussed in any other milieu. Supervisors might wish to share their own

CAUTION

Pay attention to your attitude about CEU requirements. Be sure to model excitement and enthusiasm for current reading, articles, and books, attending continuing education seminars, and conferences.

career development experiences in the field, recommend readings, or suggest self-exploration exercises. One exceptional idea is to put together a panel of different practitioners and have them discuss how they got where they are and what they have learned on the way. This topic might be used for a brown bag lunch program or spread out over a number of sessions.

Those who supervise paraprofessionals have a fertile ground for mentoring in the area of career development. Some supervisees may only need a few supportive comments such as "I think you have real ability or talent" to get on with their education, while others will require more step-by-step guidance. No matter what, supporting and guiding supervisees to develop their potential can supply rich rewards for supervisors.

The supervisor can also support supervisees getting involved in the larger society. There is a tremendous need for mental health professionals to be advocates for social services in their community. Practitioners need to take their caring and compassion for those in need outside the office by serving on the board of a nonprofit organization, the school board, a city council, or by running for other public office. Further, counselors, therapists, and others with advanced training in relationships and sensitivity for multicultural differences can and should be playing a much larger role as social activists for peace and justice in the world (Gerstein & Moeschberger, 2003).

TAKING CARE OF THE CARETAKER

As the demands placed on those in the health professions and social services increase, learning how to nurture oneself over the lifetime of a career is a continuing challenge. Protinsky and Coward (2001) found that the "topic of nurturing and maintaining the self throughout a career is mostly ignored in graduate programs and is virtually nonexistent in research studies on experienced therapists" (p. 375). In much of the supervision literature, there is rarely a mention of this important topic. Yet ethical codes and standards caution all practitioners to monitor their health and stress level and take care of themselves so as not to unintentionally harm clients. Hence the issue of learning how to take care of oneself and develop healthy strategies to avoid burnout and compassion fatigue should be high on the list of supervision topics. Rapid Reference 9.5 lists a number of suggestions for managing stress.

A number of studies of seasoned practitioners show the importance of finding a balance between work life and outside life (Dlugos & Friedlander, 2001; Protinsky & Coward, 2001; Sherman & Thelen, 1998). Common strategies described were setting clear boundaries between work and outside lives, exercising,

≡ *Rapid Reference 9.5*

Taking Care of the Caretaker

- Redefine the word *help*.
- Help supervisees set boundaries.
- Acknowledge, normalize, and process feelings.
- Avoid isolation. Develop a team approach.
- Help supervisees find meaning in life and work.
- Provide continuing supportive feedback.
- Apply anxiety reduction techniques as necessary.
- Encourage supervisees to acknowledge feelings of grief and sadness.
- Help supervisees rebuild basic assumptions about the world, people, and safety if shattered by experiences with clients.

exploring hobbies, having friends, engaging in activities that refresh and rejuvenate, taking periodic vacations, belonging to a consultation network, and finding mentors who both provide reassurance and act as catalysts for growth.

Taking a sabbatical is another time-honored means for individuals to regenerate and increase their productivity. While usually only available to those in academia, the media is reporting positive results for managers and other personnel who take a few months off from their business. Job sharing, flexible scheduling, and mandatory vacation breaks are also good ideas for those in high-stress jobs.

Stress, Burnout, and Compassion Fatigue

Stress management, burnout prevention, and compassion fatigue are topics that should be of concern to all clinical supervisors. All three are considered significant issues for everyone in the health and social service fields, regardless of education level or experience. The causes for stress and resulting burnout or compassion fatigue may be quite different depending on the level of responsibility and type of work involved. Supervisors and administrators may be stressed out by the demands of the job, the impact of rules and regulations, and problems of time management, whereas supervisees may experience stress arising from the demands of clients and issues such as danger, crisis management, and suicide. Inexperienced supervisees may be more vulnerable to compassion fatigue, which results from trying to help those who are suffering from traumatic events,

≡ Rapid Reference 9.6

Helping Supervisees Manage Stress

- Encourage supervisees to ask for help before they are completely over-whelmed and exhausted
- Offer tips for time management right from the start
- Be empathic
- Normalize thoughts and feelings that can be triggered by crisis situations
- Share wisdom such as how you have learned to balance work and stay fresh and invigorated
- Model desired behavior
- Explore irrational thoughts and demands for perfection
- Pay attention to inexperienced supervisees' ability to set boundaries and practice self-care (i.e., do they stay late all of the time, skip lunch, take work home on weekends)

while, on the other hand, burnout may be more of a problem for those who are experienced and have been working for a long time.

Supervisors have an important role in helping supervisees avoid burnout and compassion fatigue. They need to take an active role in helping all supervisees set boundaries, learn how to go home and have a life, as well as how to find satisfaction in what they are doing, even when their clients do not make large scale changes or find a pot of gold at the end of the rainbow. Rapid Reference 9.6 lists ways supervisors can assist supervisees with managing stress.

Burnout is a term used to describe the physical and emotional exhaustion of an individual produced by prolonged job stress and a reduced sense of accomplishment on the job. Usually burnout in the health professions is triggered by a sense of being caught in the middle between serving the needs of the clients and the structures and policies of an organization. Indicators of burnout can be tardiness, absenteeism, job apathy, irritability, cynicism, lack of caring about clients, and even illness. A list of burnout symptoms is specified in Rapid Reference 9.7.

One approach supervisors can take to help supervisees prevent burnout is to provide them a safe place to process thoughts and feelings. Depending on the situation and the relationship, supervisors concerned about burnout could encourage supervisees to redefine career and work goals, search for new challenges, or, in some instances, even seek outside help, such as EAP or counseling for extra support.

≡ *Rapid Reference 9.7*

Symptoms of Burnout

Physical Symptoms
Exhaustion, fatigue, sleep difficulties, headaches, upset stomach, colds

Emotional Symptoms
Irritability, anxiety, depression, guilt, sense of helplessness

Behavioral Symptoms
Callousness, defensiveness, pessimism, aggressiveness, substance abuse

Work-Related Symptoms
Poor work performance, absenteeism, tardiness, wanting to quit, poor concentration

Interpersonal Symptoms
Withdrawal, intellectualizing, perfunctory communication, dehumanizing

Compassion fatigue (Figley, 1995) is a different phenomenon from burnout in that it is the result of caring deeply, which can make the caregiver emotionally vulnerable and cause exhaustion. Caretakers, counselors, and rescue workers all are at risk of suffering from compassion fatigue as they attempt to help those who are suffering terribly, such as victims of violence or long-term abuse. Personal history can also contribute to compassion fatigue and create what Figley (1995) termed *secondary trauma* as supervisees attempt to help clients who have similar background issues to their own. For example, counselors who work with victims of child abuse and who have had the same childhood experience would be considered at risk for secondary or vicarious trauma.

Symptoms of compassion fatigue run the gamut and include a sense of helplessness and confusion, depression, tiredness, social isolation, disruption of daily routine, suspicion or feelings of persecution, excessive worrying about clients, intrusive thoughts about clients that are difficult to shut down, and loss of sleep.

Guilt can also be a significant factor with compassion fatigue. Guilt can take the form of feeling unworthy, a failure, at fault, responsible, sinful, evil, wrong, ashamed, remorseful, or blameworthy. Guilt may result from any circumstance, real or perceived, in which supervisees fail to live up to their own expectations or standards.

Figley (2002) suggested two important supervisory activities to prevent compassion fatigue: teaching supervisees how to disengage from work and teaching them how to find satisfaction in their work. *Disengagement* is the boundary-setting

> ## CAUTION
> ....
> Supervisors should serve as role models for supervisees in how to take care of themselves and avoid burnout and compassion fatigue. Therefore, ask yourself what you are doing to disengage from work, relax, and rest; what strategies do you use to deal with stressful circumstances; how are you modeling boundary setting and self-care for your supervisees; and what keeps you fresh and excited about work.

process whereby professionals learn to leave client problems at the office and to take time off. *Finding satisfaction* means redefining the word *help*, being able to see success in helping people for whom there is little one can do to relieve pain and suffering. It is also important for supervisors to normalize supervisees' feelings, provide a safe place for them to process feelings, assist them to avoid isolation, and offer continuing supportive feedback.

Adapting a narrative approach is another recommended strategy for supervisors to teach supervisees in order to prevent compassion fatigue and secondary trauma (Etherington, 2000). The narrative approach to therapy, a contemporary reworking of Roger's client-centered therapy, asks counselors and therapists to encourage clients to tell their stories from their own viewpoints as a means to promote change. This method shifts the focus away from the counselor as being responsible for client change to clients having the resources to heal themselves.

Osborn (2004) took a very different tactic on the topic of stress management and burnout prevention. She preferred counselors, therapists, and other health professionals build endurance or *stamina* by cultivating strengths and resources as a means to resist stress, rather than the reactive position implied by the terms "coping" and "burnout prevention" (p. 319). In her article, she listed seven suggestions for on- and off-the-job activities that contribute to building stamina. These can be found in Rapid Reference 9.8. It is interesting to note that her suggestions about how to build stamina mirror the findings from research on resiliency and personal hardiness.

SUPERVISION OF SUPERVISION

One important question for all practitioners to address is whether in fact there should ever be an end to supervision. In other words, in order to be fully competent and ethical, should one always be seeking more supervision? Many authors and experts in the area of clinical supervision stress the need for experienced supervisors to seek ongoing supervision and training as a valuable aid to develop

≡Rapid Reference 9.8

Seven Suggestions to Develop Stamina

Selectivity: To become selective in what one can know and do and to understand the need for limits and be comfortable with those limits

Temporal sensitivity: To see time not as an enemy but in collaborative terms so that one makes the best use of whatever time one has within organizational and regulatory restraints

Accountability: To practice according to a sound theoretical and ethical model that supports one's actions with clients

Measurement and management: To protect and conserve resources, such as energy and compassion, by setting limits and acting selectively, consulting with trusted colleagues, having a network of supportive, positive people, and engaging in meaningful off-work activities or hobbies

Inquisitiveness: Maintaining a sense of curiosity and wonder about human behavior

Negotiation: Having a sense of internal control or self-efficacy such that one is able to negotiate work to gain flexibility and an opportunity for innovation

Source: Osborn (2004).

awareness of supervisory blind spots (Green et al., 2001; Yerushalmi, 1999). Further, consultation with other professionals is always the suggested strategy for the maintenance of ethical practice. In fact, discussions with experienced supervisors

DON'T FORGET

In order to be an ethical practitioner, supervisors need to seek out regular consultation or supervision of supervision.

indicate that most would like to have ongoing supervision of their supervision (Campbell, 2001–2005).

It follows then that clinical supervisors must look closely at how they are going about seeking supervision or consultation on their supervisory practice. They must ask themselves, "How can I still grow in my skills and expertise now that I am at this advanced level? What form should this take?" Most often, an individual supervisor seeks out another clinical supervisor to discuss informally issues and concerns about a troubling supervisory situation. However, it is strongly recommended that group supervision of supervision be an integral part of any training model because such a group will generally improve the overall quality of supervision.

Peer Consultation Groups

Supervision-of-supervision groups, or peer supervision groups, are considered a valuable alternative to formal supervision as a means for experienced clinicians to receive the benefits of consultation with peers. Such groups can serve as an important part of professional development, especially for those in private practice or school settings where an ongoing opportunity for consultation with other supervisors is limited.

Readers should note that referring to these supervision-of-supervision groups as peer consultation groups is technically more accurate because in the majority of cases, membership is voluntary, and rarely is there any power differential among group members or any real structured evaluative feedback about supervision skills included at this advanced level. It is simply a sharing of suggestions and concerns. However, to make them more meaningful, it is a good idea to create such a structure and include more formal evaluative feedback or even use a rating scale. Additionally, a highly regarded practitioner could be asked to serve more in a supervisory role with the group, giving feedback as well as suggestions.

A peer consultation group could be built in numerous ways: through an organizational context, a professional organization, or even a local university. That is, three or more clinical supervisors within an organization could periodically get together and talk about issues, concerns, difficulties, and successes with their supervisees. Or a group could be formed outside an organization drawing on diverse members of a professional community. In fact, having diversity among group members can increase the benefit if handled correctly. A number of state licensing boards and some national organizations (e.g., the NBCC and the AAMFT) keep a list of approved supervisors that could be used as a means to build a more diverse group. Networking at workshops and conferences is another means to locate potential members. Regardless, if clinical supervisors believe in the value of such an activity, they can make it happen.

Just as in other groups, there are a number of important factors to consider in making this experience truly worthwhile. First is the makeup of the group and where the group will be held. Usually, groups independent of work settings are easier to manage and more successful than those held in house, but this certainly doesn't have to be the case. Also, some homogeneity of group membership in terms of client population and work setting is suggested as it helps members to quickly bond and see the usefulness of the group, but, again, diversity of membership could, if handled correctly, augment the success of the group. A second and very pressing need to consider when forming a peer consultation group is the structure of the group. To be most effective, members would need to take time at the beginning to discuss their needs and their goals for the group and settle on some kind of a basic structure.

Members of the peer consultation group, just like members of a supervision group or group therapy, will have to deal with issues of inclusion, boundary setting, rules, and expectations. Good questions for these groups to consider are "Will there be informal leadership that rotates among members? Will everyone get equal time to present cases, or will members' level of need at the meeting dictate? How will we handle feedback so we give support to each other?" Rapid Reference 9.9 lists topics for consideration by a peer consultation group.

CAUTION

If members do not take time out in the beginning to create a formal structure for the peer supervision group, the group can degenerate into a time for gossiping and complaining rather than a forum for consultation about cases.

≡Rapid Reference 9.9

Structuring the Peer Consultation Group

- Share goals and establish group purpose.
- Decide on a time for meeting.
- Discuss the group-member roles and leadership function.
- Agree on the use of time in the group and group process.
- Discuss the expectations of members in the group to come prepared and keep to group purpose.
- Establish how members will give feedback to each other in the group.
- Include a discussion at the beginning of the peer supervision group about each member's comfort level with corrective feedback.
- Discuss how to handle disagreements.
- To improve benefit, include taping, role-play, and other more direct means for supervision beyond self-report about client cases.
- Appoint a group observer to monitor the group process and keep the group focused.
- Establish an evaluation method for the group so periodically you can stop and review the group's effectiveness.
- Make the peer supervision group a time-limited group experience, and give it an end date. There are many benefits for doing so.

A peer consultation group for clinical supervisors has understandable benefits (Bernard, Hackney, & Wilkerson, 2004; Green et al., 2001). Participating in such a group can help increase self-awareness, foster professional growth, and improve motivation. These groups also promote ethical practice by helping supervisors combat isolation and loneliness. Talking with other supervisors in a safe format improves problem solving, promotes learning, and provides validation for actions. For example, if a supervisor has to terminate a supervisee, processing thoughts and feelings associated with this experience can have a healing effect. Additionally, if the clinical supervisor is impaired, burned out, or otherwise struggling, the peer group can provide support and encouragement to make changes.

However, just as with other groups, in order to reap these benefits, considerable attention has to be paid to member needs and expectations, boundary setting, rules, and group structure. The more diverse the group membership, the more attention needs to be paid to how to handle that fact. It is important to maintain flexibility and openness to different points of view, search for commonality among members, and avoid rigid adherence to the rightness of any one model of practice. Safety issues, confidentiality, and agreement on how problems between members or other disagreements will be handled are also essential to the success of the group.

One outstanding but rarely instituted idea to improve the value of a peer consultation group is to have each supervisor bring in a videotape of one of their supervision sessions and use that as a means to generate feedback and make improvements. Another profitable strategy to employ in large organizations where there are a number of supervisors and supervisees is to borrow the fishbowl technique from the field of organizational development. To create a fishbowl, supervisees sit on the outside of a group of supervisors and observe them as they consult with each other about a case. Watching highly trained and experienced supervisors trade ideas and viewpoints and hash out differences of opinion, can serve as a powerful learning experience on the value of consultation at all levels of professional development.

Impaired Supervisors

Much is written and discussed about impairment in supervisees, but what about the same problem with supervisors? Sometimes problems with supervisors can be categorized as bad or lousy supervision (see Chapter 1 for discussion of effective and ineffective supervisors). In a number of such situations supervisors may simply be unaware that they are unsuccessful or doing anything wrong. Bad supervision may just be an outcome of poor training in supervision or misunderstandings about expectations or roles. After all, differences and disagreements are natural and normal in any relationship, and it may not necessarily be a sign of serious problems. Ideally in such circumstances, supervisees might take it upon themselves to speak up about difficulties, and the supervisor would be open to such feedback. Or if training in supervision were required, most problems with supervisors, such as lack of attention to supervision or absence of constructive feedback, would be resolved.

However, Ellis (2001) has suggested there is another category of supervisor behavior that goes far beyond just what could be considered bad or lousy supervision when supervisors misuse their power and act in ways that are deeply harmful, even traumatizing, to supervisees. According to Ellis, activities such as overstepping boundaries (sexual intimacy with supervisees); misusing power (using supervision to meet the supervisors personal needs); being vindictive; responding to supervisees with malice and derision; demeaning them publicly and privately; and showing blatant prejudice toward people of color, the opposite gender, different sexual orientation, age, or different discipline and education level can result in short- or long-term emotional trauma to supervisees and, in some instances, even result in supervisees leaving the field. Rapid Reference 9.10 reminds supervisors about harmful supervisor behaviors.

Such harmful behavior on the part of supervisors presents a serious challenge to the ethical-practice model for clinical supervisors because a supervisee's trust hinges on a perception of the supervisor's good will and fairness, and such trust is vital to supervisees' openness and risk-taking in supervision. However, in instances of harmful, exploitive

CAUTION

There is an important distinction between corrective feedback that may be difficult or even painful for supervisees to hear but necessary for their professional growth and feedback that is meant to shame or demean them. Feedback should always be done in the best interests of supervisees, not to meet the needs of the supervisor.

Rapid Reference 9.10

Harmful Supervisor Behavior

- Misusing power
- Overstepping sexual boundaries
- Being vindictive
- Acting maliciously with intent to harm
- Being derisive—showing contempt for supervisees
- Demeaning supervisees in public
- Acting in a blatantly prejudiced manner

behavior on the part of supervisors, it may be difficult to uncover. Supervisees who have low power and choice might be reluctant to speak up for fear of reprisals. In highly charged situations, feedback from a person of less power to one of greater power rarely works (Muratori, 2001). Supervisors who are behaving problematically may be highly resistant to any feedback from their supervisees and, if confronted, will retaliate even more. And even if a supervisee were willing to speak, finding a safe means to do so may not be available. It follows then that an important aspect of excellent supervision is to provide all supervisees with a safe means to speak up about any unethical behavior or misuse of power on the part of supervisors.

Ethical codes and standards for all mental health disciplines state clearly that if a psychologist, counselor, therapist, or social worker knows a colleague is acting unethically, they must talk to the person about this behavior or, in some instances, bring it to the attention of that person's licensing board. In other words, mental health practitioners are supposed to police themselves. Therefore, the question on the table for all mental health professionals to address is "How would you know a clinical supervisor was behaving in an improper or unethical manner with a supervisee? If you did know, how would you proceed?"

The answer to this question is only partly satisfactory. For example, in large organizations, anonymous feedback from supervisees about a supervisor's unethical behavior might be possible, whereas in private practice, small agencies, and rural settings, assuring safety and anonymity might be difficult, making it less feasible to unmask an unethical supervisor. A further complication might be that there are no established procedures in place to attempt to prevent such behavior in the first place.

Some other recommendations to approach problematic behavior on the part of supervisors are as follows: (1) Stress training in supervision and ongoing supervision of supervision, (2) ask all clinical supervisors to participate in a supervision-of-supervision group on a regular basis. Use structured review sheets, taping, or live observation as a part of the supervision-of-supervision plan, (3) make the usage of a supervisor feedback rating scale a standard requirement for everyone, (4) prominently post the ethical standards and codes for clinical supervisors from each discipline, (5) provide an anonymous ethical complaint box, (6) identify a safe person for supervisees to speak to about any unethical behavior on the part of supervisors, and (7) encourage administrators to speak up about the importance of ethical behavior on the part of all supervisors.

Rapid Reference 9.11 summarizes suggestions to counteract harmful behaviors in supervision.

> ## ≡Rapid Reference 9.11
>
> ### Ideas to Address the Problem of Bad or Harmful Supervisors
>
> * Provide more training for supervisors
> * Prepare both supervisors and supervisees for their roles
> * Encourage supervisees to speak up about unethical behavior
> * Publish ethical standards for supervisors
> * Require supervision for supervisors
> * Use a written informed consent and contract agreement to establish expectations and support ethical practice
> * Reconsider evaluation procedures to get more objective data about supervisees' competence
> * Establish procedures for resolving conflicts that promote fair treatment
>
> Sources: Ellis (2001) and Veach (2001).

Whenever the supervisor in question is licensed by a state board to practice, another, though somewhat controversial, recommendation is for supervisees to contact the licensure board of any licensed clinical supervisor for help and suggestions on how to proceed. Licensure boards across the country are concerned about unethical behavior on the part of any clinical supervisor and encourage such contact. If the supervisee is a member of national professional organizations such as ACA, APA, NASW, or AAMFT, they are encouraged to call the member help line to seek advice.

> ## DON'T FORGET
>
> In any situation that involves licensed practitioners, questions concerning ethical behavior can always be addressed to that practitioner's licensing board. Additionally, members of any national professional organization in the mental health field or anyone who holds malpractice insurance with these organizations can call the member help line for advice.

ENDING SUPERVISION

In many instances, clinical supervision is a time-limited experience with a prescribed conclusion. After a certain number of hours, supervision ends; interns graduate, and postdegree interns receive a license or certificate to practice. How supervision concludes and what is done to mark this significant event may be overlooked with all the business surrounding the moment. From a career development standpoint, much benefit can be derived from orchestrating a formal ending experience for all supervisees. Additionally, with this activity, supervisors model how to terminate counseling or psychotherapy with clients.

The most common means to end supervision is to hold an evaluation session where both supervisor and supervisee discuss their experience, benefits, and successes along with suggestions for change. Paper-and-pencil evaluation instruments and rating scales are the usual catalyst for this discussion.

During this final supervision meeting, supervisors might ask supervisees to share one thing they will take away from the experience that will be helpful to them in their professional development. A scaling question could be added to spur serious self-evaluation on the part of those at the end of postdegree supervision: "On a scale of 1 to 10, how ready do you think you are to be a self-supervising practitioner?"

Another topic to explore with supervisees at the end of supervision is any of their ideas to improve the supervision experience. For example the supervisor can ask "Let's imagine that you are now a clinical supervisor. What do you see yourself doing as a supervisor? How might it be similar and how might it be different from what you have experienced here with me?"

One issue that frequently comes up at the conclusion of supervision is the giving of gifts to commemorate the experience. Ethically, most mental health practitioners are advised not to accept gifts from clients, but with supervision, the ethical guidelines are not clear on this point. It is really up to the individual supervisor to establish rules for gift giving. Supervisees may choose to give supervisors a small memento, such as a mug or picture to commemorate the relationship, or a luncheon party is held to honor the end of the journey. This is rarely seen as a problem. If the supervisee is a graduate student, supervisors may be invited to the graduation and celebrate that way. With group supervision, there are a host of rituals that can be borrowed from group therapy in order to conclude the supervision experience. For example, supervisees who are graduating may be requested to give feedback to each member of the group as a parting present. If the supervision group itself is ending, everyone in the group, including the supervisor, is invited to give this type of positive feedback.

However, others, especially those involved in a lengthy supervision relationship for licensure purpose, will frequently want to do more. Obviously this can become a touchy subject if not discussed openly early on in supervision. Some experienced supervisors circumvent the entire problem by having a plaque on which they place the names of all the supervisees who successfully complete their licensure hours. Others have a standard practice of taking pictures of everyone at the end of supervision and creating a collage for the office wall. Those who like to work with metaphors could ask their supervisees to create a symbol that represents their supervision experience and bring it to the last session. Regardless of the choice, it is advised that supervisors establish with supervisees how to mark the formal conclusion of supervision.

But what about situations when clinical supervision is a standard part of an organization for all employees, and unless a supervisee is fired or takes another job, there is no formal conclusion ever to the experience? Should formal ending times to supervision be set periodically anyway? The answer is an unequivocal yes for many reasons. Endings allow for change and encourage evaluation. Endings give structure to supervision and can help make the experience more beneficial. They also give people permission to make changes in a way that does not appear negative. For example, if at the end of every year, supervision concludes, and everyone is encouraged to evaluate the experience and then has permission to change the structure of supervision, reform groups or teams, or even to change supervisors or supervisees, it can make these changes seem more positive and less personal. The suggestion to have a set ending time for all supervision groups, even open-ended ones, is especially recommended. When people know something is going to conclude, it propels them to action that they might not take if no ending is in sight. For supervisors, thinking about supervision in units of time will promote goal setting and definitely improve the effectiveness of the supervision time.

Putting It Into Practice

Case Example

Melissa works in a large agency that specializes in families and children with trauma and has recently been promoted to supervisor. One of her friends, Sheila, another counselor who has been at the agency for 15 years, is going through a very messy divorce and custody battle. Sheila had admitted to Melissa (before Melissa was promoted) that as a result of the divorce, she was having lots of trouble focusing on her work. Her mind wandered in sessions, and sometimes she blanked out when clients were talking. However, Sheila divulged that she did not think any of this was a real a problem for her as she already knew what most of the clients were going to say anyway.

Melissa also had begun to notice that Sheila's objectivity was being compromised. In staff meetings when client cases were being discussed, Sheila immediately cites a potential for abuse by the father and recommends he immediately be prevented contact with the children.

(continued)

Now that Melissa is Sheila's supervisor, she is in a tough spot. Ethically, she knows she has to confront Sheila about what is going on because it is definitely affecting her work with clients at the agency. However, she still is Sheila's friend and so is very worried about all the things that are happening to Sheila outside of work. She decides to take Sheila to dinner and see if she can encourage her to seek some outside counseling.

Melissa started the conversation about Sheila needing counseling by citing Sheila's self-disclosure about blanking out with clients; Sheila became enraged. She said she felt betrayed by Melissa, that she was taking information she had been given as a friend and was using it against her at work. Melissa was horrified and tried to placate her friend. She told Sheila to forget what she said about needing counseling. Being friends was more important. The dinner ended with both women in tears.

Teaching Point: Melissa recognized the ethical issues at stake with Sheila and the need to intervene as part of her new role as supervisor. However, she did not establish clear boundaries for the discussion. By talking about a work problem over dinner and not in the office, it confused roles and relationships. It would be better to hold the meeting at the office to establish her new role as supervisor with Sheila. Second, Melissa made a mistake when she brought up information obtained through friendship outside the office rather than keep the focus of the discussion on Sheila's current behavior in staff meetings. Third, even though the conversation went poorly, Melissa cannot back off from her role as supervisor to preserve the friendship when such clear ethical issues are involved. Sheila, as an experienced practitioner should know what is expected of her ethically when under a situation of extreme personal stress and should take responsibility to insure no harm comes to any client as a result of her personal life circumstances.

CONCLUSION

Within the experience of supervision a number of unvarying themes are present, regardless of the setting, population served, education, experience level of supervisors and supervisees, and stage of the supervisory relationship: the need for goals and structure, self-awareness, attention to issues of safety and trust, and open communication. Whether one is setting up the supervision relationship or continuing to meet years later, these themes are still powerful factors in success. Research, as well as anecdotal material, keeps returning to the importance of the relationship in supervision: the need for supervisors to be open and clear about the expectations and requirements; be aware of their own thoughts, feelings, and needs as well as those of their supervisees; and to keep monitoring the quality of the relationship throughout supervision.

When examining the ethical standards for supervisors, the occurrence of these themes stand out. For example, in order to build the working relationship and to treat supervisees with fairness and respect, supervisees need to be informed from the beginning about the goals, tasks, and requirements of supervision. The use of an informed consent agreement and orientation are the two recommended strategies to engage in at the beginning of any supervision experience to accomplish this task. However, it is strongly suggested that supervisors continue to return to a discussion of the goals and tasks for supervision even at later stages of development.

As has been discussed throughout this book, what is really asked for is transparency about the supervision process—a clearing up of the mysteries that could create anxiety and interfere with the effectiveness of supervision. Also, it requires supervisors' self-awareness and self-monitoring of the relationship and just some plain garden variety common sense about human beings. It is sometimes truly amazing how expert professionals in the behavioral and mental health field who can manage sessions with some of the most difficult and complicated clients completely park their relationship skills at the door when taking on the role of clinical supervisor! They would never treat their clients (nor probably their friends and family) the way they treat their supervisees. The old adage of treat people the way you want to be treated continues to be true in supervision, and this simple truth, if followed, will carry supervisors farther than any amount

CAUTION

Ten Myths about Clinical Supervision

1. If I am experienced counselor or psychotherapist, I can be successful and effective as a supervisor.
2. True clinical supervision is strictly review of cases. If you give handouts or teach, that is training, not supervision.
3. If supervision is not going well, it is the supervisee's fault.
4. Supervision is only for the inexperienced and beginners. If you have to be supervised, it means you are deficient or incompetent.
5. Because supervisors are all professionals, diversity issues do not have to be addressed.
6. The best feedback is direct. Tell it like you see it. There is no need to coddle supervisees.
7. A supervisee's thoughts and feelings are not relevant to learning in supervision.
8. Supervisors are experts, so it is important to make that clear and to never admit mistakes or that you don't know something.
9. Because supervisees are totally responsible for the actions of their supervisees, the supervisor's suggestions should not be questioned.
10. In order to avoid dual relationships and becoming your supervisee's therapist, you shouldn't use your counseling and therapy skills in supervision and never go into the area of the supervisee's personal feelings or beliefs.

of course work or training. Having said that, however, advanced training and course work in supervision, along with supervision of supervision, is still the best professional development strategy for ethical practice in supervision.

In closing, it is hoped this book has stimulated readers to continue to explore supervision, to seek out supervision of their supervision, to try out new strategies and ideas, and to strive to do the right thing with their supervisees, no matter the obstacles. The goal is worth the struggle.

🪶 TEST YOURSELF 🪶

1. **The main task of the advanced stage is to help supervisees move to a more collegial or collaborative supervisory relationship.** True or False?

2. **When working more collaboratively, the supervisor would**
   (a) tell the supervisee what to do and how to do it.
   (b) ask the supervisee what they have thought of trying rather than giving one's advice when problems occur with a client.
   (c) not say anything.
   (d) agree with everything the supervisee suggests or does.

3. **Process comments and process questions are excellent skills to increase collaboration.** True or False?

4. **One of the easiest ways to encourage self-evaluation on the part of supervisees is to use scaling questions.** True or False?

5. **In group supervision, during the advanced stage of supervision, the supervisor would want to**
   (a) use a group-dynamics or teambuilding model for group supervision.
   (b) encourage group support and positive group interactions.
   (c) do the same things he or she did all along in supervision without regard to change.
   (d) do a and b.
   (e) do b and c.

6. **The main reason to use solution-focused questions in supervision is they make supervisees do all the work and, therefore, save the supervisor's energy.** True or False?

7. **Professional growth and development are also an important focus in the advanced stage.** True or False?

8. **In order to practice ethically,**
   (a) all supervisors should engage either in consultation or supervision of their supervision.
   (b) it is not necessary for supervisors to seek consultation with other professionals.
   (c) supervisors should consider engaging in personal therapy to avoid negative bias or impaired judgement.
   (d) supervisors should just relax and enjoy the fact that they know everything.
   (e) do a and c.
   (f) do b and d.

9. **List two ideas for helping supervisees grow professionally.**

10. **List the seven suggestions to develop stamina and endurance.**

11. **Some of the benefits of a peer consultation group are**
    (a) increasing self-awareness.
    (b) fostering professional growth.
    (c) improving motivation.
    (d) combating isolation and loneliness.
    (e) all of the above.

12. **Name three types of supervisor activities that are considered harmful to supervisees.**

13. **Suggestions to address the problem of bad or harmful supervisors are to**
    (a) require training for supervisors.
    (b) post ethical guidelines for clinical supervisors.
    (c) require supervision for supervisors.
    (d) do all of the above.
    (e) do none of the above.

14. **It is not necessary to do anything special at the conclusion of supervision because everyone is just glad to get it over with.** True or False?

15. **One good idea for the conclusion of clinical supervision for postdegree licensure is to**
    (a) ask supervisees to give you a really nice gift.
    (b) tell supervisees to take you to a very expensive restaurant as a means to show gratitude for your giving them a good evaluation.
    (c) ask supervisees to share one thing they will take away from the experience.
    (d) to skip the last meeting as good-byes are always difficult.

(continued)

16. Burnout

    (a) is the same thing as compassion fatigue.

    (b) is defined as feeling a reduced sense of accomplishment and loss of meaning in work.

    (c) is only found in older practitioners.

    (d) is more likely to be a problem with smokers.

Answers: 1. True; 2. b; 3. True; 4. True; 5. d; 6. False; 7. True; 8. e; 9. Share your own professional growth; attend workshops and conferences, read current research; take supervisees to CEU programs and conferences; ask them to give a paper or program with you at a conference; 10. Selectivity, temporal sensitivity, accountability, measurement and management, inquisitiveness, and negotiation; 11. e; 12. Overstepping boundaries, such as sexual intimacy with supervisees; misuse of power; vindictiveness; responding to supervisees with malice and derision; demeaning supervisees publicly; blatant prejudice toward people of color, gender, sexual orientation, age, or different discipline or education level; 13. d; 14. False; 15. c; 16. b

References

American Psychiatric Association. (2000). *Diagnostic and statistical manual of mental disorders* (4th ed., text revision). Washington, DC: Author.

Anderson, S. A., Schlossberg, M., & Rigazio-diGilio, S. (2000). Family therapy trainees: Evaluations of their best and worst supervision experiences. *Journal of Marital and Family Therapy, 26*(1), 79–91.

Arnstein, R. L., & Balsam, R. (2001). Supervision for the supervisor. In R. Balsam (Ed.), *Psychodynamic psychotherapy: The supervisory process* (pp. 301–318). Madison, CT: International Universities Press.

Association for Counselor Education and Supervision. (1990). Standards for counseling supervisors. *Journal of Counseling and Development, 69,* 30–32.

Association for Counselor Education and Supervision. (1993). *Ethical guidelines for counseling supervisors.* Alexandria, VA: Author.

Baker, S. B., Exum, H. A., & Tyler, R. E. (2002). The developmental process of clinical supervisors in training: An investigation of the supervisor complexity model. *Counselor Education and Supervision, 42*(9), 15–30.

Baldo, T. D., Softas-Nall, B. C., & Shaw, S. F. (1997). Student review and retention in counselor education: An alternative to Frame and Stevens-Smith. *Counselor Education and Supervision, 36,* 245–253.

Bandura, A. (1986). *Social foundations of thought and action: A social cognitive theory.* Englewood Cliffs, NJ: Prentice Hall.

Bandura, A. (1997). *Self-efficacy: The exercise of control.* New York: Freeman.

Barbuto, J. E. (1997). A critique of the Myers-Briggs Type Indicator and its operationalization of Carl Jung's psychological types. *Psychological Reports, 80,* 611–625.

Barnes, K. L. (2004). Applying self-efficacy theory to counselor training and supervision: A comparison of two approaches. *Counselor Education and Supervision, 44*(9), 56–80.

Bernard, J. M. (1997). The discrimination model. In C. E. Watkins (Ed.), *Handbook of psychotherapy supervision* (pp. 310–327). New York: Wiley.

Bernard, J. M., & Goodyear, R. K. (2004). *Fundamentals of clinical supervision* (3rd ed.). Boston: Pearson.

Bernard, J. M., Hackney, H., & Wilkerson, K. (2004). *Requisite skills for engaging in peer supervision.* Presentation at the 2004 American Counseling Association Annual Convention, Kansas City, MO.

Bischoff, R. J., Barton, M., Thober, J., & Hawley, R. (2002). Events and experiences impacting the development of clinical self confidence: A study of the first year of client contact. *Journal of Marital and Family Therapy, 28*(3), 371–382.

Bittel, L. R., & Newstrom, J. W. (1990). *What every supervisor should know* (6th ed.). New York: McGraw-Hill.

Boer, P. M. (2001). *Career counseling over the internet: An emerging model for trusting and responding to online clients.* Mahwah, NJ: Erlbaum.

Borders, L. D. (1997). Subtle boundary issues in supervision. In B. Herlihy & G. Corey (Eds.), *Boundary issues in counseling: Multiple roles and responsibilities* (pp. 73–75). Alexandria, VA: American Counseling Association.

Borders, L. D., & Brown, L. L. (2005). *The new handbook of counseling supervision*. Alexandria, VA: American Counseling Association.

Borders, L. D., & Usher, C. H. (1992). Post-degree supervision: Existing and preferred practices. *Journal of Counseling and Development, 70,* 594–599.

Bordin, E. S. (1983). A working alliance based model of supervision. *The Counseling Psychologist, 11,* 35–42.

Bradley, L. J., & Gould, L. J. (2001). Psychotherapy-based models of counselor supervision. In L. Bradley & N. Ladany (Eds.), *Counselor supervision: Principles, process, and practice* (3rd ed., pp. 147–180). New York: Brunner-Routledge.

Bradley, L. J., & Ladany, N. (Eds.). (2001). *Counselor supervision: Principles, process, and practice.* (3rd ed.). New York: Brunner-Routledge.

Bridges, N. A. (1999). The role of supervision in managing intense affect and constructing boundaries in therapeutic relationships. *Journal of Sex Education and Therapy, 24,* 218–225.

Burns, D. D. (1989). *The feeling good handbook: Using the new mood therapy in everyday life*. New York: William Morrow.

Cameron, S., & turtle-song, I. (2002). Learning to write case notes using the SOAP format. *Journal of Counseling and Development, 80,* 286–292.

Campbell, J. (2000). *Becoming an effective supervisor: A workbook for counselors and psychotherapists.* Philadelphia: Accelerated Development.

Campbell, J. (2001). Coaching: A new field for counselors? *Journal of Counseling and Human Development, 34,* 3.

Campbell, J. (2001–2005). Clinical Skills for Behavioral Health Managers: Ethical and best practice issues. Cross-country seminars.

Cardona, J. R. P., Harris, S. M., Brock, A., & Sandberg, J. G. (2002). Sexual attraction and training in the MFT field: Taboo or learning experience? *Journal of the Texas Association for Marriage and Family Therapy, 7*(1), 13–20.

Chen, E. C., & Bernstein, B. L. (2000). Relations of complementarity and supervisory issues to supervisory working alliance: A comparative analysis of two cases. *Journal of Counseling Psychology, 47*(4), 485–497.

Christensen, T. M., & Kline, W. B. (2001a). Anxiety as a condition for learning in group supervision. *Journal for Specialists in Group Work, 26*(4), 385–396.

Christensen, T. M., & Kline, W. B. (2001b). The qualitative exploration of process-sensitive peer group supervision. *Journal for Specialists in Group Work, 26*(1), 81–99.

Chung, Y. B., Baskin, M. L., & Case, A. B. (1998). Positive and negative supervisory experiences reported by counseling trainees. *Psychological Reports, 82,* 762.

Chung, Y. B., Marshall, J. A., & Gordon, L. L. (2001). Racial and gender biases in supervisory evaluation and feedback. *The Clinical Supervisor, 20,* 99–111.

Clingerman, T. L., & Bernard, J. M. (2004). An investigation of the use of e-mail as a supplemental modality for clinical supervision. *Counselor Education and Supervision, 44*(2), 82–95.

Cobia, D. C., & Boes, S. R. (2000). Professional disclosure statements and formal plans for supervision: Two strategies for minimizing the risk of ethical conflicts in post-master's supervision. *Journal of Counseling and Development, 78,* 293–296.

Cobia, D. C., & Pipes, R. B. (2002). Mandated supervision: An intervention for disciplined professionals. *Journal of Counseling and Development, 80,* 140–144.

Coleman, D. (2001). A coach's lessons learned. In C. Fitzgerald & J. G. Berger (Eds.), *Executive coaching: Practices and perspectives*. Stanford, CA: Davies-Black.

Constantine, M. G. (1997). Facilitating multicultural competency in counseling supervision. In D. B. Pope-Davis & H. L. K. Coleman (Eds.), *Multicultural counseling competences: Assessment, education and training, and supervision* (pp. 310–324). Thousand Oaks, CA: Sage.

Cook, E., Berman, E., Genco, K., Repka, R., & Shrider, J. (1986). Essential characteristics of master's level counselors: Perceptions of agency administrators. *Counselor Education and Supervision, 34,* 146–152.

Corey, M. S., & Corey, G. (2002). *Groups: Process and practice* (6th ed.). Pacific Grove, CA: Brooks/Cole.

Daniels, J. A., & Larson, L. M. (2001). The impact of performance feedback on counseling self-efficacy and counselor anxiety. *Counselor Education and Supervision, 41*(12), 120–130.

Davis, K. M. (2003). Teaching a course in school-based consultation. *Counselor Education and Supervision, 42*(6), 275–286.

Davy, J. (2002). Discursive reflections on a research agenda for clinical supervision. *Psychology and Psychotherapy: Theory, Research and Practice, 75*(2), 221–238.

Dlugos, R. F., & Friedlander, M. L. (2001). Passionately committed psychotherapists: A qualitative study of their experience. *Professional Psychology: Research and Practice, 32*(3), 298–304.

Doehrman, M. J. G. (1976). Parallel processes in supervision and psychotherapy. *Bulletin of the Menninger Clinic, 40*(1), 3–10.

Edwards, J. K., & Chen, M-W. (1999). Strength-based supervision: Framework, current practice and future directions. *Family Journal-Counseling and Therapy for Couples and Families, 7*(4), 349–357.

Edwards, T. M., & Heshmati, A. (2003). A guide for beginning family therapy group supervisors. *American Journal of Family Therapy, 31*(4), 295–304.

Ellis, M. V. (2001). Harmful supervision, a cause for alarm. Comment on Gray et al. (2001) and Nelson and Friedlander (2001). *Journal of Counseling Psychology, 48*(4), 401–406.

Ellis, M. V., Krengel, M., & Beck, M. (2002). Testing self-focused attention theory in clinical supervision: Effects of supervisee anxiety and performance. *Journal of Counseling Psychology, 49*(1), 101–116.

Ellis, M. V., & Ladany, N. (1997). Inferences concerning supervisees and clients in clinical supervision: An integrative review. In C. E. Watkins, Jr. (Ed.), *Handbook of psychotherapy supervision* (pp. 447–507). New York: Wiley.

Enyedy, K. C., Arcinue, F., Puri, N. N., Carter, J. W., Goodyear, R. K., & Getzelman, M. A. (2003). Group supervision of school psychologists in training. *American Psychologist, 57,* 1060–1073.

Estrada, D., Frame, M. W., & Williams, C. B. (2004). Cross-cultural supervision: Guiding the conversation toward race and ethnicity. *Journal of Multicultural Counseling and Development, 32,* 307–319.

Etherington, K. (2000). Supervising counsellors who work with survivors of childhood sexual abuse. *Counselling Psychology Quarterly, 13*(4), 377–389.

Falvey, J. E. (2002). *Managing clinical supervision: Ethical practice and legal risk management.* Pacific Grove, CA: Brooks/Cole.

Falvey, J. E., Caldwell, C. F., & Cohen, C. R. (2002). *Documentation in supervision: The focused risk management system (FoRMSS).* Pacific Grove, CA: Brooks/Cole.

Figley, C. R. (1995). *Compassion fatigue: Coping with Secondary Traumatic Stress Disorder in those who treat traumatized.* New York: Brunner/Mazel.

Figley, C. R. (2002, May). *How to work with traumatized families.* Paper presented at the Jewish Family Services Professional Conference, Houston, TX.

Fisch, R., Weakland, J., & Segal, L. (1982). *The tactics of change: Doing things briefly.* San Francisco: Jossey Bass.

Fitch, T. J., & Marshall, J. L. (2002). Using cognitive interventions with counseling practicum students during group supervision. *Counselor Education and Supervision, 41*(6), 335–342.

Forrest, L., Elman, N., Gizara, S., & Vacha-Haase, T. (1999). Trainee impairment: A review of identification, remediation, dismissal, and legal issues. *Counseling Psychologist, 27,* 627–686.

Foster, V. A., & McAdams, C. R. III. (1998). Supervising the child care counselor: A cognitive developmental model. *Child and Youth Care Forum, 27*(1), 5–19.

Frame, M. W. (2000). The spiritual genogram in family therapy. *Journal of Marital and Family Therapy, 26*(2), 211–216.

Frame, M. W., & Stevens-Smith, P. (1995). Out of harm's way: Enhancing monitoring and dismissal processes in counselor education programs. *Counselor Education and Supervision, 35,* 118–129.

Frawley-O'Dea, M. G., & Sarnat, J. E. (2001). *The supervisory relationship: A contemporary psychodynamic approach.* New York: Guilford.

Freitas, G. J. (2002). The impact of psychotherapy supervision on client outcome: A critical examination of 2 decades of research. *Psychotherapy: Theory/Research/Practice/Training, 39*(4), 354–367.

Friedlander, M. L., & Ward, L. G. (1984). Development and validation of the supervisory styles inventory. *Journal of Counseling Psychology, 4,* 541–557.

Furr, S. R., & Carroll, J. J. (2003). Critical incidents in student counselor development. *Journal of Counseling and Development, 81,* 483–489.

Gaubatz, M. D., & Vera, E. M. (2002). Do formalized gatekeeping procedures increase programs' follow-up with deficient trainees? *Counselor Education and Supervision, 41*(6), 294–306.

Gehring, T. M., Widmer, J., Baenziger, O., & Marti, D. (2002). Quality of work and need for supervision among physicians and nurses of a pediatric intensive care unit. *Clinical Child Psychology and Psychiatry, 7*(4), 505–608.

Gerstein, L. H., & Moeschberger, S. L. (2003). Building cultures of peace: An urgent task for counseling professionals. *Journal of Counseling and Development, 81,* 115–120.

Getz, H. G. (1999). Assessment of clinical supervisor competencies. *Journal of Counseling and Development, 77*(4), 491–497.

Getz, H. G., & Agnew, D. (1999). A supervision model for public agency clinicians. *Clinical Supervisor, 18*(2), 51–62.

Getz, H. G., & Protinsky, H. O. (1994). Training marriage and family counselors: A family-of-origin approach. *Counselor Education and Supervision, 33,* 183–190.

Glasser, W. (2004). Panel discussion. American Counseling Conference Convention. Kansas City, MO.

Goodyear, R. K. (1998). Research and practice: Implications of the SCMCT: Observations and comments. *Counseling Psychologist, 26*(2), 274–284.

Gould, L. J., & Bradley, L. J. (2001). Evaluation in supervision. In L. Bradley & N. Ladany (Eds.), *Counselor supervision: Principles, process and practice* (3rd ed., pp. 271–303). New York: Brunner Routledge.

Gottlieb, M. C. (2004, September). *Ethical issues for practitioners in a complex world.* Continuing education seminar presented by the Houston Psychological Association, Houston, TX.

Granello, D. H. (2000). Encouraging the cognitive development of supervisees: Using Bloom's taxonomy in supervision. *Counselor Education and Supervision, 40,* 31–46.

Granello, D. H. (2003). Influence strategies in the supervisory dyad: An investigation into the effects of gender and age. *Counselor Education and Supervision, 42,* 189–202.

Gray, L. A., Ladany, N., Walker, J. A., & Ancis, J. R. (2001). Psychotherapy trainees' experience of counterproductive events in supervision. *Journal of Counseling Psychology, 48*(4), 371–383.

Green, S., Shilts, L., & Bacigalupe, G. (2001). When approved is not enough: Development of a supervision consultation model. *Journal of Marital and Family Therapy, 27*(4), 515–525.

Greer, J. A. (2002). Where to turn for help: Responses to inadequate clinical supervision. *The Clinical Supervisor, 21*(1), 135–143.

Griffith, B. A., & Frieden, G. (2000). Facilitating reflective thinking in counselor education. *Counselor Education and Supervision, 40,* 82–93.

Haber, R. (1996). *Dimensions of psychotherapy supervision*. New York: Norton.

Haley, J. (1976). *Problem solving therapy*. San Francisco: Jossey Bass.

Halgrin, R. P. (2002). Special Section: Issues in clinical supervision. *The Clinical Supervisor, 21*(1), 111–114.

Hantoot, M. S. (2000). Lying in psychotherapy supervision: Why residents say one thing and do another. *Academic Psychiatry, 24,* 179–187.

Hardy, K. V., & Laszloffy, T. A. (1995). The cultural genogram: Key to training culturally competent family therapists. *Journal of Marital and Family Therapy, 21*(3), 227–237.

Harris, S. M. (2001). Teaching family therapists about sexual attraction in therapy. *Journal of Marital and Family Therapy, 27*(1), 123–128.

Hart, G. M., & Nance, D. (2003). Styles of counselor supervision as perceived by supervisors and supervisees. *Counselor Education and Supervision, 43*(12), 146–158.

Hawkins, P., & Shohet, R. (2003). *Supervision in the helping professions* (2nd ed.). Berkshire, UK: Open University Press.

Hayes, R. L., Blackman, L. S., & Brennan, C. (2001). Group supervision. In L. Bradley & N. Ladany (Eds.), *Counselor Supervision: Principles, process, and practice* (3rd ed., pp. 183–206). New York: Brunner Routledge.

Haynes, R., Corey, G., & Moulton, P. (2003). *Clinical supervision in the helping professions*. Pacific Grove, CA: Brooks/Cole.

Hays, D. G., & Chang, C. Y. (2003). White privilege, oppression, and racial identity development: Implications for supervision. *Counselor Education and Supervision, 43,* 134–145.

Helmeke, K. B., & Prouty, A. M. (2001). Do we really understand? An experiential exercise for training family therapists. *Journal of Marital and Family Therapy, 27*(4), 535–544.

Helms, J. E., & Cook, D. A. (1999). *Using race and culture in counseling and psychotherapy: Theory and process*. Boston: Allyn & Bacon.

Hensley, L. G., Smith, S. L., & Thompson, R. W. (2003). Assessing competencies of counselors-in-training: Complexities in evaluating personal and professional development. *Counselor Education and Supervision, 42*(3), 219–230.

Herlihy, B., & Corey, G. (1997). *Boundary issues in counseling: Multiple roles and responsibilities*. Alexandria, VA: American Counseling Association.

Hersey, P., & Blanchard, K. H. (1996). Revisiting the life cycle theory of leadership. *Training and Development Journal,* 43–47.

Horney, K. (1950). *Neurosis and human growth*. New York: Norton.

Housman, L. M., & Strake, J. E. (1999). The current state of sexual ethics training in clinical psychology: Issues of quantity, quality, and effectiveness. *Professional Psychology: Research and Practice, 30*(3), 302–311.

Hulse-Killacky, D., & Page, B. (1994). Development of the corrective feedback instrument: A tool for use in counselor training groups. *The Journal for Specialists in Group Work, 19*(4), 197–210.

Hyrkaes, K., & Lehti, K. (2003). Continuous quality improvement through team supervision supported by continuous self-monitoring of work and systematic patient feedback. *Journal of Nursing Management, 11*(3), 177–188.

Ivey, A. E., & Ivey, M. B. (1999). *Intentional interviewing and counseling* (4th ed.). Pacific Grove, CA: Brooks/Cole.

Kagan, H., & Kagan, N. (1997). Interpersonal process recall: Influencing human interaction. In C. E. Watkins, Jr. (Ed.), *Handbook of psychotherapy supervision* (pp. 296–309). New York: Wiley.

Kagan, N. (1980). *Interpersonal process recall: A method of influencing human interaction*. Class presentation. Houston, TX: University of Houston.

Kaiser, T. (1997). *Supervisory relationships: Exploring the human element*. Pacific Grove, CA: Brooks/Cole.

Kaiser, T. L., & Barretta-Herman, A. (1999). The supervision institute: A model for supervisory training. *Clinical Supervisor, 18*(1), 33–46.

Kanz, J. E. (2001). Clinical-Supervision.com: Issues in the provision of online supervision. *Professional Psychology: Research and Practice, 32*(4), 415–420.

Kerl, S. B., Garcia, J. L., McCullough, S., & Maxwell, M. E. (2002). Systematic evaluation of professional performance: Legally supported procedure and process. *Counselor Education and Supervision, 41*(6), 321–334.

Knapp, S., & VandeCreek, L. (2003). An overview of the major changes in the 2002 APA ethics code. *Professional Psychology: Research and Practice, 34*(3), 301–308.

Kormanski, C. (1999). *The team: Explorations in group process.* Denver, CA: Love.

Kuehll, B. P. (1995). The solution-oriented genogram: A collaborative approach. *Journal of Marital and Family Therapy, 21*(3), 239–250.

Ladany, N., Brittan-Powell, C. S., & Pannu, R. K. (1997). The influence of supervisory racial interaction and racial matching on the supervisory working alliance and supervisee multicultural competence. *Counselor Education and Supervision, 36,* 284–304.

Ladany, N., Constantine, M. G., Miller, K., Erickson, C. D., & Muse-Burke, J. L. (2000). Supervisor countertransference: A qualitative investigation into its identification and description. *Journal of Counseling Psychology, 47*(1), 102–115.

Ladany, N., Ellis, M. V., & Friedlander, M. L. (1999). The supervisory working alliance, trainee self-efficacy, and satisfaction. *Journal of Counseling and Development, 77*(4), 447–455.

Ladany, N., & Friedlander, M. L. (1995). The relationship between the supervisory working alliance and trainees' experience of role conflict and role ambiguity. *Counselor Education and Supervision, 34,* 220–231.

Ladany, N., Hill, C. E., Corbett, M. M., & Nutt, E. A. (1996). Nature, extent, and importance of what psychotherapy trainees do not disclose to their supervisors. *Journal of Counseling Psychology, 43,* 10–24.

Ladany, N., Inman, A. G., Constantine, M. G., & Hofheinz, E. W. (1997). Supervisee multicultural case conceptualization ability and self-reported multicultural competence as functions of supervisee racial identity and supervisor focus. *Journal of Counseling Psychology, 44,* 284–293.

Ladany, N., Lehrman-Waterman, D., Molinaro, M., & Wolgast, B. (1999). Psychotherapy supervisor ethical practices: Adherence to guidelines, the supervisory working alliance, and supervisee satisfaction. *The Counseling Psychologist, 27*(3), 443–475.

Ladany, N., Marotta, S., & Muse-Burke, J. L. (2001). Counselor experience related to complexity of case conceptualization and supervision preference. *Counselor Education and Supervision, 40*(3), 203–219.

Ladany, N., & Muse-Burke, J. L. (2001). Understanding and conducting supervision research. In L. Bradley & N. Ladany (Eds.), *Counselor supervision: Principles, process, and practice* (3rd ed., 304–329). New York: Brunner-Routledge.

Ladany, N., O'Brien, K. M., Hill, C. E., Melincoff, D. S., Knox, S., & Petersen, D. A. (1997). Sexual attraction toward clients, use of supervision, and prior training: A qualitative study of predoctoral psychology interns. *Journal of Counseling Psychology, 44,* 413–424.

Ladany, N., & Walker, J. A. (2003). Supervision self-disclosure: Balancing the uncontrollable narcissist with the indomitable altruist. *Journal of Clinical Psychology, 59*(5), 611–621.

Ladany, N., Walker, J. A., & Melincoff, D. S. (2001). Supervisory style: Its relation to the supervisory working alliance and supervisor self-disclosure. *Counselor Education and Supervision, 40*(6), 263–276.

Landsberg, M. (1997). *The Tao of coaching.* Santa Monica, CA: Knowledge Exchange.

Langan, M., & Milioti, D., Jr. (2002, October). *The power of metaphor: A method of enhancing student development.* Paper presented at ACES National Convention: Celebrating our past while shaping our future, Park City, UT.

Lee, R. L., Nichols, D. P., Nichols, W. C., & Odom, T. (2004). Trends in family therapy supervision: The past 25 years and into the future. *Journal of Marital and Family Therapy, 30*(1), 61–69.

Lehrman-Waterman, D., & Ladany, N. (2001). Development and validation of the evaluation process within supervision inventory. *Journal of Counseling Psychology, 48*(2), 168–177.

Lerner, H. G. (1989). *The dance of intimacy.* New York: Harper & Row.

Lerner, H. G. (1997). *The dance of anger.* New York: Harper & Row.

Ligiero, D. P., & Gelso, C. J. (2002). Countertransference, attachment, and the working alliance: The therapist's contribution. *Psychotherapy: Therapy, Research, Practice, Training, 39*(1), 3–11.

Linton, J. M. (2003). A preliminary qualitative investigation of group processes in group supervision: Perspectives of master's level practicum students. *Journal for Specialists in Group Work, 28*(3), 215–226.

Locke, L. D., & McCollum, E. E. (2001). Clients' views of live supervision and satisfaction with therapy. *Journal of Marital and Family Therapy, 27*(1), 129–133.

Lowe, R. (2000). Supervising self-supervision: Constructive inquiry and embedded narratives in case consultation. *Journal of Marital and Family Therapy, 26*(4), 511–521.

Lyddon, W. J., Clay, A. L., & Sparks, C. L. (2001). Metaphor and change in counseling. *Journal of Counseling and Development, 79*(2), 269–274.

Magnuson, S., Norem, K., & Wilcoxon, S. A. (2000). Clinical supervision of prelicensed counselors: Recommendations for consideration and practice. *Journal of Mental Health Counseling, 22*(2), 176–188.

Magnuson, S., & Shaw, H. E. (2003). Adaptations of the multifaceted genogram in counseling, training and supervision. *Family Journal-Counseling and Therapy for Couples and Families, 11*(1), 45–54.

Magnuson, S., & Wilcoxon. (1998). Successful clinical supervision of prelicensed counselors: How will we recognize it? *Clinical Supervisor, 17*(1), 33–45.

Magnuson, S., Wilcoxon, S. A., & Norem, K. (2000). A profile of lousy supervision: Experienced counselor's perspectives. *Counselor Education and Supervision, 39,* 189–202.

Manzanares, M. G., O'Halloran, T. M., McCartney, T. J., Filer, R. D., Varhely, S. C., & Calhoun, K. (2004). CD-ROM technology for education and support of site supervisors. *Counselor Education and Supervision, 43*(3), 220–231.

Marshall, R. J. (1999). Facilitating cooperation in group supervision. *Modern Psychoanalysis, 24*(2), 181–186.

McCarthy, P., Sugden, S., Koker, M., Lamendola, F., Maurer, S., & Renninger, S. (1995). A practical guide to informed consent in clinical supervision. *Counselor Education and Supervision, 35,* 130–138.

McCollum, E. E., & Wetchler, J. L. (1995). In defense of case consultation: Maybe "dead" supervision isn't dead after all. *Journal of Marital and Family Therapy, 21,* 155–166.

McGee, M., & Burton, R. (1998). The use of co-therapy with a reflecting mirror as a supervisory tool. *Journal of Family Psychotherapy, 9*(4), 45–60.

McGoldrick, M., & Gerson, R. (1985). *Genograms in family assessment.* New York: Norton.

McMahon, M., & Simons, R. (2004). Supervision training for professional counselors: An exploratory study. *Counselor Education and Supervision, 43*(6), 301–309.

Middleman, R. R., & Rhodes, G. B. (1985). *Competent supervision: Making imaginative judgments.* Englewood Cliffs, NJ: Prentice Hall.

Moorhouse, A., & Carr, A. (2001). A study of live supervisory phone-ins in collaborative family therapy: Correlates of client cooperation. *Journal of Marital and Family Therapy, 27*(2), 241–249.

Morran, K. D., Kurpius, D. J., Brack, C. J., & Brack, G. (1995). A cognitive-skills model for counselor training and supervision. *Journal of Counseling and Development, 73,* 384–396.

Munson, C. E. (2002). *Handbook of clinical social work supervision* (3rd ed.). Binghamton, NY: Haworth.

Muratori, M. C. (2001). Examining supervisor impairment from the counselor trainee's perspective. *Counselor Education and Supervision, 41,* 41–56.

Muse-Burke, J. L., Ladany, N., & Deck, M. D. (2001). The supervisory relationship. In L. Bradley & N. Ladany (Eds.), *Counselor supervision: Principles, process, and practice* (3rd ed., pp. 28–62). New York: Brunner-Routledge.

Myers, I. B., McCaulley, M. H., Quenk, N. L., & Hammer, A. L. (1998). *MBTI manual: A guide to the development and use of the Myers-Briggs Type Indicator* (3rd ed.). Palo Alto, CA: CPP, Inc.

National Association of Social Workers. (1999). *Code of ethics.* Washington, DC: Author.

National Board for Certified Counselors, Inc. (1999). Approved clinical supervisor certification requirements. Retrieved September 16, 1999, from http://www.nbcc.org/acs/requirements.htm

Nelson, M. L., & Friedlander, M. L. (2001). A close look at conflictual supervisory relationships: The trainee's perspective. *Journal of Counseling Psychology, 48*(4), 384–395.

Nelson, M. L., Gray, L. A., Friedlander, M. L., Ladany, N., & Walker, J. A. (2001). Toward relationship-centered supervision: Reply to Veach (2001) and Ellis (2001). *Journal of Counseling Psychology, 48*(4), 407–409.

Neufeldt, S. A. (2001). Educating supervisors: A constructivist approach to the teaching of supervision. In K. Eriksen & G. McAuliffe (Eds.), *Teaching counselors and therapists: Constructivist and developmental course design* (pp. 169–184). Westport, CT: Bergin & Garvey.

Neufeldt, S. A. (2003). *The portable mentor: Expert guide to a successful career in psychology.* New York: Kluwer Academic/Plenum Publishers.

Neufeldt, S. A., & Nelson, M. L. (1998). Research in training clinics: A bridge between science and practice. *Journal of Clinical Psychology, 54*(3), 315–327.

Neukrug, E., Milliken, T., & Walden, S. (2001). Ethical complaints made against credentialed counselors: An updated survey of state licensing boards. *Counselor Education and Supervision, 41*(9), 57–70.

Nevill, D., and Super, D. (1985). *Values scale.* Palo Alto, CA: Consulting Psychologists Press.

Nickell, N. J., Hecker, L. L., Ray, R. E., & Bercik, J. (1995). Marriage and family therapists' sexual attraction to clients: An exploration study. *American Journal of Family Therapy, 23,* 315–327.

Noelle, M. (2002). Self-report in supervision: Positive and negative slants. *The Clinical Supervisor, 21*(1), 125–134.

Norcross, J. C. (2002). Empirically supported relationships. In J. C. Norcross (Ed.), *Psychotherapy relationships that work* (pp. 3–16). New York: Oxford University Press.

Osborn, C. J. (2004). Seven salutary suggestions for counselor stamina. *Journal of Counseling and Development, 82*(2), 319–328.

Page, B. J., & Hulse-Killacky, D. (1999). Development and validation of the corrective feedback self-efficacy instrument. *Journal for Specialists in Group Work, 24*(1), 37–54.

Page, B. J., Piertzak, D. R., & Lewis, T. F. (2001). Development of the group leader self-efficacy instrument. *Journal for Specialists in Group Work, 26*(2), 168–184.

Page, B. J., Pietzak, D. R., & Sutton, J. M. (2001). National survey of school counselor supervision. *Counselor Education and Supervision, 41*(2), 142–150.

Patton, M. J., & Kivlighan, D. M. (1997). Relevance of the supervisory alliance to the counseling alliance and to treatment adherence in counselor training. *Journal of Counseling Psychology, 44*(1), 108–115.

Peace, S. D., & Sprinthall, N. A. (1998). Training school counselors to supervise beginning counselors: Theory, research and practice. *Professional School Counseling, 1*(5), 2–8.

Pearson, B., & Piazza, N. (1997). Classification of dual relationships in the helping professions. *Counselor Education and Supervision, 37,* 89–99.

Perls, F. (1969). *Gestalt therapy verbatim.* Moab, UT: Real People Press.

Peterson, M. (1993). Covert agendas in supervision. *Supervision Bulletin, 6*(1), 1, 7–8.

Powell, D. J. (1993). *Clinical supervision in alcohol and drug abuse counseling: Principles, models, methods.* New York: Lexington Books.

Prieto, L. R., & Scheel, K. R. (2002). Using case documentation to strengthen counselor trainees' case conceptualization skills. *Journal of Counseling and Development, 80,* 11–21.

Prochaska, J. O., Norcross, J. C., & DiClemente, C. (1994). *Changing for good.* New York: William Morrow.

Protinsky, H., & Coward, L. (2001). Developmental lessons of seasoned marital and family therapists: A qualitative investigation. *Journal of Marital and Family Therapy, 27*(3), 375–384.

Raichelson, S. H., Herron, W. G., Primavera, L. H., & Ramirez, S. M. (1997). Incidence and effects of parallel process in psychotherapy supervision. *Clinical Supervisor, 15*(2), 37–48.

Rambo, A. H., Heath, A., & Chenail, R. J. (1993). *Practicing therapy: Exercises for growing therapists.* New York: Norton.

Ratliff, D. A., Wampler, K. S., & Morris, G. H. (2000). Lack of consensus in supervision. *Journal of Marital and Family Therapy, 26*(3), 373–384.

Rau, D. R. (2002). Advanced trainees supervising junior trainees. *Clinical Supervisor, 21*(1), 115–124.

Ray, D., & Altekruse, M. (2000). Effectiveness of group supervision versus combined group and individual supervision. *Counselor Education and Supervision, 40*(9), 19–30.

Remley, T. P., & Herlihy, B. (2005). *Ethical, legal, and professional issues in counseling* (2nd ed.). Upper Saddle River, NJ: Merrill/Prentice Hall.

Rogers, C. R. (1951). *Client-centered therapy.* Boston: Houghton Mifflin.

Roman, C. (2000). *Coaching: Principles and practice.* Course handouts. Washington, DC: George Washington University.

Rosenfield, M. (2002). Electronic technology for social work education and practice: The application of telephone technology to counseling. *Journal of Technology in Human Services, 20*(1–2), 173–181.

Rubin, I. (2000). Patient safety and managerial malpractice: What's the connection? New York: Temenos®, Inc. Unpublished manuscript.

Russell, R., & Petrie, T. (1994). Issues in training effective supervisors. *Applied and Preventive Psychology, 3,* 27–42.

Ryde, J. (2000). Supervising across difference. *International Journal of Psychotherapy, 5,* 37–48.

Saccuzzo, D. P. (2002). Liability for failure to supervise: Let the master beware. *The National Register of Health Service Providers in Psychology,* (13), 1–14.

Saccuzzo, D. P. (2003). Liability for failure to supervise: Let the master beware. Part 2. Ethical basis for standard of care in supervision. *The National Register of Health Service Providers in Psychology,* (13), 1–19.

Samuel, S. E., & Gorton, G. E. (1998). National survey of psychology internship directors regarding education for prevention of psychologist-patient sexual exploitation. *Professional Psychology: Research and Practice, 29,* 86–90.

Schwartz, R. C., Liddle, H. A., & Breunlin, D. C. (1988). Muddles in live supervision. In H. A. Liddle, D. C. Breunlin, & R. C. Schwartz (Eds.), *Handbook of family therapy training and supervision* (pp. 183–193). New York: Guilford.

Schultz, J. C., Odokie, J. N., Fried, J. H., Nelson, R. E., & Bardos, A. N. (2002). Clinical supervision in public rehabilitation counseling settings. *Rehabilitation Counseling Bulletin, 45*(4), 213–222.

Scott, K. J., Ingram, K. M., Vitanza, S. A., & Smith, N. G. (2000). Training in supervision: A survey of current practices. *Counseling Psychologist, 28*(3), 403–422.

Schechtman, Z., & Wirzberger, A. (1999). Needs and preferred style of supervision among Israeli school counselors at different stages of professional development. *Journal of Counseling and Development, 77*(3), 456–464.

Sherman, M., & Thelen, D. (1998). Distress and professional impairment among psychologists in private practice. *Professional Psychology: Research and Practice, 29,* 79–85.

Shulman, L. (1993). *Interactional supervision.* Washington, DC: NASW Press.

Soo, E. S. (1998). Is training and supervision of children and adolescent group therapists necessary? *Journal of Child and Adolescent Group Therapy, 8*(4), 181–196.

Starak, Y. (2001). Clinical supervision: A Gestalt-humanistic framework. *Gestalt! Gestalt Global Corporation, 5*(1), 1–10.

Staton, A. R., & Gilligan, T. D. (2003). Teaching school counselors and school psychologists to work collaboratively. *Counselor Education and Supervision, 42*(3), 162–176.

Steven, D. T., Goodyear, R. K., & Robertson, P. (1998). Supervisor development: An exploratory study in changes in stance and emphasis. *Clinical Supervisor, 16*(2), 73–88.

Steward, R. J., Breland, A., & Neil, D. M. (2001). Novice supervisees' self-evaluations and their perceptions of supervisor style. *Counselor Education and Supervision, 41*(12), 131–140.

Stinchfield, T. A. (2004). Clinical competencies specific to family-based therapy. *Counselor Education and Supervision, 43*(4), 286–300.

Stoltenberg, C. D. (1998). A social cognitive—and developmental—model of counselor training. *Counseling Psychologist, 26*(2), 317–323.

Stoltenberg, C. D., McNeill, B. W., & Delworth, U. (1998). *IDM supervision: An integrated development model for supervising counselors and therapists.* San Francisco: Jossey-Bass.

Storm, C. L., & Todd, T. C. (1997). *The reasonably complete systemic supervisor resource guide.* Boston: Allyn & Bacon.

Storm, C. L., Todd, T. C., Sprenkle, D. H., & Morgan, M. M. (2001). Gaps between MFT supervision assumptions and common practice: Suggested best practices. *Journal of Marital and Family Therapy, 27*(1), 227–239.

Stozier, A. L., Barnett-Queen, T., & Burnett, C. K. (2000). Supervision: Critical process and outcome variables. *The Clinical Supervisor, 19*(1), 21–39.

Sutter, E., McPherson, R. H., & Geeseman, R. (2002). Contracting for supervision. *Professional Psychology: Research and Practice, 33*(5), 495–498.

Teyber, E. (1997). *Interpersonal process in psychotherapy.* Pacific Grove, CA: Brooks/Cole.

Todd, T. C., & Storm, C. L. (1997). *The complete systemic supervisor: Context, philosophy, and pragmatics.* Boston: Allyn & Bacon.

Torres-Rivera, E., Phan, L. T., Maddux, C., Wilbur, M. P., Garett, M. T., & Tlanusta, M. (2001). Process versus content: Integrated personal awareness and counseling skills to meet the multicultural challenge of the twenty-first century. *Counselor Education and Supervision, 41*(1), 28–40.

Towler, J. (1999). Supervision in uninformed settings. In *Counselling supervision in context. Counselling supervision* (pp. 177–200). London, UK: Sage.

Treadwell, T. W., Kumar, V. K., Stein, S., & Prosnick, K. (1997). Sociometry: Tools for research and practice. *Journal for Specialists in Group Work, 22,* 52–65.

Tuckman, B. W., & Jensen, M. A. (1977). Stages of small group development revisited. *Group and Organizational Studies, 2,* 419–427.

Veach, P. M. (2001). Conflict and counterproductivity in supervision—when relationships are less than ideal: Comment on Nelson and Friedlander (2001) and Gray et al. (2001). *Journal of Counseling Psychology, 48*(4), 396–400.

Walsh, K., Nicholson, J., Keough, C., Pridham, R., Kramer, M., & Jeffrey, J. (2003). Development of a group model of clinical supervision to meet the needs of a community mental health nursing team. *International Journal of Nursing Practice, 9*(1), 33–39.

Watkins, C. E., Jr. (Ed.). (1997). *Handbook of psychotherapy supervision.* New York: Wiley.

Watkins, C. E., Jr. (1998). Psychotherapy supervision in the 21st century: Some pressing needs and impressing possibilities. *Journal of Psychotherapy Practice and Research, 7*(2), 93–101.

Weaks, D. (2002). Unlocking the secrets of good supervision: A phenomenological exploration of experienced counsellor's perceptions of good supervision. *Counselling and Psychotherapy Research, 2*(1), 33–39.

Webb, J. D., & Wheeler, S. (1998). How honest do counselors dare to be in the supervisory relationship? An exploratory study. *British Journal of Guidance and Counseling, 26,* 509–524.

West, P. L., Mustaine, B. L., & Wyrick, B. (2002). Apples and oranges make a nice start for a fruit salad: A response to Culbreth and Borders (1999). *Journal of Counseling and Development, 80*(1), 72–76.

Wetchler, J. L., Piercy, F. P., & Sprenkle, D. H. (1989). Supervisors' and supervisees' perceptions of the effectiveness of family therapy supervisory techniques. *American Journal of Family Therapy, 17,* 35–47.

Whiffen, R. (1982). The use of videotape in supervision. In R. Whiffen & J. Byng-Hall (Eds.), *Family therapy supervision: Recent developments in practice.* New York: Academic Press.

Whiston, S. C., & Coker, J. K. (2000). Reconstructing clinical training: Implications from research. *Counselor Education and Supervision, 39,* 228–253.

White, M., & Russell, C. (1995). The essential elements of supervisory systems: A modified study. *Journal of Marital and Family Therapy, 21*(1), 33–53.

White, V. E., & Queener, J. (2003). Supervisor and supervisee attachments and social provisions related to the supervisory working alliance. *Counselor Education and Supervision, 42*(3), 203–228.

Whiting, P. P., Bradley, L. J., & Planny, K. J. (2001). Supervision-based developmental models of counselor supervision. In L. Bradley & N. Ladany (Eds.), *Counselor supervision: Principles, process, and practice* (3rd ed., pp. 125–146). New York: Brunner Routledge.

Worthen, V., & McNeill, B. W. (1996). A phenomenological investigation of "good" supervision events. *Journal of Counseling Psychology, 26,* 64–73.

Worthington, E. L. (1987). Changes in supervision as counselors and supervisors gain experience: A review. *Professional Psychology: Research and Practice, 18,* 189–208.

Wulf, J., & Nelson, M. L. (2000). Experienced psychologists' recollections of internship supervision and its contributions to their development. *The Clinical Supervisor, 19*(2), 123–145.

Yalom, I. D. (1989). *Love's executioner.* New York: Harper Perennial.

Yalom, I. D. (1995). *The theory and practice of group psychotherapy* (4th ed.). New York: Basic Books.

Yerushalmi, H. (1999). The roles of group supervision of supervision. *Psychoanalytic Psychology, 16*(3), 426–447.

York, C. D. (1997). Selecting and constructing supervision structures: Individuals, dyads, co-therapists, groups, and teams. In T. C. Todd & C. L. Storm (Eds.), *The complete systemic supervisor: Context, philosophy, and pragmatics* (pp. 320–333). Boston: Allyn & Bacon.

Annotated Bibliography

Campbell, J. (2000). *Becoming an effective supervisor: A workbook for counselors and psychotherapists.* Philadelphia: Accelerated Development.

This workbook will make an excellent companion to any book on supervision. Its strengths lie in the numerous self-awareness exercises and examples of materials useful to beginning as well as more advanced supervisors. Although written primarily to those working with postdegree supervision for licensure, it has a wealth of practical information for anyone working as a supervisor, inside or outside an academic setting.

Falvey, J. E. (2002). *Managing clinical supervision: Ethical practice and legal risk management.* Pacific Grove, CA: Brooks/Cole.

This book looks at clinical supervision from the aspect of ethical and legal risk management. There is a companion book, Documentation in Supervision, *that contains a large number of forms that can be used in supervision to fulfill the risk management philosophy that is presented. Those readers who wish to explore supervision from the aspect of risk management will find these two books indispensable.*

Hawkins, P., & Shohet, R. (2000). *Supervision in the helping professions: An individual, group and organizational approach* (2nd ed.). Maidenhead, England: Open University Press.

This book is a very rich resource of ideas and information about the application of supervision in organizational systems with excellent discussion of team, group, and peer supervision. The authors present a number of challenging ideas on supervision and its purpose within organizations that should stimulate thinking on the part of any reader.

Munson, C. E. (2002). *Handbook of clinical social work supervision* (3rd ed.). New York: The Haworth Social Work Practice Press.

This is an in-depth and detailed handbook for social work supervisors that covers such topics as the history of social work supervision, supervision in different settings, administrative activities for supervisors, theory and techniques, evaluation, as well as supervisory style.

Todd, T. C., & Storm, C. L. (1997). *The complete systemic supervisor: Context, philosophy, and pragmatics.* Boston: Allyn & Bacon.

Although this book is designed to teach supervision to marriage and family therapists, everyone who is interested in the application of systems theory to supervision can find helpful information and ideas. To the uninitiated, the book gives an excellent overview of systems theory and how to construct supervision from a systems viewpoint.

Index

About the Authors

Jane M. Campbell, Ph.D., NCC, ACS, is a licensed psychologist in the state of Texas, a clinical member of AAMFT (American Association of Marriage and Family Therapists), and a National Board for Certified Counselors Approved Clinical Supervisor. Over a long career in the field of mental health, she has been in private practice and the schools as well as on the faculties of the University of Houston and University of Houston-Clear Lake. In the late 1990s she was a visiting assistant professor at George Washington University. Dr. Campbell has presented on the local, state, national, and international level on supervision as well as brief psychotherapy intervention strategies, ethics, and grief counseling. In 2000, she published *Becoming an Effective Supervisor: A Workbook for Counselors and Psychotherapists,* which is based on her experience teaching a 40-hour course for those seeking certification as supervisors in the state of Texas. For the past 5 years she has been crisscrossing the nation teaching clinical supervision to broad audiences in the mental and behavioral health field. Dr. Campbell can be found at drjmcamp@aol.com.

Barbara Herlihy, Ph.D., NCC, LPC, is a professor of counselor education at the University of New Orleans. She is the co-author of six books on ethics in counseling and psychotherapy. She is also the author or co-author of numerous articles and book chapters on ethical issues, supervision, multicultural counseling, and feminist therapy.